Uses of Economics

Also in the British Association series:

Economics and Technical Change

edited by E. M. Hugh-Jones

The Managed Economy

edited by Alec Cairncross

Conflicts in Policy Objectives

edited by Nicholas Kaldor

British Association for the Advancement
" of Science.

Uses of Economics

Papers presented to Section F (Economics) at the 1971 Annual Meeting of the British Association for the Advancement of Science

Edited by G. D. N. Worswick

Basil Blackwell Oxford 1972

ISBN 0 631 14360 2

Library of Congress Catalog Card No. 72-77974

Printed in Great Britain by
Burgess & Son (Abingdon) Ltd.
and bound by
The Kemp Hall Bindery, Oxford.

Contents

Introductory Note

THE MAIN BODY of papers in this book consists of the lectures given in Section F (Economics) of the British Association for the Advancement of Science at the annual meeting held at Swansea in September 1971. They have been supplemented in two ways.

In the first place the British Association, for the first time in its history, had as its President a professional economist. The Committee of Section F felt that it would be appropriate as well as eminently desirable to mark the occasion by including the Presidential Address given by Sir Alec Cairncross. We were glad to have his agreement and give pride of place to his lecture on Government and Innovation.

A second unusual feature is the inclusion of the record of a Symposium on Traffic and Towns which was organised jointly by Section F and Section G (Engineering). Professor K. M. Gwilliam, Director of the Centre for Transport Studies in the University of Leeds, introduced speakers whose short papers are reproduced here, and directed the very lively discussion. The latter was too lengthy to reproduce in full, but Professor Gwilliam has prepared a summary of the main points which emerged.

In planning a Section F programme it is customary to invite the President to state a theme and to invite other speakers to give papers on topics relating to it. On this occasion I declared that I intended to ask why, despite the development of high-powered techniques, the performance of economics seemed to remain so meagre. Anticipating that I might have some harsh things to say about mathematical economics and econometrics I suggested that the Section might invite a mathematical economist, an econometrician and an economic statistician to talk about recent developments in their special fields. This would fill out the opening address, and enable the mathematician and the econometrician to put right any judgements in that address which they considered mistaken or unfair. The remaining lectures were to be on topics illustrating the use of economics, and the proposal of a Symposium on Traffic and Towns fitted this programme well.

The first part of this scheme did not come out quite in the form originally intended, owing to the failure of the planners to foresee the possibility that the lecturers invited might agree with the opening address, or, at any rate, not disagree sufficiently as to wish to take up the cudgels. As Professor Johnston observed, the critical remarks in that address were directed only at *some* econometricians, which, he felt, let him out and enabled him to present a model of the wage bargaining process which might prove to be more realistic than that which is implicit in recent econometric analysis. Professor Bliss reminded us that some of the presidential grumbles were not new, and suggested that progress in economics is to be seen as much in the reformulation of questions as it is in the provision of definitive answers. Meanwhile, Mr Berman was able to give an encouraging report on recent advances in British official economic statistics and new developments in their organisation. Though not conforming exactly to the original conception, the papers of Professor Bliss and Mr Berman, with my own, form one group. But I have transferred Professor Johnston's paper to the second group on the uses of economics. How does economics look to the actors on the economic stage? Mr Radice and Mr Rybczynski gave some answers from a Trade Union and business point of view. Finally, we had a progress report from Mr Cleary of a research project of the greatest importance to the town in which we were meeting, namely 'The Economic Consequences of the Severn Bridge'.

Authors were told that, in preparing their lectures for publication, they were free to alter their texts in any way. This discretion has been used sparingly, but the texts printed here may not be identical with the lectures as delivered at Swansea. The large programme of lectures required a good deal of organisation and I would like to express my appreciation for all the work put in by the Recorder of Section F, Mr Alan Peters.

G. D. N. Worswick

1

Government and Innovation

Sir Alec Cairncross†, KCMG, FBA

I

FOR MANY YEARS it has been the practice of the British Association to call on a natural scientist, almost invariably a Fellow of the Royal Society, to deliver this address. No professional economist has ever done so before and no one with any claim to be regarded as a social scientist has done so since 1935 when Lord Stamp spoke on 'The Impact of Science upon Society'. An economist, elevated to such dizzy isolation, must find it hard to decide what to say to his colleagues in other disciplines. It would perhaps be legitimate, when so many non-economists have used this occasion for an address on economics, to reciprocate by looking at the activities of the natural scientists through the eyes of an economist. But with the caution natural to one who has spent nearly twenty years in the civil service, I have hedged a little and stopped half-way, choosing a subject half of which at least is home ground.

My subject is the role of the government in innovation and I shall be using innovation in a limited sense to mean the generation and absorption of technological change. I shall not be talking about the advancement of science as such, dear though that subject may be to this Association. My concern will be less with science and what goes on in the laboratory than with technology and making things for the final consumer, individual or corporate. The question that I want to ask is essentially a political one: what can a government usefully do to accelerate technological development? I shall bring in science only to the extent that it is drawn upon by technologists and so affects economic activity. To this extent—but only to this extent—I shall be reviewing how the government of an individual country like Great

† Master, St Peter's College, Oxford; and President of the British Association, 1970–71.

Britain can harness the application of scientific knowledge to social and economic advancement.[1]

These are familiar themes, on which, as on all great matters, there is nothing very new to be said. I do not stand before you as an innovator. The issues involved are of great practical importance to us all and it is better to debate them in this Association rather than, as commonly happens with questions to which no one knows the answer, on political platforms. Not that the Association has neglected them. As far back as 1952 it set up a Committee at the Belfast meeting 'to study the problems of speeding up in industry the application of the results of scientific research'. This led eventually to a series of important studies of technical progress by two distinguished economists, Professor Charles Carter, now Vice-Chancellor of the University of Lancaster, and Professor Bruce Williams, now Vice-Chancellor of the University of Sydney. Since then the Association has returned to the subject on a number of occasions and governments have taken it up with more enthusiasm than discernment.

II

Let me begin by asking why we should want technological innovation at all. Indeed some of you may wonder whether we do want it and whether it does more harm than good. I might reply with Bronowski that, on the grand scale of evolutionary history, technology has made man what he is so that 'to quarrel with technology is to quarrel with the nature of man'.[2] It was the unprecedented step 'from using rudimentary tools . . . to making them and keeping them for future use that . . . sent man off breakneck at a speed unmatched in three billion years of terrestrial life'.[2] In the more humdrum terms of economics it is natural to want technological innovation if it is on balance useful: if it adds to the wealth of the country or relieves poverty and hardship. The case for more rapid technological innovation broadly coincides with the case for faster economic growth. You

[1] I am indebted to Mr. M. Fores for clarification of the distinction between science and technology. See, for example, his 'Price, Technology and the Paper Model' (*Technology and Culture,* October 1971). For another view of technology, linking it with invention and 'sub-invention', see Jacob Schmookler, *Invention and Economic Growth*, Harvard University Press, 1966, pp. 5–9.

[2] J. Bronowski, 'Technology and Culture in Evolution', *Cambridge Review,* 8 May 1970, p. 141.

may not find this case persuasive or you may think that, with increasing affluence, there are good grounds for a less wholehearted dedication to the pursuit of wealth. If so, I hope that you will bear with me if I do not turn aside to argue the pros and cons but pass them sternly by. I am going to assume that, rightly or wrongly, governments want faster growth and that it is this that kindles their interest in science and technology.

I do want to insist, however, that technological change has been the mainspring of economic and social progress over the past two centuries, and that it remains the chief source of our increasing affluence. Whatever may be said to pooh-pooh or deride economic growth—and economists are not behindhand in these flights—no one would want us to go back to the mode of living of 1770, still less to the lower standards to which present population would be reduced if we abandoned every improvement in technology since then.

Perhaps we should remind ourselves more often that income levels have risen fourfold here and in other industrial countries in less than a century and that the greatest beneficiaries have been the manual workers at the bottom of the social scale. It is not because we work harder or longer that we are better off than our forefathers: hours of work are much shorter and the physical effort involved is generally a great deal less. We are better off because of the enhancement of productivity that rapid technical change has made possible. It is mainly this that has produced the rise in the living standards of the mass of the population, hardly perceptible from year to year but adding up to a revolution in each successive generation. In spite of social disasters of all kinds—wars, revolutions, slumps—by which from time to time the improvement in income per head has been interrupted, this improvement now continues at an increasing pace which in no major industrial country is less than 2–3% per annum—well above any previously sustained rate of advance. Even in Britain, where the low rate of growth is a matter of reproach, productivity is rising three times as fast as in the nineteenth century when we led the field.

It would be absurd to attribute the whole of this improvement to technological innovation. Something is due also to the expansion in world markets, the accumulation of capital, better education, new methods of business organisation, and so on. But all of these take second place to advances in technology and some are themselves largely the fruit of those advances. There would have been little expansion in world trade, for example, without the steamship. More rapid capital accumulation would be to little purpose without a progressive improvement in new equipment. And so on.

If one looks back, it is the introduction of new products and new techniques that increasingly dominates the process of growth. Technical change, once discontinuous and erratic, is now sweeping us along and transforming our environment and style of life.

If this is what dominates the process of economic development, it is obviously of first-class importance to know how more rapid technological innovation can itself be fostered by deliberate policy. Which of the different elements involved—and obviously there are quite a number—can the government usefully influence? How should it set about influencing them? These are not questions to which a conclusive and unanimous answer is ever likely to be given: we are dealing with political attitudes as well as hard facts. Attitudes change from one generation to the next and so does the scope for government action. Some people are predisposed to believe that government action could accelerate economic progress while others are sceptical.

A hundred years ago the dominant philosophy was that governments should stand aside and not get in the way of individual effort to translate more skill and knowledge into a more efficient use of resources. The function of government was seen as one of maintaining a social and political framework within which technical change could occur rapidly, prompted by the spur of profit and the pressure of competition. The framework might be adjusted as technological and social factors interacted, creating new needs and fresh tensions, but innovation was left to take place sporadically within the private sector of the economy in response to commercial pressures and opportunities.

In these circumstances technological innovation in Britain and abroad owed little to government support in any form. It would be difficult to name any invention of importance in civilian life made by a government employee or at government expense in Britain before the Second World War. It is true that efforts were made in various countries and at various times to encourage new industries; but this rarely meant singling out some departure in technology for official support. One well-known exception was the prize offered by the British Government at the beginning of the eighteenth century for the development of an improved chronometer. The Government was also, by virtue of its spending power, in a position to assist the more rapid diffusion of technical improvements. An example of this was the use of mail subsidies to Cunard in the 1840's by the British Post Office which accelerated the introduction of a passenger steamship service across the Atlantic. But in general the government regarded patents as the appropriate way of encouraging the innovator and competition as the appropriate way of promoting rapid diffusion of the innovation.

To all this defence provided a major exception. From a very early period governments were interested in promoting inventive activity and accelerating changes in the design of weapons for defensive purposes. Where they were the buyers, they had a direct interest in seeing to it that the products offered to them were in advance of those available to potential enemies. This did not mean that governments were very successful in their efforts to improve weapons by additional expenditure. Indeed many of the more important developments took place almost in defiance of governments, as is apparent, for example, in the case of the Spitfire in the 1930's. But, successful or not, the objective of governments usually embraced the need to improve weapons technology long before any similar objectives were expressed in relation to private industry.

Over the past century defence has come to seem less the exception than the rule. Governments are now as anxious to see civil industry adopt the latest technology as they are to be up-to-date in the military sphere. What is much more to the point, they are far more deeply involved in what civil industry does and far less willing to assume that what it does from self-interest will produce the best results. Without quite nationalising so-called private industry they have semi-nationalised a great deal of it. They have accepted the role of managing the entire economy in the interests of full employment, economic growth, and other broad objectives of policy. In discharging this role they have greatly enlarged the public sector of the economy: in the United Kingdom, for example, public authorities employ one man in four and over 40 per cent of the national income passes through their hands. The state has thus acquired wider functions, wider powers and greater leverage on the economy.

For the first time technological innovation as a major source of economic growth has become an object of conscious government policy. This has coincided with two important developments with which I should like to deal at some length. The first is the growth of a widespread belief in the power of governments to use science for economic ends. The second is the growth of expenditure on research and development and of attempts to help private industry by government expenditure on technological innovation.

III

Popular faith in the economic potential of science is not hard to understand. It found forcible expression in Mr. Wilson's speech in this very town seven years ago. Many people have argued that if governments can put a man on the moon or produce atomic bombs by mobilizing the scientific and technical brainpower of the country they should be capable by a similar concentration of resources of eliminating human poverty and distress. It is often suggested that if it was right in wartime to build up teams of scientists and spend heavily on the development of new weapons of destruction it must be equally right to follow a similar strategy for the purposes of peace. To those who think along those lines it hardly matters that the *British* government has yet to launch a satellite successfully, much less put a man on the moon, or that there is a rather fundamental difference between a single consumer and a single project with a clearly defined objective and innumerable consumers wanting a multiplicity of things and exercising their preferences in unpredictable ways. Science is thought of as the modern Aladdin's lamp which, if rubbed the right way, can work miracles.

This belief in science—and I mean science rather than technology—has been given added intensity in Britain by the disappointment felt in the rate of economic growth over the past 20 years. Comparisons are drawn with countries that were in ruins only a few years ago and have now achieved higher levels of output per head than the United Kingdom without ceasing to chalk up a faster rate of growth from year to year. There is less recognition that the divergence between British and continental rates of growth is of long standing, extending back for almost a century, or that the British record since the war compares very favourably with that of earlier periods in which we now take pride. It is still widely felt that industry has fallen down on the job. What more natural than to turn to science in which Britain has an outstanding record and press the government to let science come to the rescue of the economy.

If indeed science could do the trick the British government would be well placed to take the action necessary. It is by far the largest employer of staff with a scientific training. If all government demands are added up, they absorb two out of three of those qualified scientists and technologists in Britain who work in industry or in government research establishments. About two-thirds of all expenditure on research and development is financed by the state and of this the amount spent on defence alone exceeds the total spent by (private) civil industry on research and development.

There are, of course, many people who would be sceptical of the ability of governments to make the right use of scientists and technologists. They would say that if the rate of growth has been disappointing, this is because governments try to do too much already. The last thing that governments are equipped to do is to promote industrial innovation. They can never spot the real winners because they are far too clumsy, ignorant and bureaucratic. Instead they are likely to go in for expensive prestige projects that tie up scarce design teams until another government comes in and scraps the whole affair. Do not let us be blinded by this talk of science, they might say, when nothing could be more unscientific than a government.

I have some sympathy with this view. I would not dispute that we should be on our guard against the tendency in modern life to call for government action whenever things are thought unsatisfactory. It is an illusion to suppose that governments can do everything or that government action is always for the best. They have their limitations like every other human agency and these limitations are most evident when we ask too much of them. If we want to encourage innovation we must face the possibility, to put it no higher, that there is very little that governments can do about it or at least that they would be well advised to find indirect rather than direct ways of operating on it. We must take governments as we find them, not as idealized, infallible do-gooders.

But we cannot shut our eyes to the powers and responsibilities that governments already possess. The greater the area of the economy which is owned or controlled by the government, the greater, almost by definition, must be its role in technological development. To take the extreme case of a collectivist economy like the U.S.S.R. where the whole of industry is owned by the government, who else but the government can apply scientific knowledge to industrial innovation? In a mixed economy like Britain, the government's powers may be less extensive but it is in a strong position to influence almost every industry of any importance whether by providing a market for its output or by offering financial assistance for specific purposes or by abating taxation or by taking measures to regulate competition, limit prices, and so on. It is unthinkable that where the government has such influence it should deliberately refrain from bringing it to bear on technological development and from seeking to increase industrial productivity by encouraging innovation.

But is it science that the government should be seeking to make use of for this purpose? This is far from self-evident. What science yields is knowledge but knowledge by itself need not give rise to any improvement in the practical arts. This is obviously true, in the short run at least, of advances in pure science. But even in applied science much of the research that is undertaken may have no immediate application or, where it has, may be of no economic value.

Historically there is little to show that the process of innovation owed much directly, even if it owed a great deal indirectly, to advances in scientific knowledge. The key figures were the inventor and the business man, who might be the same person, and might or might not be steeped in the relevant scientific literature. Inventions, whether patented or not, were dominated by the need to solve practical problems rather than by some recent scientific discovery. In a study of nearly 1000 important inventions undertaken by Professor Schmookler he found no single instance in the four American industries which he investigated—petroleum refining, paper making, railways and farming—in which a scientific discovery between 1800 and 1957 was cited as the factor initiating the invention. In almost all of them the stimulus was 'a technical problem or opportunity conceived largely in economic terms'.[3]

At the beginning of the nineteenth century it was France, not Britain, that led Europe in the sciences but it was Britain that was the acknowledged leader in technological innovation.[4] Until comparatively recently science remained very much in the background and technology, although it drew on science, responded far more to market pressures. Up to the Second World War quite a sketchy knowledge of science was sufficient even in some of the science-based industries. In the days of subsonic flight, a recent study of the aircraft

[3] J. Schmookler, *op. cit.*, p. 67.
[4] T. S. Kuhn, in *The Rate and Direction of Inventive Activity* (National Bureau of Economic Research, Princeton University Press, 1962), p. 453.

industry points out, 'it was possible to build an aeroplane . . . that would perform adequately if inefficiently without paying much attention to science'.[5] Whittle's invention of the jet engine was based on a cadet's knowledge of engine design.[6] Wankel's rotary piston engine was the work of a man with no university training.

You may think this exceptional but it is in fact far more typical of innovation than satellites and moon travel. New concepts and designs are by no means exclusively the work of university-trained scientists or even of university-trained engineers. In the 1950's half the patents taken out in the United States were issued to non-graduates. It is also an illusion to suppose that innovations originate almost entirely in large research and development departments. The trend may well be in that direction to judge from the rising proportion of patents that are taken out by companies rather than by individual inventors. But the individual inventor remains responsible for a surprising number of the major inventions of the 20th century.[7] Although of diminishing importance in the newer industries where the links between science and technology tend to be closest, he continues to play an important part in industrial innovation. Whereas independent inventors in the United States account for only 3 per cent of chemical and 9 per cent of electrical inventions covered by new patents, they account for no less than 88 per cent of mechanical inventions.[8]

New concepts have usually to be embodied in a working model and tested out in a pilot plant. But even then, nothing may come of them; about half the ideas reaching the stage of a working model are subsequently abandoned. The crucial decision is to embark on full-scale commercial production and it is usually at this stage that large amounts of capital are involved with the attendant risk of outright loss. Projects that have been fully tested up to this point will be looked at by business men from the same point of view as other investments bearing similar risks and without much regard to the element of new scientific knowledge embodied in them.

When we turn from the generation of technological change to its diffusion we have to think in international terms. Innovation in any one

[5] Ronald Miller and David Sawers, *The Technical Development of Modern Aviation*, Routledge and Kegan Paul, London, 1968, p. 254.

[6] ibid., p. 253.

[7] J. Jewkes, D. Sawers and R. Stillerman, *The Sources of Invention*, Macmillan, London, 1969.

[8] R. R. Nelson, M. J. Peck and E. D. Kalachek, *Technology, Economic Growth and Public Policy*, Broonings Institution, Washington, 1967, p. 58*n*.

country does not rest on the base of invention in that country alone. It is an axiom that most inventions are made abroad. No country need limit itself to using its own inventions since it can licence or improve on inventions made elsewhere. Even if it is not so quick off the mark as enterprises in the country where the invention is made there is typically a period of many years—rarely less than ten—from the date of first commercial application to use by all the major firms in that country.[9] Since the rate of diffusion tends to be slow there is usually some opportunity, if other conditions are favourable, to catch up with the competitors or at least stay in business with them.

I should not wish to imply that diffusion is no more than replication of what has been done elsewhere. New machines and new processes, for example, have to be adapted to local circumstances including differences in relative costs, market opportunities and local attitudes. What takes place in the process of diffusion is a form of reinvention essentially similar to invention itself. The process calls for highly skilled staff that is capable of spotting what might be borrowed and improved upon and can insure that it is appropriate not only to local conditions at the time but to conditions as they change in the course of time.

It is a mistake, particularly if one is thinking in national terms, to put the emphasis on major inventions when these may well form only a limited part of the whole process of technological development, while mini-invention—the gradual piece-meal improvement of existing processes and products that goes forward all the time—is easily overlooked and is likely to add up to a much more significant contribution to the total. No one invented the ship, the locomotive, the motor car or the aeroplane. But all of them have undergone a gradual and continuous evolution in design as one new concept after another was subjugated to the needs of modern transport. What we are discussing, therefore, is not a few conspicuous leaps of creative imagination but the adaptation of new ideas to market requirements and the bringing to bear on these ideas of technological competence and commercial initiative and enterprise.

This part of my argument leads to three main propositions.

First of all those who put their faith in science as the means of our economic salvation exaggerate the part played by the body of formulated knowledge in the generation of technological change. They

[9] E. Mansfield, *Industrial Research and Technological Innovation*, Norton, New York 1968, p. 204.

underestimate the importance of unformulated knowledge: of skill born of experience, of insight and perseverance in grappling with the unforeseen, of inventiveness and imagination in design. Scientific knowledge is only one ingredient in the solution of engineering problems and very often by no means the most important. It goes without saying that the input of science has risen progressively in relation to other industrial inputs and this is reflected in the increasing employment of scientists in modern industry. Scientists may well be indispensable to industrial success; and industry may make too little use of them or use them ineffectively. These are not matters that I wish to dispute. What I do suggest is that if we want more rapid technological innovation the contribution that science can make may prove to be a limited one.

Secondly, while science follows its own logic, the problems to which technology responds are set by market forces. It is the consumer, including the industrial consumer and public authorities acting as buyers, who decides whether an innovation is really worth while and it is his wants, disclosed or divined, responsive or unresponsive to selling pressure, that stimulate the generation and still more the diffusion of new technology. So it is consumer demand rather than advances in scientific knowledge that gives innovation its motive force.

Thirdly, consumer demand operates on innovation through industrial management. It is the responsibility of management to organise economic activity and decide when and how to introduce new products and processes. If the government wants faster innovation, therefore, it is industrial management that it must try to influence. It may seek to do so in specific ways such as encouraging more expenditure on research and development. But it is likely to find that the chief need is to ensure that the management of individual businesses is enterprising and efficient and uses resources wisely in the face of opportunity and risk. Science adds to the range of resources on which management can draw and opens up fresh opportunities not unlike those offered by mineral deposits not yet exploited or not yet even located. The use of these opportunities, like the use of new mineral deposits, depends on the managerial assessment of risks and returns. Faster innovation means reducing the risks, raising the returns and improving the capabilities of management. But to say this is to say that innovation is like any other aspects of industrial efficiency: the prescription for greater efficiency and faster innovation is broadly speaking the same.

IV

This brings me to the second point of my argument. What are we to make of the growth of large scale research and development and of the science-based industries that make use of it? Does this not change the whole basis on which industry rests and put the relationship between government and industry on a quite different footing? If the government undertook more research and development on behalf of private industry in its own establishments or commissioned it from private firms, could this not be a major contribution to technological development? Are we not in danger of falling behind other countries by neglecting these possibilities?

There is no doubt of the vast scale on which research and development is now conducted. In the United States an expenditure of less than $600 million in 1940 had grown by 1966 to $22,600 million or from 0·6 per cent of G.N.P. to over 3 per cent. The United States employs on R. and D. about 2·5 times as many scientists and engineers as Western Europe. NASA alone has a budget twice as big as the total amount that is spent on all research and development in the United Kingdom. Even if one looks exclusively at expenditure by civil industry, however financed, U.S. expenditure is ten times as great as British and even higher in relation to any other industrial country. A single American company, IBM, spends as much on R. and D. alone as the British computer industry spends on producing computers.

Such a disproportion has alarmed many commentators who see in it the portent of an increasing domination of world markets in the research-intensive industries by the United States and a corresponding subordination of European industry unless it responds as a single technological community.[10]

But has the emergence of R. and D. on the grand scale really transformed the situation? I think that the answer is no, or at least not yet.

First of all, whether massive investment in R. and D. is crucial to industrial success or not, there is simply no possibility of matching the American level of expenditure. The amounts involved are far too large for this. It is not as if the scale of research and development in Britain were out of keeping with other features of the British economy

[10] See, for example, Christopher Layton, *European Advanced Technology,* Allen and Unwin, London, 1969.

or low in comparison with continental countries. The margin of ten to one by which American R. and D. exceeds British corresponds to the relative dimensions of the two economies as measured, for example, by G.N.P. If the outlay on research and development is smaller in Britain, so is the size of the market, the average scale of production, length of run, volume of investment, and so on. Unless these things are changed too, a big increase in R. and D. might prove indigestible within the limits of British business conditions.

The growth of R. and D., moreover, is highly concentrated in a small group of industries. In the United States nearly two-thirds of the total expenditure comes from federal funds and is directed largely towards defence and space projects. Two manufacturing industries—aircraft and missiles and electrical equipment and communication—employ well over half the scientists and engineers engaged in industrial R. and D. and four other industries—chemicals, machinery, motor vehicles and instruments—account for most of the rest. Only about 5 per cent of the total expenditure represents applied research out of their own funds by firms in industries other than aircraft and missiles and electrical equipment and communication.[11] Very little R. and D. is undertaken outside manufacturing industry. The figures for Britain are not very different.

Experience in industries where success seems to have been on the side of the big research and development departments should not blind us to the fact that there is nothing inevitable about this success. Taking industry as a whole, the evidence suggests that there is no inherent advantage in size and no inevitable tendency towards an increasing preponderance of larger firms over smaller, even if the average firm is getting bigger all the time. The rate of innovation, industry by industry, does not appear to be conspicuously faster in the larger firms. There is a good deal of evidence that the pioneers are not the biggest firms or those that are best equipped with research and development facilities. On the contrary, it is quite common when a new industry takes shape for the smaller firms to make the running, growing into big firms as the industry grows.

Nor should we assume that innovation takes place only within the research-intensive industries; far from it. It may take the form of adaptation to new equipment, materials and processes developed elsewhere. The most striking development in textiles may be the use

[11] Jewkes, Sawers and Stillerman, *op. cit.*, p. 196.

of synthetic fibres which the textile industry did not develop; in packing, the use of polythene and polystyrene; in various service industries, the use of computers. The more this is so, the less does the competitive position of British industry rest on its success in the research-intensive industries.

There is certainly no correlation between a country's expenditure on R. and D. and its rate of economic growth. The level of productivity in America may be higher than here (and for that matter in a lot of other industrial countries), but it is not rising faster than here. On the other hand, Japan, which spends only half as much on R. and D. as Britain, has experienced a fantastically more rapid improvement in productivity. The rate of economic growth is not governed by the relative importance of research-based industries although the time may come when a country's progress could be hampered through lack of adequate economic potential in those industries.

As the example of Japan shows, it is possible to supplement domestic expenditure on R. and D. by making use of imported technology. What costs money is not the kind of knowledge available in text books or in learned journals but industrial know-how which comes from heavy development expenditure and tends to be a closely guarded secret—often not even patented for fear of putting competitors on the track. This know-how can nearly always be tapped by production under licence. While the disadvantages of licensing go well beyond the expense incurred, the benefits may be seriously underestimated. They include the power to start further along the line and save time in working out what is already known to competitors; the power to select from among the fruits of development elsewhere what seems best adapted to local circumstances; and the power to concentrate a limited staff on adaptation and improvements that would not otherwise have been incorporated. In short, licensing does not dispense a business from spending heavily on development but does enable it to spend with more hope of keeping up-to-date, and in research-intensive industries this is vital.

The alternative is to allow U.S. subsidiary companies to establish themselves in Britain and introduce U.S. innovations directly. This is, on the whole, the policy pursued so far. It tends to be viewed uneasily because of the dependence on foreign capital that is involved and the consequent surrender of control. But if British industry lags behind and foreign innovations are denied entry through subsidiary companies, they enter in another way through imports and this also amounts to surrender of control. It is the failure to innovate successfully that represents the true dependence on foreign capital whatever shape the dependence takes.

Experience to date bears out the conclusion that it is not easy for a government to speed up technological innovation by encouraging R. and D. It may begin by exhorting industrial management (and I include the nationalised industries and other public bodies in this) to spend more on R. and D. than they would if left to themselves. This by itself is not likely to be very effective unless it goes on to make more R. and D. worth while by subsidising it, or making grants (for example, to research associations), or offering generous tax treatment.

How far it should go must be a matter of judgement and circumstances. Industry probably underinvests in R. and D. because it does not appropriate all the benefits to set against its costs. Part of the gains from innovation leak away in lower prices to the consumer, higher wages to the worker and higher taxes to the government. This alone would justify some financial support for R. and D. on a non-selective footing. I also see quite a strong case for the kind of joint venture in which NRDC now engages and for acquiescing in a net loss on the money advanced if it helps to quicken the pace of innovation.

Financial support may also be claimed because of the sheer size of the outlay required. No commercial enterprise in Europe could face unaided the cost of developing the Concorde. Only a government could afford to run such a risk. It is safe to say that even in the United States no single enterprise would meet out of its own resources the whole cost of developing a supersonic aircraft. But this is (fortunately) a rare example. Other development expenditures involve less of a plunge or the minimum scale is not such as to rule out commercial development, often by quite a small firm.[12]

R. and D. carried on in government establishments on behalf of private industry raises issues of a different kind: issues of industrial organization. Some of this R. and D. can be justified on ordinary economic grounds as a form of useful specialisation. As a rule, however, there is a great deal to be said for leaving it to industry to carry out its own R. and D. It is always hard to improve efficiency from

[12] 'Despite some well-known exceptions like nylon, the magnitude of R. and D. expenditures necessary to develop most innovations is not beyond the financial capacity of small and medium-sized firms.' D. G. Mueller and J. E. Tilton 'Research and Development Costs as a Barrier to Entry', *Canadian Journal of Economics,* Feb. 1970, p. 373.

outside: and efficiency in innovating is no exception. The same logic that suggests a decentralisation of production units to meet consumer needs suggests a similar decentralisation of development in those units. Development has to be exposed to pressure from the ultimate consumer if its purpose is to serve the consumer. Even in war-time the success of Rolls Royce in engine development owed a good deal to the direct contact which they maintained with the squadrons using their engines in aerial combat.

V

Concentration on R. and D. is less helpful to innovation than concentration on industrial efficiency for true industrial efficiency must embrace the ability to innovate successfully. This still leaves an important role for government. There are many ways in which it can contribute to industrial efficiency, even from outside, and so encourage the more rapid diffusion of new technology towards which its strategy should be directed first and foremost. It alone can adapt the educational system to the needs of an industrial society undergoing rapid and continuous technological change. It can try to maintain competitive pressure and get rid of restrictive practices, particularly those that stand in the way of innovation. It can take action to reduce uncertainty, stimulate investment and improve the level of management. I do not propose to discuss such action in detail since it has often been described and has in particular been amply covered by Carter and Williams. I will confine myself to three brief considerations.

First of all, the rate of diffusion obviously depends on the speed with which new equipment can be constructed and brought into use. It is one thing to defer judgement before embarking on an innovation but quite another to be handicapped by delays that eat into profits and postpone the next stage in the process. It seems to me that these delays have been one of the chronic weaknesses of British industry throughout the post-war period and that getting things done more quickly should take high priority as an objective of policy.

Diffusion also depends heavily on education and ease of communication, two inter-related factors within the scope of government action. Let me take them in turn.

The more scientific knowledge enters into technological change, the more important is adequate provision for education in science. But because of the prestige attaching to research, and to science as opposed to technology, it is no use thinking that all that is required is an increase in the numbers and influence of trained scientists. It could be positively injurious to economic development to concentrate on educating as scientists a higher proportion of the top talent of the country. For this might mean insulating them from industrial and commercial problems and encouraging them to apply themselves to those fascinating conundrums in which pure theory is so rich.

If we confine ourselves to technologists (including those scientists who become technologists) what is needed is not so much more technologists as better technologists and better training for them. There is too low a proportion of graduate technologists in British industry by comparison with other countries and too few of the ablest children opt for a training in technology.

This is not just a matter of the availability of staff for research and development. Innovation concerns the whole of industry from management to manual worker and from laboratory to final consumer. The smooth planning of an innovation into production and its subsequent presentation to customers at the right time and in the right form is bound to be greatly assisted by an adequate technological background in the design, production control and marketing departments. If British industry underinvests it is perhaps in this direction that underinvestment is most marked. This is turn may be because too few men of the necessary ability and training are available to fulfil these responsibilities.

Next, ease of communication. There is general agreement that a new technology is spread mainly through the movement of ideas men from one application to another, often in a quite different field. The circulation of ideas on paper is a less effective means of communication. There are many ways in which greater mobility would be helpful: above all we stand in need of greater movement between industry, government and academic life. Such movement is just as important at a low level as among those with an established reputation.

One particular form of circulation that might be more fully developed is that between the science and technology departments of the universities and polytechnics and industrial establishments. These contacts could be doubly valuable in showing academic staff the range of problems that would have wide commercial application and in allowing industry to benefit from new ideas. New scientific and technical knowledge is not always communicated with most advantage at board level and the value of casual advice given by word of mouth without careful study is often dubious. What is needed is far more of the kind of systematic contact lower down between professional scientists in industry and academic life that is typical of the best American practice.

VI

Looking at government policy towards innovation in Britain since the war I am tempted to argue, provocatively and dogmatically, that the problem was misconceived, the strategy mistaken, the tactics unsatisfactory and yet that none of this made much difference since the pace was set by an unfavourable social climate over which the government had little control.

First of all, the problem. Post-war discussion was dominated by what were thought to be the achievements of science in wartime. In fact these achievements were in large measure the achievements of scientists rather than of science and, what is more, scientists acting as technologists, that is, helping to produce military hardware. The necessary scientific knowledge was largely available before the war; it was the engineering knowhow that had to be created. Cost, which interests the civilian consumer a good deal, was a secondary consideration: the development of the atomic bomb, for example, cost about $1500 million and the outcome was uncertain until the first bomb was successfully exploded. Governments tended to draw the conclusion that heavier expenditure on science would yield a dividend in GNP and their emphasis on science increased as time went on. But the basis weakness lay in engineering: in the lack of appreciation in British industry of the value of outstanding design engineers and the simultaneous lack of interest in the schools in an engineering career.

Next, development strategy. It seems to me a serious error in strategy for the United Kingdom to have put so much effort into the research-intensive industries in the post-war period. Unlike some of our industrial competitors we measured ourselves against the United States in just those products where large-scale research needs to be combined with a large and growing market and where in consequence we were at a disadvantage. In nuclear energy, aerospace, computers, and so on, our achievements may stand out in comparison with continental countries. But they have not enabled us to meet American competition with much success abroad or even, very often, in our own home market. It might have been wiser to have concentrated on less ambitious targets, adapting and improving on imported designs, squeezing into the interstices rather than trying to cover the whole range of market requirements, and spreading our limited scientific man-power more evenly over industry. Such a conclusion is suggested, not just by the experience of Germany and Japan which were denied the opportunity of following our example, but also of Sweden and the Netherlands which have been remarkably successful in limited sectors of high technology industry. Perhaps too, we should reflect, in the light of Italy's experience, on the need to put at least as much emphasis on good design as on scientific competence.

At the level of tactics I would draw attention to two connected problems. There was a tendency to over-emphasise the generation of technological change as against its absorption: and anxiety to boast of *British* achievements in the development of nuclear energy, for example, when we might well have waited to come later into the race. At the same time, there was a tendency to exclude civil industry from participation in development work carried out by government agencies and yet look to industry to find commercial applications at a later stage for the fully developed project: again I am thinking primarily of nuclear energy. This does not look like a well-conceived division of labour between the central authorities and individual managements.

Finally, the social climate. The innovating manager in Britain has a hard time of it compared with other countries. He has to contend with government regulations that absorb his time, with restrictions imposed by his workers or by his competitors, with public apathy, with the slowness with which things get done. Innovation is a form of investment and when the economic and social climate is uncongenial to investment it is naturally discouraging to innovation too. If the whole community were dedicated to economic growth and all that it involves I should expect the rate of innovation to respond automatically and to sustain faster economic growth. But I cannot help suspecting that interest in growth is fainter than we pretend.

VII

Any modern government, concerned to achieve a faster rate of economic growth, will look with favour on technological innovation. But it would be unwise to form large expectations of what it might do by direct action to promote it. There is no obvious accord between government and innovation. The one stands for control, law, uniformity: the other for creativeness, non-conformity, uniqueness. In a sense innovation is a form of heresy, an expression of discontent with the established order of things: no easy object of official encouragement. 'Science' as a distinguished scientist once told me 'is a subversive activity that flourishes best when nobody is looking'. In some ways the same is true of innovation. It comes far more from below than above. It may respond to the promptings of governments but it depends much more on the whole ambience of economic activity: the predispositions and presuppositions of the public, which governmental acts in a democratic community tend to reflect. If the consumer and the worker want more innovation they will probably get it, just as they will get faster growth if this is the one thing above all others that they want. If they do not get it, it may be because they are half-hearted in wanting it and pay lip-service to ideas which they repudiate by their acts.

2

Is Progress in Economic Science Possible?*

G. D. N. Worswick†

A Flourishing Science

BY ALL THE outward and visible signs economics is in a very flourishing state and enjoys a satisfactory rate of growth.

In 1966 the National Register of Scientific and Technical Personnel obtained information about their salaries from some 200,000 individuals in full-time civilian work in the United States. The register identified 13 major professions and, among these, economists had the highest median salary of $13,000, by comparison with a median salary of $12,000 for all registrants.[1] For some economists this evidence alone would be sufficient demonstration of the progress of their science. It hardly needs to be said that there are no equivalent figures for the United Kingdom where, in any case, we allow just a little more room for non-monetary measures of value. Concerning these we do have some evidence. Whereas in 1938 only one in seven of the members of the Council of the Royal Economic Society was a Lord or a Knight, in 1971 nearly one in four was so dignified and this comparison understates the change. For in the old days once you got on the Council you stayed on, whereas nowadays there is a

* After I had begun to prepare this lecture I found myself twice overtaken by presidential conveyances moving very fast in the same general direction: first by Professor Leontief in his Presidential address to the American Economic Association, which is published in the *American Economic Review* for March, 1971, and later by Professor Phelps-Brown, President of the Royal Economic Society, in his Presidential address to the Society in July, 1971, which is published in the *Economic Journal* for March, 1972. It was gratifying to find such distinguished support for some, at any rate, of the arguments I have been using and it was tempting to embellish my own text with some of their very telling observations. However, although the general direction is the same the arguments and conclusions are not identical. It seemed better therefore to give my own argument in my own words.

† Director of the National Institute of Economic and Social Research; and President of Section F, 1970–71.

[1] N. A. Tolles and E. Melichar, *Studies of the Structure of Economists' Salaries and Income*, American Economic Review Supplement, December 1968, p. 56.

regular circulation of membership, which has the effect of reducing the average age and *ceteris paribus* reducing the average incidence of nobility. Nowadays there are more economic Lords outside the Council than in it. But it could perhaps be said that nobility is not what it was, so let us apply other tests.

In 1961, 11·3% of all A level passes in England and Wales were in chemistry and by comparison only 2·4% in economics. But by 1969, chemistry had fallen to 7·0% while economics had come up to 5·3%. Similar remarkable figures could be cited for university degrees, not only in economics but in all the social sciences.

As late as 1964, the number of full time economists in government service was less than 40, whereas nowadays it is some 250. Yet, despite paying salaries apparently higher than in universities, the government still has difficulty in recruiting enough senior economists.[2]

The number of books and journals increases almost daily. Nor is this simply a question of the increase in the volume of activity. There has been an enormous increase in diversity, which is reflected in the appearance of more and more specialised journals devoted to some particular branch of the subject. The two most striking developments since the end of the second world war are the emergence and expansion of the economics of development and of econometrics. There has too, so some would say, been a clarification of the status of economics and of the economist. Nowadays the student learns in his first year not to confuse a fact with a value judgement. Thus it might seem that in terms of the volume, diversity and clarity of the subject matter and of the opulence and social standing of many of its practitioners, whether in universities, government, business, developing countries, or commuting by jet aeroplane between two or more of them, economic science is flourishing.

But is there Advance?

And yet one cannot avoid some uneasiness. The standards are high, the intellectual battalions are powerful, but notwithstanding the appearance of formidable progress in techniques of all kinds the performance of economics seems curiously disappointing the moment one puts a few test questions, such as:

[2] Cf. Civil Service Commission. *Annual Report*, 1970, p. 15.

1. What are the causes of inflation in the United Kingdom at the present time? Do we really know whether what we have been lately experiencing is simply a logical consequence of an exchange rate adjustment or a major upheaval in society?

2. Do we really know whether devaluation improves the balance of payments, and for how long?

3. Already growth theory has itself become big enough to have its own specialisms, but how much light has this economic theory thrown on the question why the growth rate in the United Kingdom and the United States has been so much slower than elsewhere?

4. Can we in practice distinguish a monopoly profit from a reasonable rate of return?

5. Does free trade help or hinder economic development?

That economic science may not provide complete answers to such questions is understandable and acceptable, but are we any nearer to answering them than we were ten or twenty years ago?

If it is argued that the opulence of its practitioners is no conclusive demonstration of the progress of the science, even more strongly might it be objected that poor economic performance or policies are not necessarily evidence of the lack of it. Opening a debate in the House of Lords on the 19th January 1971, the Lord Privy Seal observed: 'However reluctant some academic economists are to admit the existence of cause and effect, the fact is that the Six Community countries have all enjoyed a far better rate of growth since the formation of the Community than Britain has enjoyed in EFTA'. One can but suppose that the noble Lord was unaware that the members of the Six had enjoyed a faster rate of growth than Britain before the formation of the Community as well. Confronted with such glorious 'nonsequence'—and other examples abound—economists might well ask to be excused any responsibility for policy. As for economic performance, it is not logically necessary that scientific exploration should invariably unearth possibilities of amelioration: it is not for nothing that economics acquired the title of the 'gloomy science'.

These are good reasons why, when things go wrong, the entire blame should not be laid at the door of the economists. But they cannot be wholly exonerated; nor indeed should they seek to be. 'The ideas of economists and political philosophers', said Keynes, 'both when they are right and when they are wrong, are more powerful than is commonly understood. Indeed the world is ruled by little else'.[3] All the great economists of the past have been reformers and there are few contemporary economists who would not claim that their work and their ideas are intended to contribute in some degree, however indirectly, to the improvement of a firm, an industry, a national economy or the world as a whole. And if it is said that some do not claim this, there are very few who explicitly proclaim the uselessness of their work, with the vigour with which G. H. Hardy once attempted to justify pure mathematics.

While most contemporary economists would probably acknowledge the ultimate reforming ends of their work they would play down the role of the economist as preacher, telling us, in Graaff's words,[4] 'at what level the National Coal Board ought to set the price of coal' and play up his role as positive scientist, predicting 'the probable consequences of setting it at various different levels'. I shall return at the end of this lecture to the question of welfare economics. Meanwhile I wish to pursue the aspect of the economist as positive scientist. What follows is, I hope, a fair summary of how most economists nowadays conceive this role.

Economics as Positive Science

We wish to account for some facts, e.g. why prices are rising or why there is unemployment: but the facts alone do not arrange themselves in such a way as to provide the explanation. We need to have some theory about how the economic system works. The range of possible theories is very wide and so we express always a strong preference for any theory which will do two things against two separate theories which will do one thing each.

Obviously we shall not choose a theory which will not explain the facts immediately confronting us, and the theory becomes interesting when, besides explaining these facts, we can deduce from it hypotheses about other facts which we have not yet looked at. Examination of these new facts may then confirm the hypotheses (or not contradict them) and thus strengthen our attachment to our economic theory. On the other hand if the new facts conflict with the hypotheses so deduced we must go back to the theory and seek some modification which will lead to accordance with the new facts without disturbing the accord with the original facts from which we started.

[3] *General Theory of Employment, Interest and Money*, Macmillan, 1936, p. 383.
[4] J. de V. Graaff, *Theoretical Welfare Economics*, Cambridge, 1957, p. 171.

With this picture in mind we conceive progress in economic science as consisting of a dialogue, or inter-action, between facts and theory, the latter being strengthened or modified according as new data come to light and according as they agree or disagree with hypotheses deduced from the theory.

So far this simple account might apply to any science: there is as yet nothing peculiar to economics. The more familiar of the features distinguishing economics (and other social sciences) from other sciences is the unavailability, except in an attenuated form, of experiment, so that testing hypotheses is more difficult. A less frequently stressed, though probably more important, feature is the nature of economic facts. Many quantities which appear in economic literature, such as numbers employed, or tons of steel, look very like familiar physical facts, but there is a subtle and all-important difference. The physical quantities of steel, or labour are only proxies for economic 'values' or 'utilities'. This distinction is vital: failure to make it can have detrimental consequences, both for policy, as for example in the discussion of the relation between wages and productivity, and for theory, as in the measurement of capital. Important though this problem is, however, the ability to distinguish economic facts must here be taken for granted.

Specialisation within Economics

Adam Smith vividly explained the power of specialisation and the division of labour—and the scientific process just described clearly lends itself to specialisation. Thus, there could be economic statisticians who specialise in the collection of economic data, and it is no more necessary for them to have knowledge of economic theory, than for enumerators of the census of population to be demographers. At the other end of this spectrum there might be people of imagination with a gift for formulating 'models' and then deducing in some detail how they work. In between we might have another category of specialists, econometricians, who are particularly good at studying how to arrange the data so as to make valid tests of the hypotheses being put forward.

The theory of production examines the way in which different specialisms are, or can be, combined to achieve a given product, and it studies the mechanisms which exist, or would have to be created, to elicit the different specialisms in suitable proportions. In the competitive model, if there is a shortage of a particular grade of skilled worker, wages will be bid up, and stimulate new workers to acquire the relevant skill. Even in the world of industry the mechanisms for bringing into line the demand for and supply of different kinds of skill do not always work smoothly, but at least there are industrialists who know what the appropriate combinations are and thus, as it were, organise the demand. But are there any mechanisms which will bring about a correct balance between economic statisticians, econometricians and economic theorists (to mention only the three specialisms distinguished above for illustration) so as to secure the fastest advance of economic science? To ask this question is to imply that the advance of science consists of an increase of knowledge or understanding of real economies, which is analogous to an increase in industrial production. I find the analogy acceptable, the more so that it enables one to expose an important ambiguity in the concept of scientific progress. Whereas we would probably not accept, as an increase of production, an increase in the output of windscreens[5] which are simply put on one side and never actually embodied in cars (over and above some normal stock of spares against accident), there is not the same inhibition in the case of the economic specialisms which contribute to economic science. It is quite possible, that is to say, that there could be a proliferation of theorems, none of which help to illuminate questions about the real world and that there could be what looks like spectacular progress in economic theory and yet no progress at all in economic science in the broader sense.

The Contribution of Economic Theory

Anyone who has attempted to keep pace with even some small part of the enormous output of theoretical literature must have asked himself at times, what exactly is it *about*? Consider as a first example the theory of economic growth, which has taken the form of the elaboration of a great variety of economic models whose behaviour is examined and whose performance is contrasted with that of other models. There is no question but that these models throw up fascinating problems, taxing one's intellectual powers to the full, but there is very little of it which is of any help in answering such questions as

[5] Or the creation of entirely new kinds of windscreens.

why growth rates differ among countries and between periods. 'Given the assumptions common to the models (no government, no international trade and so on), this is not surprising, and it may reasonably be argued that most model-builders have not been trying to do this anyway.'[6] But if not, what have they been trying to do? Facts hardly ever occur in this literature: the nearest we get is what Professor Kaldor has called stylised facts, which sometimes means no more than convenient assumptions without which determinate solutions of theoretical problems could not be obtained. As Hahn and Matthews observed at the end of their masterly survey of this literature, 'But it is essentially a frivolous occupation to take a chain with links of very uneven strength and limit one's energies to strengthening and polishing the links that are already relatively strong'.[7]

This tendency in economic theory to polish strong links is not confined to growth theory. It is arguable that the notion of equilibrium has been deleterious in economics. Lionel Robbins told us that there was no penumbra of approbation about equilibrium.[8] Perhaps so, but a great many economic theorists give the impression that disequilibrium is a pretty bad state to be in. But apart from the penumbra the difficulty has been to relate equilibrium economics to empirical facts. How do we know whether we have an equilibrium or not? Consider too the question of the short-run and the long-run. As teachers we tell our pupils that it is naïve to ask how many months or days constitute a short-run; these are, we say, relative terms, and they give us insights into the behaviour of prices or outputs. But in the end, if we are concerned with real questions these short and long-runs must be given real durations, whether in days, months or years. Yet, while there is an enormous literature on the existence of equilibria in all kinds of situations there is very little quantitative study of the time paths of adjustment to equilibrium.

Equilibrium plays a role too in the theory of allocation and in the context of allocative efficiency. This theory normally postulates that entrepreneurs or managers make optimal decisions: confronted with the prices of inputs they combine them in unique combinations to produce a given output, to which the cost of production is also

[6] F. H. Hahn and R. C. O. Matthews, 'The Theory of Economic Growth: A Survey', *Economic Journal*, December 1964.
[7] *loc. cit.*
[8] *Nature and Significance of Economic Science*, Macmillan, 1932.

uniquely related. But anyone who has worked with empirical data from firms in an industry is frequently struck, not by the fact that all the firms produce their outputs at much the same cost, but by the extraordinarily wide range of costs and profits. Over five years ago Professor Leibenstein gave a name to the concept of X-efficiency, indicative of the differing efficiency with which managers combined similar groups of inputs, and he argued that X-inefficiency was far more prevalent, and important, than the allocative inefficiency of traditional micro-economics. Nevertheless theorems in the traditional allocative economics go on being generated all over the place as though X-efficiency had never been heard of.

There now exist whole branches of abstract economic theory which have no links with concrete fact and are almost indistinguishable from pure mathematics. Indeed, it might be more correct to say that there have come into being new branches of mathematics whose distinguishing feature is that some of the axioms and some of the terminology show traces of the ancestry of this particular branch of mathematics, which originated in the distant past in some real economic question. Whether, as in mathematics, the progress in this kind of economic study constitutes a process of discovery of what, implicitly, is already there, or a process of creation of something entirely new, there is no doubt that progress of this kind is taking place and much of what goes on in the pages of *Econometrica* or the *Review of Economic Studies* is as much or as little progress as what goes on in mathematical journals[9]. But much of it does not constitute progress in economic science in the broader sense which I outlined earlier. There are those who would say that this judgement is obtuse. Science, they would argue, does not proceed in an orderly fashion tackling one problem at a time, successfully designing appropriate theoretical models to illuminate unfolding areas of fact. Allowance must be made for speculation and inspiration: you never can tell when one such piece of abstract reasoning may not turn out to be a powerful solvent in the most unexpected quarters. Of course you never can tell. But more than the occasional chance success is needed to sustain this argument: it would have to be demonstrated that

[9] In mentioning two examples, I do not wish to exclude other journals: the kind of work to which I am referring appears in a great many places. Nor would I interpret 'mathematical' narrowly. My concern is with the proportion of the abstract—whether expressed in verbal long-hand, or symbolic short-hand—to the concrete.

more scientific advance is achieved by those who steadfastly avert their eyes from the facts than by those who face them.

The Contribution of Econometrics

Surely such a comment cannot be made about econometrics: by its very name it is concerned with measurement, so how could it become detached from the facts. But the remark that Samuelson once made about economists that: 'We are like highly trained athletes, who never run a race'[10] can, I think, be fairly made about some econometricians. They are not, it seems to me, engaged in forging tools to arrange and measure actual facts so much as making a marvellous array of pretend-tools which would perform wonders if ever a set of facts should turn up in the right form. Thus what was said above about the detached mathematical nature of much economic theory also goes for some econometric theory as well. But it must also be recognised that econometrics has been a powerful force in bringing economic theory back into touch with reality. Indeed it is the econometricians, as much as any, who have advanced the idea, outlined above, of economics as a positive science. For some economists indeed, 'the testing of hypotheses' has become virtually synonymous with the specification of a set of mathematical equations and the estimation of their coefficients, the strength or weakness of the hypothesis being indicated by various tests of statistical significance.

The idea of economics as positive science makes predictability the test of its performance, the prediction of relationships in situations not previously observed, as well as the prediction of future events, which in some ways is the acid test. The volume of applied econometric work is enormous and any judgement of progress is highly subjective. But it is my impression that the predictive power of econometrics is rather low, certainly very much lower than what one expects in natural sciences, and that progress in the establishment of firmer bases for economic relationships, if it occurs at all, is going at a very slow pace. I have time only to give one example of what I mean.

The rate of industrial investment plays a major role in the *General Theory* of Keynes. Investment in his model is determined by the rate of interest and the marginal efficiency of capital. Another theory of

[10] *Foundations of Economic Analysis*, Harvard, 1947.

the same period is the accelerator, linking the capital stock to output, or investment (which is the change in the capital stock) to the change in output. These theories can be regarded as alternatives or they can be combined in a variety of ways. Given the strategic importance of investment in macro-economic theory it is natural that much effort has been devoted to finding empirical investment functions. The quantity and quality of relevant data vary from one country to another and as so often the data appears to be more plentiful for the United States; certainly greater research efforts have been made there than elsewhere. Recently Professor Jorgenson and his colleagues[11] have reported on the performance of four alternative econometric models which were selected as being representative of a larger variety of functions which have been tried for the United States. They were fitted (for the purpose of comparison) to the same data for 15 industry groups for the period from the fourth quarter of 1949 to the fourth quarter of 1964. As a standard of performance they were all four compared with an auto-regressive scheme. It turned out that only one of the models beats the auto-regressive scheme, in the sense that it performs better in 11 industries and worse in only 4, whereas the auto-regressive scheme does better in a majority of the industries for all the other models and in one case for an overwhelming majority. If our interest is exclusively with *forecasting* investment for a year or two ahead, then anticipatory data, *i.e.* the results of asking firms what their short-term investment plans are, perform vastly better than any of the models.

The fact is that econometric models are not, as a rule, sharp instruments for discriminating between hypotheses. One has only to think of the recent controversies concerning the money supply, or to ask how many consumption functions are still in play. Such methods are better at telling us what is not the case, than at telling us what is.

That this is so should not come as too much of a surprise. In almost every economic question, which appears to lend itself to econometric treatment, there is a multiplicity of potential explanatory variables. Ask what determines whether family A saves more than family B, or whether firm X is more likely to install a new invention than firm Y, and it is easy to write down a couple of dozen candidate explanatory variables in each case. How then are most equations encountered in

[11] Dale W. Jorgenson, Jerald Hunter and M. Nadiri, 'A Comparison of Alternative Econometric Models of Quarterly Investment Behaviour', *Econometrica*, March 1970.

econometric work restricted to half a dozen variables or less? Partly because candidate variables are put aside when no suitable measures happen to be available and partly because researchers naturally exercise judgement in selection of what they believe to be the most important or relevant variables. Even if damage is not done in this narrowing down process we come up against an even more serious problem. It is customary to postulate a structure, which is represented by the parameters of a set of equations and it is usually required, for the purposes of estimation, that these parameters should not alter within the estimation period; but sometimes we find, after the event, that we might have been wiser to postulate that one or other of our parameters was in fact a variable, inter-related to the other chosen variables. Very often the only way to sort things out is to have more observations, but this is of little help if we have already made use of such observations as there are. One aspect of this is that we often succeed in picking up a trend just at the moment when it is about to change.

Much of what I am now saying has been said before and often more eloquently. But if there is truth in it, if econometrics is only rather a blunt tool for the development of positive economics, it behoves its practitioners to go cautiously and to make sure that all the necessary qualifications are suitably stressed, if only to avoid misunderstanding.

The Strange Case of the Phillips Curve

Consider the Phillips curve. The idea that, *ceteris paribus*, there might be some association between the level of unemployment and the rate of increase of money wages is not new. Certainly it was familiar to the British economists advocating Keynesian full employment policies during the 1940s. They did not expect this relation to be at all precise[12] but the publication in 1958 of A. W. Phillips' paper[13]

[12] 'There is no inherent mechanism in our present system, which can with certainty prevent competitive sectional bargaining for wages from setting up a vicious spiral of rising prices under full employment.' W. H. Beveridge, *Full Employment in a Free Society*, George Allen & Unwin, London, 1944, p. 199.

'If there is considerable unemployment there will be a general downward pressure on money wages; if there is full employment the upward pressure is too great. There must, it might be argued, be a unique level of employment which will

footnote continued on p. 32

put a different complexion upon things, for it was bound to appear, whatever his explicit or implicit qualifications, that he was expounding a simple economic or perhaps, more precisely, econometric law. Using data from 1861 to 1913 Phillips estimated a single equation relating the change in wage rates to the level of unemployment. He then asserted that the wage history of the inter-war years, given the levels of unemployment which actually occurred, 'could have been predicted fairly accurately from a study of the pre-war data, if any one had felt so inclined to carry out the necessary analysis', and he concluded his article with the statement that 'It seems from the relation fitted to the data that if aggregate demand were kept at a value which would maintain a stable level of product prices, the associated level of unemployment would be a little under 2½%' (this was on the assumption that real productivity rose annually at 2% a year). Since throughout the post-war period unemployment had been rather less than 2% and since also price inflation had been continuous at a rate of around 3%, sometimes faster and sometimes slower, the policy implications of Phillips' paper were obvious, and to some people attractive. The idea that 2½% unemployment would stop inflation could be linked with another idea, propounded by Professor Paish, that a higher level of unemployment would be favourable to economic growth. Putting these two ideas together made for a very attractive prescription for governments, worried by the persistence of inflation in Britain with its damaging consequences for the balance of payments and becoming increasingly concerned that the growth of the British economy was too slow. In a comment upon Phillips' paper in the following year[14] Knowles and Winsten argued that such a 'daring simplification of what is generally thought to be a highly complex problem' should be subjected to a searching analysis which they proceeded to supply. But despite this and other warnings there seems no doubt that the idea that some relatively small increase in unemployment would be sufficient to stop inflation came to be

bring out precisely the "correct" rise in money wages, which does not lead to a steady rise in prices. . . . But this "critical" level of employment, even if it could be found and kept under control, which is doubtful, may be relatively low, and so involve considerable waste of resources.' G. D. N. Worswick in *Economics of Full Employment* (Institute of Statistics), Blackwells, Oxford, 1944, p. 65.

[13] A. W. Phillips' 'The Relationship between unemployment and the rate of change of money wage rates in the United Kingdom 1861–1957', *Economica*, November 1958.

[14] 'Can the Level of Unemployment Explain Changes in Wages', *Bulletin of the Oxford University Institute of Statistics*, May 1959.

widely believed in official circles. Much of the subsequent econometric work in this field has in fact been highly critical, but some of it has retained traces of the pristine determinism of the original article, and by the irony of publication delays continues to appear at a time when accelerating inflation was being accompanied by rising unemployment and virtually every Phillips curve ever invented had jumped off the page.[15]

What makes the Phillips case important is not the statistical failure which, though dramatic, is not uncommon in econometric work, but the fact that the initial results were given such a build-up. Somewhere along the line a quite unjustified stability and precision were imputed to relationships of this type, so that they acquired an altogether disproportionate significance in the minds of policy makers.

How did it happen?

It is worth turning aside for a moment to ask how this can have come about. Whose fault was it? The immediate culprits were those 'communicators' who seized on the article by Phillips and upon subsequent studies and dressed them up for public presentation. You know the kind of thing: 'Back room economists at the University of Middlesex have discovered an econometric law which in the next few years will transform the conduct of economic policy'. But the professionals cannot be absolved altogether from responsibility. Some of them, when confronted with negative results, promptly assemble even more formidable batteries of econometric engines for a new assault when they might have been better employed in asking questions about the quality and suitability of the data. Then, there is a tendency to notice only 'positive' results. If an equation is tested over 10 industries and the coefficient of some variable turns out to be not significant (by some statistical test) in 9 cases and significant in 1, how often does our author observe 'there does not seem to be much in

[15] This is an exaggeration. There must be hundreds of Phillips curves of different specifications, for different countries, estimated over different periods. What I have here in mind is a number of wage equations developed at the National Institute of Economic and Social Research. These equations use vacancies, and the change in vacancies, rather than the more usual unemployment, earlier work having suggested that vacancies 'did better' than unemployment in explaining wage movements. Such equations fitted quite well until 1969, but in 1970 gave prediction errors more than five times the standard error of the equation. (See *National Institute Economic Review*, no. 55, February 1971, p. 40.)

this idea'? We are just as likely to find a remark such as: 'It is encouraging to see our hypothesis so clearly supported in the steel industry'. This natural tendency to make the most of one's efforts is reinforced by the belief that journal editors would not be interested in publishing negative results. Nor can this belief be entirely without foundation, for it is very rare to find published articles which make no claim to positive results. One effect of this bias is to give the newcomer and the outsider the impression that applied econometrics is much more successful than is in fact the case. Finally there exists among some econometricians and some editors a doctrine of econometric escalation whereby if one believes that a particular piece of econometric work is unsatisfactory, the rules of the game require that even heavier econometric weapons have to be mobilised. The employment of lower levels of weaponry, such as a critical analysis using only the English language, is considered off-side.

Does the Imbalance matter?

There is, I have suggested, at present an imbalance among the specialisms which go to make economic science. It would be too neat to say that progress in economics occurs fastest in those areas which are furthest removed from reality, but there is sufficient in the charge to cause discomfort. Too much of what goes on in economic and econometric theory is of little or no relevance to serious economic science. If this is not a fair judgement some of the other speakers in this year's Section F may put me right. But even if the judgement be accepted, does the imbalance do any harm? Does the fact that some economists play abstract games of little relevance and others engage in meretricious quantification prevent serious economists from going about their business? The danger is that university courses in economics will become increasingly mathematical and increasingly concerned with technique to the exclusion of the subject matter itself. Such an imbalance is perhaps less dangerous for students going on to be professional economists than for those going on to posts in business or government. The former, when they do eventually come to try out their techniques on real problems, may learn to accept the constraints of the real world and adjust their methods accordingly, although one sees a disturbing amount of 'research' which is no more than exercising. But the latter, those going into government and business, finding such a large gap between what they have learned and the realities with which they are now confronted, may be inclined to dismiss all, and not merely some, of what they have learned as of no conceivable relevance to their future work. The more the impression is allowed to persist that economics is an exact science, or if not already one, then with the aid of mathematical models and the computer is about to become one, the more damage will be done to the subject when it fails to live up to exaggerated expectations.

If the imbalance exists and is regarded as serious, how is it to be rectified? Certainly academic economists need to pay more attention to the provenance of the statistical data which they put into their models. They need to give more thought to the contexts in which their models might conceivably be used, and they need to make a great effort to resist the blandishments of scholastic conjurors and to re-direct the subject into relevant and practical channels. Let me say at once however that I do not think that correcting the imbalance will be easy, nor will its effect be to make economics any easier. I am not arguing that we can do without abstract theory altogether. The working out of the logic of relevant models is a necessary component of the scientific process. Nor am I suggesting that all we need by way of econometric apparatus is a few simple regressions. Relevance does not entail relaxation.

The Inevitability of Gradualness

Correction of the imbalance would surely accelerate progress in positive economic science, in the understanding of how actual economic systems work and respond to varying stimuli. Nevertheless that progress is bound to remain slow. The more familiar difficulties will still remain: the multiplicity of potentially relevant variables, the difficulty of obtaining accurate data, and the inability to conduct experiment, except occasionally and in the most attenuated form. But the most fundamental difficulty is that however much we improve our knowledge of the data we shall still not be able to rely upon its remaining unchanged. In the last resort our data are human beings, or, if you like, the responses of human beings to varying stimuli. Human beings have the awkward ability of being able to learn and modify their behaviour. Consider the business cycle. By studying the past behaviour of different economies we may learn the causes of fluctuations in economic activity. But if we correctly understand the causes this may indicate to us those modifications in monetary or fiscal policy which would, in principle, eliminate the fluctuations. Governments might not be wholly successful in practice, however, so that some fluctuations remain. Obviously in such a case it would be a mistake to try to account for these residual fluctuations exclusively in the terms in which we accounted for the original ones, for we must now take into account the fact that monetary and fiscal policy is being conducted on principles different from those which previously existed. The understanding of movement in this type of situation, where there is known to be conscious intervention, is a more complex question than understanding fluctuations where there is no such *deus ex machina.*[16] Nor is this the end of the story. It is arguable, though not easy to prove, that business behaviour itself can be modified merely by the knowledge that, in future, governments will intervene in predictable ways in certain types of situation. An economic variable may be determined, not only by the other variables normally expected to influence it, but by a unique history as well, in a manner which does not occur, with anything like the same force, in natural science. The coefficients which appear as constants in our equations do not have the durability of constants of natural science, such as specific gravity or the elasticity of metals. I do not share the view that the low predictive performance of economic science simply arises from its comparative youthfulness. I am prepared to believe, and certainly hope, that the National Institute forecasts a hundred years hence will be better than they are today, but I suspect that my successor will be saying that the main improvement comes from knowing more accurately where the economy actually is, because his data are more accurate and up-to-date than the ones we have today, than because the crystal ball he uses for gazing into the future is all that much less cloudy than the one we use at the moment.

The answer then to my question: 'Is progress in economic science possible?' is Yes—but slow. We must reconcile ourselves to remaining inexact scientists.

[16] When I started doing economics, fluctuations were blamed on the system and the Government was called upon to intervene; nowadays stop/go is blamed on the Government and people call on it to stop intervening!

Is Positive Science Enough?

That looks like the proper place to stop but there is one final matter which I should raise. I have not in this lecture so far questioned the current view that the economist's main function is that of positive scientist. Yet I am not sure that we are right to place so much stress upon this aspect of our function to the exclusion of other possible ones. In saying this I am not, as a cynic might observe, simply looking for a more exciting role for the economist, since he cuts such a poor figure as a positive scientist. The contemporary view is that it is not for the economist to say what policies ought to be, but to indicate the probable consequences of different policies. The logic of this view is quite simply that no policy prescriptions can be made which do not ultimately entail value judgements, and that economists as such have no special qualifications which give them the right to impose their value judgements upon others. But while this logical distinction is of great importance, and should never be lost sight of, it does not follow that in order to preserve his scientific integrity, anyone calling himself an economist should be required to refrain from expressing his own value judgements, or should be required to avoid getting involved in any way in the generation of economic policy. Even if positive economics were an exact science, the idea that the generation of policy could be exclusively decided by the layman or the politician, who would then simply ask the economist to explain the consequences of alternative policies, has never been wholly convincing. Even to present policies in such a way that it is easy to distinguish between the factual and the value elements itself requires expertise, which economists are well fitted to provide. How much more is this so, when positive economics is not exact but hedged with uncertainty.

At present, we leave the design of new policies too much to governments, academic economists being content with the role of critic. Of course, some division of labour is essential: I am not suggesting that all academics should become politicians or civil servants as well, but I think there is a need for more academics to generate fully fledged policy models which are not simply abstract accounts of how some problem might be solved in an ideal world, but which come to grips with practical administrative details and take account of social attitudes which might well be 'irrational' but nevertheless preclude particular types of solution.

If economists tackle practical problems in this way, they may well find themselves trespassing on the territory of other specialists, political scientists, sociologists or whatever. So be it. If they get deeply involved they would do well to call in expert assistance. The position of economists simply as positive scientists pre-supposes that there exists someone who is able to piece together the somewhat rickety planks of positive economics with the equally rickety planks from other disciplines to produce good policies. But this piecing together is itself a rather specialised job which economists are as well equipped as any to undertake, provided they bear constantly in mind that the houses they build are for others to inhabit as well, who may not always share the same tastes.

3

Prices, Markets and Planning

C. J. Bliss†

FOLLOWING on the Presidential Address the theme of Section F of the British Association this year is progress in economic science. It is an absorbing theme and it would not be difficult to devote a whole paper to a commentary on, and a response to, the arguments that the President has laid before us. The task which the present paper attempts is however a more prosaic one. This is to examine the development of the economist's understanding of the operation of a price system and, in particular, his understanding of the relation between a price system and the allocation of resources in an efficient and rational manner. The questions involved are questions of economic theory, although they impinge, but only after considerable modification, upon live debates about planning practice and economic organisation.

If there is general and continuing progress in economic science then we ought to observe its cumulative effect in this area, for the evaluation of the operation of a free and ideal price system is one of our subject's oldest concerns. Naturally, when one takes such a long view, it could hardly be denied seriously that there has been substantial progress, if only in the coherence and sophistication of theory. Yet if one were to count as progress only the provision of clear and definite answers to specific questions the rate of return on the time and energy that has been invested in these speculations would not perhaps seem very impressive. There has indeed been a great deal of anti-progress; not infrequently the consequence of more careful and imaginative theorising has been to teach us that things that we once thought we knew are not necessarily so. As knowledge and technique increase, and the ability of the economist to answer any specific questions expands, he understands more and more that the questions posed to him by the public are not simply the technical questions of

† Professor of Economics, University of Essex.

the kind that he can readily answer. Socrates was said to be wiser than all men because he knew that he knew nothing, which should remind economists that part of such wisdom as they have resides in their recognition that economic questions are very often complicated and involve many considerations and may admit of no straightforward answer. Nowhere more than with respect to economic issues does Josh Billings' dictum apply.

> 'The trouble with people is not that they don't know but that they know so much that ain't so.'

It would not be absurd to claim that economic science was progressing when economists 'established' that free trade is the best commercial policy and that it continued to progress when the claims of free trade as the universally best policy were systematically demolished. The first stage is the clear formulation and understanding of an argument; the second stage is the understanding of its limitations that arises from setting the favourable case against a background of examples of situations where a departure from free trade would be appropriate for one of the many reasons that economists now recognise. Economic theory should not be chided for a failure to produce simple, clear-cut and unchanging answers to large questions—that is not its business. On the other hand it is the business of economic theory to be of some help in dealing with the problems, including the intellectual problems, that the world presents, and here it frequently disappoints. No diagnosis is here offered—certainly no cure—but let us not forget that the disease is an ancient one and certainly not the product of the mathematical mode of reasoning. There is nothing new about treating economic reality by means of highly abstract models based upon recklessly simplified assumptions, as any reader of Ricardo's *Principles* knows. Again, we feel today, substituting suitable contemporary jargon, the bewilderment of Sir John Clapham's student of economics going over a hat factory.

> 'The difficulty of supplying illustrations had been brought home to him that day in the hat-factory. Whilst wandering among hollow copper cones to which hat-stuff miraculously adhered, shaping and pressing appliances, and dye vats, he had wondered—recalling the words with difficulty—whether "the increment of product due to

> the increase by a unit in the quantity of resources occupied in producing" hats is smaller (diminishing returns), or greater (increasing returns), "the greater is the quantity of resources so employed". How should he conceive his unit of resources? How his increment of product? No one had given him any help here. Must he fix on a standard hat or a standard quantity of standard hat-stuff? It is physical output, the Great Analytics repeat, with which these Laws deal; so something of the sort seems necessary. He appreciates the wisdom of talking not of hats but of commodities.'[1]

In this brilliant parody, economists are taken to task for refining theoretical concepts without relating them to reality and for developing systems that could not be related to reality. Sir John Clapham was writing 50 years ago in the *Economic Journal*, at a time when that journal did not contain any mathematical symbol in many an issue, and long before the foundation of the *Review of Economic Studies*. Whatever progress economic science may or may not make our doubts and worries about the subject are always much the same.

I. The Invisible Hand

The idea that resources are allocated in a desirable manner when the separate decisions of many individuals are co-ordinated by a price system is an old one. In its simplest form it is the notion of the Invisible Hand as proposed by Adam Smith in *The Wealth of Nations* almost two hundred years ago. Adam Smith was advocating the removal of the old mercantile controls and inhibitions to trade and arguing instead, although not entirely without qualification, for allowing the free play of self interest to determine the allocation of capital between different branches of trade and between home and foreign commerce. The public interest he believed was best promoted when men pursued their own self-interest in a free economy. Adam Smith's work was only a beginning of course; there is no detailed analysis of how free competition promotes the public interest to the greatest possible extent and, as a consequence of that lack of detailed analysis, the argument is not hedged about with the multitude of qualifications and provisos that we would now demand. Smith made

[1] Sir John Clapham, 'Of Empty Economic Boxes', *Economic Journal*, 1922.

his point by way of examples and thus arrived at a conclusion which subsequent 'progress' in economic science has severely undermined. Nonetheless we should not underestimate Adam Smith's achievement from the point of view of economic analysis. Although the ideas that he advanced were not his alone, to him belongs the credit for stating clearly, and in a form that was immediately assimilated, one of the most basic ideas of economics—this is that the behaviour of the economy is not correctly described as the sum of its component parts; it is not simply a giant version of the typical individual that makes it up. An economy might in principle allocate capital efficiently between its many competing uses although not one individual in that economy could care less whether capital was so allocated. That basic point remains true, and is not always understood even today, long after Adam Smith's advocacy of Laissez-Faire has been qualified out of existence.

Progress in the economist's understanding of the Invisible Hand was not rapid. The battle that Adam Smith had been fighting against the Mercantile System was already as good as won and with the demise of that system economists turned their attention elsewhere. It would not be very wrong to say that nothing of great significance happened in this area for about one hundred years. Further progress waited upon an intellectual breakthrough. Economists had to come to see the economic system as a collection of interrelated markets each one affecting the other—to develop, in our modern terminology, the concept of a general equilibrium—and this did not happen quickly or easily. By the time that it did happen (largely after 1870) the prevailing intellectual orientation of economists was in most cases reformist and interventionist (the mighty Pareto is an exception here) where it was not socialist. However, at this time even the critics of free-enterprise Capitalism for the most part paid it one compliment at least—they did not think that it was inefficient—that idea was to come later. Indeed one of the outcomes of the new marginal methods developed by Jevons, Menger, Marshall and others was to allow far more precise definitions of the proposition that resources are allocated under perfect-competition-equilibrium in an efficient and rational manner. By the end of the century we have clear statements of what is after all an elementary proposition—that in an ideal fully competitive equilibrium a position would be reached from which it would not be possible, given the inputs available, to increase the output of any commodity without sacrificing the output of another.

For suppose some such change were possible; this implies that it would be possible to increase the value of output produced by the economy net of all inputs used, all evaluated at the ruling equilibrium prices. This is clearly not possible unless that value can be increased for at least one producer, which is the same as saying that at least one producer could increase his profit at the original prices. This contradicts the assumption that all producers maximise profit.

To understand the conditions under which a theorem holds true is to understand the conditions under which it is false. It is no surprise then that the increased precision of general equilibrium ideas and marginal analysis was associated with a great growth in the understanding of the limitations of free competition. Thus Marshall was able to propound the proposition that increasing returns industries should be subsidised, even if he could not tell Sir John Clapham which these industries were. These cases could have been accumulated without limit and made the basis of a thoroughgoing critique of competitive Capitalism. That they were not has little to do with Economic Analysis and a lot to do with the fact that these economists were not basically hostile to the capitalist mode of economic organisation, and could see anyway no far-reaching manner of improving upon it.

II. The Theory of Socialism

Around the turn of the Century a very important intellectual advance took place and one that is central to the subject matter of this lecture. One of the uses to which the new marginal analysis could very readily be put was characterising an economic optimum, viewed here as an efficient state of the economy. It was not difficult to show that an economic optimum would require, for example, that the marginal return to any resource would be the same in every line of production in which that resource was employed. From there one can go on to show how this condition would be achieved in an ideal competitive economy in stationary equilibrium, because each producer would employ the resource up to the point where the marginal return was equal to the cost. But notice that this last point is no more than a gloss on the first, whose status is quite independent of it. The result that an efficient state of an economy requires that the marginal returns to resource inputs be equated in different lines of production has nothing to do with Capitalism, competition, market equilibrium, or indeed any mode of economic organisation; it is simply a piece of economic logic. Hence in particular, and the advance here discussed was the realisation of this point, it is a result which can be applied to characterise the optimum of an idealised socialist economy.

The economic theory of the Socialist Economy was developed between 1890 and 1910 by von Wieser, Pareto and Barone, none of whom by-the-way were socialists. The contribution was in two parts; it was shown that the optimal conditions for an idealised socialist economy were the same as those that had been derived for an equally idealised capitalist economy, and it was suggested that the socialist economy might make use of the price mechanism. This surely was the greatest of triumphs for the Invisible Hand—it was now proposed that it might guide a socialist economy. Furthermore, the suggestion did not come only from non-socialists. Between the two World Wars a debate arose about the economic possibility of Socialism, meaning in this context the question of whether the efficient allocation of resources could be achieved under the socialist form of organisation. When Hayek and von Mises and Robbins argued that an efficient allocation of resources could not be achieved without the institution of private property, and supported their claim with the argument that it would not be possible for the Ministry of Production (Barone's term for the planning authorities) to solve the millions of equations on whose solution such an allocation depended, Oskar Lange, the famous marxist economist whose training in bourgeois economics left nothing to be desired, was ready with the reply that it was only in a socialist economy that the ideal assumed conditions of the text-books would be obtained. The socialist economy, he argued, could make use of the price mechanism to solve the equations and could get the right solutions because the workings of the market in the socialist economy would not be hindered or distorted by such factors as monopoly and an unjust distribution of income.

Lange's contribution was important in that he gave a dynamic interpretation to the functioning of the price system. He saw the millions of equations as being solved by a 'trial and error' process based on the one that Walras had described in his *tâtonnement*—a system of moving prices on a trial and error basis, raising them when demand exceeded supply, lowering them when supply exceeded demand, until the balancing solution was obtained. This process, a product of the abstract speculation of an economic theorist, and bearing only the most tenuous relation to how real-life markets really function, could, according to Lange, be actually realised in the socialist economy.[2]

Looking back at this debate now it is hard to escape the feeling that the protagonists on both sides were debating, without realising it, about the Economics of Fairyland, and different Fairylands at that. It is fairly obvious that the Austrian writers and Robbins had idealised out of existence a number of gross features of the functioning of capitalist economies, notably their models always produced solutions where labour was fully employed, and their models settled down to a stationary equilibrium, while the World did neither of these things. What is perhaps less immediate, but equally true, is that Lange had abstracted out of existence the concrete problems of running and organising a socialist economy, problems which were then being tackled—but by methods that bore no relation at all to Lange's ideas—in the Soviet Union. It would be no exaggeration to say that both sides in the debate shared in common a naïve view about how the price mechanism functioned in capitalist economies, although they differed greatly in their evaluations of the outcome, and that Lange's complacency about the purely organisational problems could be attributed to his thinking that the socialist economy could take over existing market organisation and merely adapt it (e.g. by instructing producers to behave as perfect competitors, and causing incomes to depart from those that would rule under free competition).

III. Linear Programming

Let us take a step sideways now and look at a parallel development, the theory of linear programming. Linear programming is a method of solving problems where some objective is to be maximized or minimized, subject to various constraining conditions. In the linear programming case it is assumed that all the functions, the quantity to be maximised or minimised, and the various constraining functions, can be expressed in a linear form. As a simple example, consider an enterprise which has various resources at its disposal (labour,

[2] For an excellent account of this whole debate at much greater length see Abram Bergson, 'Socialist Economics' in *A Survey of Contemporary Economics* edited by Howard S. Ellis. Richard D. Irwin Inc., 1948.

equipment, materials inputs, etc.) which it can utilise to produce one output. The resources can be used in various different processes each of which produces the same output. This simple case suffices to illustrate the basic points. We suppose that a process is characterised by a list of the input requirements per unit output for each of the resources and that these are independent of the production level. This is a very restrictive assumption which excludes from consideration expenditures of the overhead type and also the case where unit variable input requirements fall as the level of production increases. In spite of this very strong linear assumption, linear programming has been found useful and widely applied. This is probably because variable input requirements are often approximately linear and overhead requirements can be ignored in the short-run, which is the relevant period in the case of many known successful applications. In the example, suppose that the aim of the problem is to produce the largest possible output from the given resources.

In contrast to the ideas outlined so far, linear programming theory sprang out of purely practical considerations. It was developed in the Soviet Union by the Russian mathematician Kantorovich, and later and independently in the West by Dantzig and Koopmans. The first successful applications were to transportation studies, problems of transporting goods from various sources to various destinations at minimum cost. With the rapid post-war development of electronic computers it is now established in many areas. Linear programming would not have held much excitement for economists as a method, although they would no doubt have employed it from time to time as a tool, had it not been for the observation that a linear programming solution has associated with it a set of variables, called dual or auxiliary variables, which have an interpretation as a certain kind of price. The interpretation of these prices is not difficult to understand and can be sketched in terms of the example.

If output is being maximized subject to the availability of certain resources then the largest output that can be obtained depends naturally upon the resources available. Hence, given a parcel of resources and a corresponding maximum output level, one can ask by how much the maximum level of output would be increased if a small addition were to be made to the quantity of one of the resources (to be specific consider labour) and the various process levels adjusted to obtain a new maximum output. The rate at which the maximum value increases as more labour is made available can be calculated and this number is the dual price of labour—or, in the Soviet terminology, the auxiliary variable associated with labour. Mathematicians would object to this explanation of the interpretation to be attached to the dual variables of a linear programme but the refinements that they would want to add are not germane to the present discussion. Furthermore, the simple explanation has the advantage of indicating the close relationship of dual variables to the marginal coefficients of standard economic analysis, which relationship is often obscured by precise definitions and presentations of dual variables. If one is maximising (or minimising) an objective, the level at which that objective is maximised will depend upon the parameters of the problem (in our example the given resource supplies) and to each parameter therefore one can attach a marginal return to increasing it, and this, essentially is what a linear programming dual variable comprises. Notice that this is a very simple notion and there is no very compelling reason looking at these marginal valuations of resources why they should be called 'prices'. However, some of the properties of linear programming dual variables make them look very like prices. As an example consider the situation where the solution to our problem of maximising output from given resources has been obtained and with it the associated values of the dual variables. Suppose now that a new process is under consideration which might be added to the processes originally available. The question is whether this new process will be of any use—i.e., whether the addition of it to the family of processes will make any difference to the solution of the problem. This question can be answered with the greatest of ease by some calculations of an accounting type using the dual variables to weight the resource inputs. The new process must be included in the optimal solution if and only if the resources required by this process to produce one unit of output cost, using the dual variables as cost coefficients, less than the value of the output. One can therefore conclude that in some sense 'prices', in fact a whole system of prices, is embedded beneath the surface of every economic problem that can be expressed as a linear programme.

The foregoing result is one that economists have found extraordinarily impressive and to which even ideological overtones have attached themselves on both sides of what used to be called the Iron Curtain. It stands as an example of the understandable fact that a really good discovery is worth making at least twice, for the discovery is merely Barone's discovery in a slightly new context. Barone it will be remembered argued that a socialist economy if it were to achieve the efficient and rational allocation of resources of the economic textbooks' descriptions of the ideal market economy would have to satisfy the very same relations (conceived in his case as marginal relations) that characterised this state. Hence, according to Barone, 'prices', including rents and capital charges, could be associated with the desirable state, giving an ideal set of socialist accounting prices. In the unlikely circumstance that the socialist economy was a completely linear one, the prices obtained by Barone would be linear programming dual prices; in that sense there was nothing basically new about the discovery, but because it was made in the context of linear programming the discovery was now perceived by a different set of people.

IV. The Formation of Prices

So far we have followed the trail of the idea of the Invisible Hand as it developed through 150 years of economic analysis. We have seen how the idea that there existed an association between the rational allocation of resources and a price system was increasingly refined, purged of purely extraneous interpretations such as any necessary association with private ownership of property, and rigorously proved. Had the questions stood still the answers would seem to have advanced a very great distance. Where Adam Smith had been content to take the detailed workings of the price mechanism for granted economists had later asked how precisely the mechanism functioned; in particular, how did the system find an equilibrium state if it started initially with markets out of equilibrium? This was a question to which Walras had addressed himself, and the answer that he had been able to obtain, though brilliant, was only in terms of a highly artificial account of the price adjustment process and one which, in essence, threw the essential problem 'out of the window'. Walras' idea, embodied in his *tâtonnement* which means 'groping', was to study the case where exchanges only took place at market clearing prices. Thus one could imagine an auctioneer calling out a complete list of prices for all outputs and inputs and counting up the supplies and demands which these prices called forth. If the prices were wrong—i.e., not all markets cleared—he would try again until he found an equilibrium set. Only then would the offers to supply and demand become actual trades. The English economist, Edgeworth, had a similar idea with his notion of 'recontracting'.

Walras' idea has been enormously influential. This may seem odd for such an extreme idealisation of trade and exchange, but it is not in fact surprising. One has to remember that the complete price system of an economy, involving as it does the actions and responses of many economic agents, is a system about as complicated as any which a science has attempted to study in detail. If we are to succeed at all in understanding how it works, and in particular in understanding its dynamics, then pretty extreme simplification will be the order of the day. Another reason why Walras' idea has been so influential is that it works, meaning that using it one can obtain some results on when the adjustment of prices will lead to equilibrium and when they may not. These results are somewhat disappointing but hungry men do not usually grumble about a meal. There is a tendency for ideas that lead to results, however slight, to win over ideas that do not—the Gossens Law of economic thought.

Recently there has been a growing realisation by economists that the idea of the Walrasian auctioneer may be more than over-simpified —it may be dangerously misleading. To posit an auctioneer is to put aside questions about competition and how it operates, about the definition of a market, and about the laws governing the formation of prices when these are set by the traders themselves. This is appropriate where trade is carried out on organised commodity or financial exchanges but it is evident that the proportion of trade that is transacted in this manner, say in Britain, is a small fraction of the gross annual turnover of all traders. For the rest of trade the prices at which trade takes place are made by the traders themselves, meaning that at least one side sets a price. This has a number of implications. One of the things which an organised commodity exchange does is that it announces 'the going price' and all interested can then know what that price is. Furthermore, and it is only in this case that a 'going' price is of any use, everyone understands that they can buy and sell freely at the going price.

Notice that this is not just the old point about whether individual buyers and sellers can influence the going price; imperfect competition and monopoly. It might be useful to consider a specific example here, an individual selling a fairly normal house in a large city. In such a case the seller might be regarded from one point of view as a perfect competitor. There are a large number of broadly similar houses sold in the city each year. What these houses will in general realise will be affected only to a negligible extent by whether this one seller decides to put his house up for sale or not. The seller may have in his mind a price for his house which he could estimate from knowledge of what somewhat similar houses have realised, or an estate agent might estimate for him. But he cannot know for sure what the right price is. Furthermore, on examination, the relevant consideration is not a right price but rather a probability of sale within a specified time period. There is really a whole range of reasonable prices for a house and the price chosen within that range will determine how quickly on average the house will sell. If the house is on a large estate of exactly similar houses the range will be narrow, if it is rather a unique house the range will be broad. In this last case one might say that the crucial point is that the market is 'thin' and that going prices only get established on 'thick' markets. This is correct. Organised commodity exchanges, such as wheat exchanges, are very 'thick'. The London Stock Exchange, to consider a classic example, quotes many shares for which it establishes a clear market price which most buyers and sellers could take as a datum. On the other hand the market that it makes for many of the shares that it quotes is rather 'thin'.

Continuing with the example of the market for houses, it will be seen that the manner in which such a market responds to change is different from the usual description to be found in textbooks, and the one implicit in the Walrasian process. Suppose that there is a fall in the demand for houses in the city. This becomes evident only slowly as sellers find that it is taking longer to sell than they had expected. However, eventually prices will come down as sellers seek to make a sale fairly promptly in the new conditions. In the meantime some houses will have been bought and sold at 'wrong' prices, meaning prices which do not correspond to equilibrium in the long run. To contrast this account with the operation of the idealised auctioneer-guided market, notice that in the case of the latter adjustment proceeds in two stages. First a uniform market price is established and then that price is adjusted until the market clears. Basic to this account is the view that the forces that bring the prices at which different transactions take place into line operate much more quickly than the forces that bring the general level of trading prices to the market clearing level. Which account is appropriate will depend upon the extent to which information about the prices which various traders are offering or demanding flows freely throughout the market. The commodity exchange is only the extreme case of a market in which the goods transacted are very homogeneous, so that a trader knows that information on other prices is immediately relevant to his transactions, and in which information on trading prices is nearly perfect. The market for houses is at the opposite extreme, sellers and buyers are badly informed, and the forces that pull different sellers' prices more or less into line, and the forces that pull down the general level of prices when there is a glut of houses for sale, are the same forces. A house-owner who has failed to sell his house at the price for which he had hoped usually has no clear idea whether the cause lies in his having asked a particularly high price relative to the prices asked for closely competing houses or whether his price is much the same as the prices asked by others but these are all too high to clear the market. In either case he will have to reduce his asking-price but the rate at which he will reduce it would be affected if he knew which cause lay behind his failure to sell.

A market which has many features in common with the market for houses is the labour market. Just as a house-owner does not place his house on a perfect house exchange which then gives to him the right price and guarantees a buyer at that price; so a man searches for a job looking at once both for an opening for the kind of labour that he offers and the right price for that labour.[3] It seems likely that a view of the labour market parallel to this one lies at the bottom of the definition of involuntary unemployment proposed by J. M. Keynes in Chapter 2 of the *General Theory*, a definition which has long puzzled students of economics and which is ignored in most presentations of Keynes' ideas. It will be remembered that Keynes distinguished between the effect of a general rise in the prices of wage goods on the supply of labour seeking work and the effect of a general fall in money wages. In a world of perfect information it is hard to see any rationale for this distinction, but where information is very imperfect it is possible that the two types of change are not perceived in the same way by individual workers or groups of workers. A fall in the money wage rate may be mistaken by each group of workers for a decline in their relative position, even though in fact all groups might

[3] For a fuller development of these ideas see G. J. Stigler, 'Information in the Labor Market', *Journal of Political Economy*, Supplement, October 1962. Also A. A. Alchian, 'Information Costs, Pricing and Resource Unemployment', in *Microeconomic Foundations of Employment and Inflation Theory*, edited by Edmund S. Phelps, Macmillan and Co., Ltd., 1971.

have suffered a similar decline, while on the other hand a rise in the prices of wage goods, affecting as it does markets where information is more freely diffused, may be correctly seen as affecting mainly the going real return to labour in general.

V. Expectations and the Future

A careful consideration of markets where there is no auctioneer, and where the diffusion of information is far from perfect, has revealed that the response of such a market to a change in the general level of demand is different from the response of a Walrasian market controlled by an auctioneer. In particular transactions will typically take place at the 'wrong' prices following a demand shift. Buyers and sellers have to adjust their estimates of the 'right' price partly as a result of experience of trying to buy or sell at current prices. This was illustrated by the discussion of the effect of a fall in the demand for houses where prices came down only because sellers learn by experience that their expectations of how long they will have to wait for a buyer are proved too optimistic and they then lower their asking prices. However this is only half the story. Just how far the prices will come down will depend upon how many sellers decide that they still want to sell in the new conditions once they have adjusted their estimates of 'right prices'. An important factor here will be their expectations. Were they firmly convinced that prices had come down, or their rate of increase been slowed down, permanently they might shrug their shoulders and sell, but in-so-far as they regard the fall as temporary they may hold off until the market picks up, which of course it may not do. As far as the current going price is concerned sellers and buyers do receive some guidance from 'the price system', conceiving that in the broadest sense, although it is not, as has been argued, the perfect guidance of the wheat exchange. Where, however, the future is concerned the price system gives no direct guidance at all.

It is here, when we come to consider the future, that the Walrasian scheme is most deceptive. Although he attempted the merest sketch of a dynamic economy the formulation adopted by Walras was, like virtually all precise economic analysis in the nineteenth century, and like a great deal since, essentially static. It was the economic theory appropriate to an unchanging economy, and it allowed insufficient role for expectations and uncertainty about the future. Because to take the Walrasian model, where there is an auctioneer for each market, and apply it to an economy that is changing over time is a translation of the original model, let us ask what form the translation would have to take to preserve the original argument as far as possible intact. Since jam today and jam tomorrow are both in some sense commodities there would have to be market for each type of jam and auctioneers to announce present prices for each type of jam. This corresponds to a futures market such as those operated for some commodities. But the coverage of futures markets in our economy is negligible. In the absence of futures markets individuals take a view about future developments, but in this case there is a complete absence of what economists, borrowing engineering terminology, have called 'negative feedback'. The price system regarded as a regulator operates through feedback; if demand runs ahead of supply prices rise more rapidly and curtail the growth of demand. When however there are no markets there is no direct feedback. What takes its place is the unguided operation of unchecked expectations. The Invisible Hand is here not merely invisible.

This discussion can be related to the ideas of J. M. Keynes' *General Theory*, particularly as interpreted recently by economic theorists. We consider the classic question of what the effect will be on an economy of an increase in the desire to forgo current consumption and save. Typically individuals who save would like to increase their consumption at some future date. If therefore there were to be a full set of futures markets for consumer goods these would experience increased activity just as the current markets were experiencing a fall in demand. The usual price regulators would then operate—current consumption would become cheaper relatively to future consumption and this would discourage some of the saving. Also making provision through investment to supply future consumption would become more profitable and demand would be switched to the investment sector, and labour would be redeployed there to some extent. In the absence of forward markets for consumption goods the effect of an increased desire to save is different—the demand removed from current markets simply disappears and this has the effect of setting in process the multiplier fall in income that Keynesian theory has familiarised us with. The operation of the price system allows unemployment and excess capacity to arise.[4]

[4] For a stimulating and readable presentation of these ideas at greater length, see Axel Leijonhufvud, 'Keynes and the Classics', *Institute of Economic Affairs, Occasional Papers* 30, London, 1969.

VI. The Theory of Socialism Again

Finally consider once again the problem of planning a socialist economy. It has been shown how, historically, economists believed that they understood the workings of the price system and that the workings of the price system, when operating ideally, would bring about an efficient allocation of resources without the necessity for a superhuman planning organisation able to solve many thousands of equations. Even a radical like Oskar Lange assumed that the apparatus for market planning existed already in a capitalist economy and that it was only a matter of adjusting the distribution of income and putting the machine in order. He supposed further that the Walrasian method of searching for the market-clearing prices by means of a *tâtonnement* would be stable—prices would converge to an equilibrium configuration. Since, given the complexity of the system, it is by no means obvious that this will happen, one might ask why Lange was not worried about this problem. As far as one can tell his failure to worry himself about the possibility of instability is to be attributed to the view that he was only proposing the adaptation of an existing system, which seemed to be stable enough. If this was Lange's view then it is of course a wholly illegitimate manner of disposing of the problem of the stability of price adjustment, for it begs the question of whether the Walrasian scheme does describe the formation of the prices that we observe in the world. In fact economic theorists now know that there is no general principle which guarantees the stability of Walras' *tâtonnement* although there is equally no reason why it might not turn out to be stable.

It has been suggested that our understanding of how the price system operates is extremely imperfect, that the Walrasian theory of price formation and price adjustment is at best a poor representation of a great deal that goes on, and that it is highly doubtful whether an invisible hand operates through the system unless it be crudely and uncertainly.

An implication of this is that to propose that socialist planning be carried out according to the textbook scheme of competitive, decentralised, price-guided behaviour is to suggest the creation of new institutions and behaviour patterns that are not ready to hand in any economy.[5]

[5] For amplification of this point in the context of the Soviet Union, see Michael Ellman, *Soviet Planning Today*, Department of Applied Economics Occasional Paper 25, Cambridge, 1971.

This last point of course does not refute the claim that socialist economies would do well to emulate the abstract ideal of price-guided decentralisation, but it does put the onus of proof on those arguing for this idea rather more strongly. It has been shown that it is not correct to claim that there is any necessary connection between the price system, here taken to mean a system where decisions are guided by the principle of profit maximization, and efficient resource allocation. The conditions for efficient resource allocation might be achieved through a price system, but they could equally be achieved by alternative methods. There is for example no inherent reason why prices should be formed by central planners and quantitative decisions taken by enterprises as the market type model proposes. Recent work has brought this point out very strongly because economists have become more and more interested in planning under conditions of decreasing costs (increasing returns to scale). The achievement of efficient allocation under these conditions is very difficult and the work undertaken so far has only gone part of the way towards solving the problem, even at the abstract level. But what has emerged already is the conclusion that a price-market system is very unsuitable for this problem. Systems which aim to achieve the necessary marginal conditions directly by quantitative allocation or rationing of inputs do much better. All this of course is still the Economics of Fairyland. The conclusions for actual economic organisation are a long way off and have yet to be worked out. But it is very sobering to think that after all this time what looked like one of the basic theorems of economic knowledge, the intimate logical connection between a system of perfect markets and the efficient allocation of resources, is no more than an example.

4

Recent Improvements in Official Economic Statistics

L. S. Berman†

I. Introduction

THIS PAPER is concerned with recent developments in official economic statistics and is devoted mainly to reviewing the progress made during the last five years or so. It describes some of the more important statistical problems which have been tackled and solved, and also those for which solutions still remain to be found. The main role of the government statistician in this area is to produce good and up to date statistics, which are sufficiently reliable to be used as a basis for assessing economic developments and for taking decisions. The final section of this paper considers how successful official economic statistics are in meeting these requirements.

Before beginning this review, I think it is worthwhile to take a rather longer look back over time than five years as the present structure of official economic statistics reflects developments over a long period. In particular, its origins can be traced back to a number of important policy decisions and events over the past thirty years. From the point of view of this paper the most important landmarks in official economic statistics seem to be the following. (A more comprehensive list is given in the appendix to this paper.)

(a) The White Paper on Employment Policy published in 1944 (Cmd. 6527). This laid down the broad lines along which official economic statistics should be developed in the post-war years.

(b) The Statistics of Trade Act (1947). This reflected the recommendations of the White Paper on Employment Policy and the Reports of the committees on the census of production and distribution (Cmd. 6687 and Cmd. 6764) and provided the general legal basis for the collection of official statistics and for obtaining the information necessary for the appreciation of economic trends.

(c) The Report of the Verdon-Smith Committee in 1954 (Cmd. 9276). This concluded *inter alia* that the census of production was of

† Assistant Director, Central Statistical Office.

little direct use to industry and recommended that the burden of censuses on the business community should be reduced.

(d) Mr. Macmillan's 'Bradshaw speech' in 1956 in which he said that 'some of our statistics are too late to be as useful as they ought to be and that we were always, as it were, looking up the train in last year's Bradshaw'. This speech was followed by the publication in January 1957 of the first official quarterly estimates of national income and expenditure and by the development of quarterly balance of payments statistics.

(e) The Report of the Radcliffe Committee on the Working of the Monetary System in 1959 (Cmnd. 827) which emphasised the need for financial statistics and led to the development of sophisticated annual and quarterly financial accounts and improved statistics of money supply and banking.

(f) The Report from the Estimates Committee on the Government Statistical Services in 1966. This was mainly concerned with the organisation of government statistics and, in particular, with the role of the Central Statistical Office. But it was also conerned with the use of computers and the need for having detailed (micro) statistics by area, industry, occupation and by commodity group. The report emphasised the need for the Government Statistical Service to provide information that industry requires and to this extent reversed the recommendations of the Verdon-Smith Committee report of 1954.

Repercussions of all these events are still being felt. For example the Estimates Committee's recommendations on organisation and on micro-statistics are still being followed through and the quarterly national income and balance of payments accounts are still being improved. References are continually being made to Mr. Macmillan's 'Bradshaw' speech when commentators discuss the timeliness of official statistics.

In considering developments in economic statistics it is convenient to distinguish between macro and micro statistics. Macro-economic statistics relate to general developments in the economy as a whole (e.g. gross domestic product, personal income and saving, total unemployment); whereas micro statistics are concerned with such things as detailed industry, commodity and area figures.

II. Macro-economic statistics

There have been no really spectacular developments in macro-economic statistics in recent years: the broad framework of the central economic statistics produced by the Central Statistical Office (CSO) is very similar now to what it was five years ago. The National Income Blue Book for 1970, for example, looks very much the same as that published in 1965. The main difference is that the later version contains figures of net capital stock at current replacement cost analysed by sector and type of asset; a more complete sector analysis of the financial accounts; and a table bringing together the three measures of gross domestic product at constant prices and an arithmetic average of them. These new features were introduced in the Blue Book for 1966 and no really significant changes have been made to the Blue Book since them.

The Balance of Payments Pink Book, on the other hand, has changed in appearance over the past five years. There have been important changes in presentation: attention is now focused once again on the current balance and on the total currency flow and not on the basic balance and monetary movements. In addition, there are now comprehensive estimates of the United Kingdom's external balance sheet, and analyses of the financing of overseas investment, trade credit extended and received, and of the overseas earnings of financial institutions and the City. There has also been a considerable increase in the amount of information shown about the invisible earnings and payments.

On the whole, the improvements that have been made to macro economic statistics in recent years have been mainly of a detailed nature. They can be divided into six broad categories.

(a) A number of the published series are now further disaggregated. For example, there is now much more detail shown in the quarterly national income and balance of payments accounts published in *Economic Trends*.

(b) New and more representative series have been introduced to take the place of less satisfactory series. One example is that new series are introduced, from time to time, into the monthly Index of Industrial Production. Another is that returns from certain Commonwealth insurance companies, which up to 1967 were excluded from the figures, are now included in the quarterly analysis of investments by insurance companies published in *Financial Statistics*.

(c) Completely new series have been introduced and published. For example, quarterly estimates of real output were published as part of the regular quarterly national income article for the first time in April 1966, and quarterly estimates of output per head and of labour costs per unit of output for groups of industries covered by the Index of Industrial Production were introduced in October 1968. Other examples are the new quarterly figures of money supply, domestic credit expansion and of the personal sector's holdings of liquid assets. More recently in April 1971 an experimental monthly index of wages and salaries per unit of manufacturing output was introduced.

(d) More series are now seasonally adjusted and revalued at constant prices. This is particularly true of the quarterly national income and balance of payments series. For example, seasonally adjusted central government and local authority current accounts were published for the first time in October 1969.

(e) There has been a conscious effort to improve the presentation and hence the usefulness of official economic statistics. For example, the October issue of *Economic Trends*, which presents long runs of quarterly national income data, has since 1969, included tables which give useful percentages derived from the National Income Blue Book. From 1970, these have been supplemented by 'growth triangles', which show for a number of important series the percentage rates of change between any two years. Another example is the publication of the Index of Industrial Production to one decimal place instead of to the nearest whole number. (Quarterly figures to one decimal place were published for the first time in 1967 and the monthly figures in 1970.) Other examples may be found in *Financial Statistics* where a great deal of effort has gone into making the rather complicated financial statistics more easily understood. Another example of improved presentation is that from October 1970 the personal savings ratio and real personal disposable income are shown as separate series in the main quarterly national income tables. A somewhat different development, which falls within this category, is the publication each month (from November 1970) of a list of the release dates of the major economic series. This list is published by the CSO in the middle of the month by press notice and gives details of the publication dates of series to be issued in the following month. The list is also published in *Economic Trends*.

(f) There has been in the past three or four years a renewed emphasis on producing more up to date and timely economic statistics.

In spite of these improvements much remains to be done. There are still large discrepancies between the two estimates of the gross domestic product at current prices based on expenditure data and income data, and between the three estimates of real output based on income, expenditure and output data. The balancing item in the balance of payments accounts, representing the net total of errors and omissions arising throughout the accounts, still persists. And the large statistical discrepancy between estimates of personal saving obtained directly by aggregating transactions in assets and liabilities and indirectly as a residual in the personal income and expenditure account has not been eliminated.

Problems of timeliness

The CSO has been giving increased emphasis in recent years to speeding up the publication of major economic indicators.

All figures are to some extent out of date. The latest published figure in a quarterly series, based on data collected quarterly, will be, on average, something like three months out of date (or 5 months late, if comparisons are made with the centre of the quarter). This is because the basic information cannot be collected until the quarter has been completed, and time must be allowed for the returns to be submitted, processed and published. Delays can be reduced by shortening the reference period. This is, of course, the reason why during the mid-1950's, even before Mr. Macmillan's 'Bradshaw' speech, it became necessary to consider compiling quarterly estimates of the national income accounts. Not only did the annual estimates provide no guide to developments during the year, but even the provisional estimates for the latest calendar year were rather unreliable.

We are trying to speed up the publication of statistics in a number of ways:

(a) By cutting down the delay between the compilation of figures and their publication. One simple device, which has been adopted, is to issue a press notice as soon as the figures become available. If the figures appear normally in a monthly publication (e.g. the *Monthly Digest of Statistics* or *Economic Trends*) this device can save two or three weeks.

(b) By tightening up administrative procedures within the CSO, the Business Statistics Office (BSO) and other Departments.

(c) By speeding up the response from industry. Various means have been resorted to, particularly by the BSO. For example, by identifying key respondents and making a special effort to chase them up, by making use of telephone calls instead of writing letters, by visiting firms, advertising in the press and giving talks to company accountants and secretaries (the form-fillers).

(d) By computerising existing procedures. This has been done with some success, for example, with the Index of Industrial Production. Previously the Index was put together in the CSO by clerical methods, but now all the component series are held on the computer and two to three days are saved in the calculation of the monthly Index. Plans are now far advanced to fully computerise the processing of the underlying basic short period production statistics at the BSO.

(e) By making preliminary estimates for the latest period by imputing from early statistical returns, or by estimating quarterly figures from two months data.

(f) By experimenting with what might be called 'leading indicators' as an early guide to movements in the series which one is trying to measure. For example, by using up to date figures of fuel consumption or man hours worked as a guide to movements in the Index of Industrial Production.

It may be noted that (a) to (d) are basically administrative methods for speeding up the publication of figures, whereas (e) and (f) are statistical methods aimed at providing additional preliminary estimates. All the various methods, of course, overlap and interact. For example, computerising existing procedures (d) facilitates the introduction of imputation techniques for providing new preliminary estimates (e) and the simple device of a press notice (a) can save additional time.

All these various methods are being used to varying extents to produce earlier estimates of the national income accounts, the balance of payments accounts and the Index of Industrial Production. Provisional quarterly estimates of national income and expenditure are now released to the press about twelve weeks after the end of the quarter to which they relate (and about five weeks before the more complete figures are published in *Economic Trends*). Previously, the press notice was first published with the more complete figures two to three weeks later than this. Similarly, the quarterly balance of payments figures are now released to the press nine to ten weeks in arrears and three to four weeks before the detailed figures appear in *Economic Trends*. Another development is that along with the monthly overseas trade figures, estimates of the 'going rate' for net invisibles and of the overseas trade figures on a balance of payments basis are now published. Thus, there is now a running monthly estimate, some ten to fifteen days in arrears, of the two components making up the balance of payments on current account.

The Index of Industrial Production has also been speeded up. By improving administrative procedures and having a slightly earlier cut-off date and by computerising the processing of data in the CSO, from the beginning of 1971 the Index has been coming out about one week earlier than hitherto. (Although the postal strike upset the publication dates from February to April.)

None of these developments is in any way spectacular, but they represent steady progress. This is, in fact, the story of macro-economic statistics in recent years.

Comparisons are frequently made with the speed with which the Americans and Canadians produce their statistics. The Office of Business Economics in the United States, for example, produces estimates of the quarterly national income accounts very much earlier than we do. The main reason for this is that their accounts are based very largely on monthly data, so it is possible to make early estimates of outturn for a calendar quarter on the basis of one or two months' figures. In the case of capital expenditure, they also take account of businessmen's investment intentions forecasts. The national income data for the United Kingdom, on the other hand, are based very largely on quarterly data. But in some cases the estimates, for example of consumers' expenditure, are based on monthly data on retail sales and other indicators so it has been possible to provide very early estimates. From the middle of 1969, preliminary estimates of consumers' expenditure have been published one month after the quarter to which they relate. From the beginning of 1971 these estimates have been issued two weeks earlier by press notice. Similarly, estimates of exports and imports of goods and services (at constant prices and seasonally adjusted), because they are based largely on monthly figures of overseas trade, have been published four weeks after the period to which they relate in *Economic Trends* since January 1971. To go further than this and publish more timely estimates of gross fixed capital formation and investment in stocks would mean changing substantially existing sources and methods of estimation.

The United States produces its monthly Index of Industrial Production very much more quickly than we do. The estimate for the latest month appears fifteen days after the period to which it relates. This is because the estimate of the Index for the latest month is based almost entirely on man-hours worked in a particular week in the month, with allowances for strikes, holidays, etc., and for underlying changes in output per man hour. The calculation is highly judgematical, but is backed up by a sophisticated computerised operation and it seems to work well. Checks on accuracy are made against actual figures of output or deliveries which may become available monthly, quarterly or annually, and also at five-yearly intervals. The CSO is aiming at further speeding up the publication of the Index of Industrial Production and is experimenting with imputation methods and leading indicators including using figures of man hours worked as a partial indicator. Having the individual series of the Index on the CSO computer is facilitating this work.

Reliability

It may be argued that too much effort is being put into improving the timeliness of series and not enough into improving their quality and reliability. What economic model builders and forecasters want are not up to date estimates of the latest position, which may be unreliable, but reliable time series stretching back over a fairly long period. But the two aims—reliability and timeliness—are not really alternatives. Our aim is to achieve both. Speeding up the flow of statistics by tightening up administrative procedures, by getting in returns more quickly, by computerising existing procedures, makes it possible to produce statistics more quickly without any loss of reliability. However, using statistical techniques to make provisional estimates by using imputation methods, leading indicators, earlier cut off points, etc., does not reduce the reliability of the whole series, but only the reliability of the latest one or two points in the series.

Many users of statistics complain about revisions to statistical series and confuse revisions with unreliability. But revisions do not necessarily mean bad statistics.

There are several types of revisions:

(a) New series become available (e.g. new series within the index of Industrial Production). The question arises, when should the new series be introduced and how far back should they be carried? They could be held up and introduced at one time, but this could lead to very large revisions and for a long way back when the changes were made. In my view it is best to introduce new series as and when they become available so as to minimise revisions. It used to be CSO practice to introduce new series into the Index only when the series was re-based, but this has now been changed.

(b) More complete coverage. Many series are based on statistics collected either both monthly and quarterly, or both quarterly and annually. Generally, the more frequently collected figures are based on a smaller sample and are less reliable than the less frequently collected series and this often means revisions have to be made to the series when the more complete statistics become available. For example, the quarterly estimates of capital expenditure by manufacturing industry for 1969 were revised following the annual census of production for that year. With regard to the Index of Industrial Production, which is based largely on monthly and quarterly series, the introduction of the new system of industrial statistics (described on pages 74 and 75) may lead to more revisions than we have had in the past, not because the monthly indicators will be worse, but because the quarterly estimates will be better.

(c) From time to time full-scale censuses are taken. These provide firmly based statistics for the period in question and often necessitate revisions to the previously published annual and quarterly series, which are based on sample data. The results of the census of distribution for 1966 and of the motor trades inquiry for 1967, for example, led to fairly substantial revisions being made to the estimates of consumers' expenditure in the National Income Blue Book for 1970.

(d) More complete returns. Obviously, the later the cut-off point for an inquiry the more reliable the series is. Here, the statistician has to make a judgement between having more complete returns and more timely data. Up to about ten years ago 'preliminary estimates' of the Index of Industrial Production and of retail sales were published. These estimates were obtained from early returns. This practice was abandoned, however, when it was found that the margins of error of the preliminary estimates were too large to be acceptable. The key to the problem is that users, for example, of the Index are seeking to identify very small month to month changes. The difference between a 1 per cent and a 4 per cent annual growth rate is less than 0·3 per cent a month but the average error in the estimated monthly change is much larger than this.

(e) New seasonal adjustment factors, which are generally introduced once a year, sometimes lead to different interpretations of the underlying movement in the series. This has led to criticisms of the monthly Index of Industrial Production. Nowadays, because the data are held on the CSO computer the seasonal adjustment factors can be re-worked once every six months to see how the seasonal adjustment factors are changing.

(f) Mistakes may be discovered in the basic source material. This may necessitate adjustments to not only the latest figures but also to back figures. Perhaps the most notorious recent example of this was the discovery of a consistent under recording of exports in early 1969 which led to the figures for exports back to 1964 being revised. A less important example noted in the National Income Blue Book for 1970 was that the item Expenditure by foreign tourists, etc., in the U.K. had previously omitted in error expenditure by overseas students in the U.K.

(g) Changes may be made to the classification of statistics. For example, the Standard Industrial Classification is revised once every ten years.

For all these reasons revisions have to be made to published statistical series. Official statisticians are, of course, not keen on revising published series as it makes life more difficult for users of statistics; it can also tend to reduce public confidence in official statistics. But it is our job to produce the best estimates and if this means revisions, so be it. On the other hand, I would be the first to admit that many revisions made to official statistics are unnecessary in the sense that they are well within the margin of error of the particular estimate. Unfortunately, it is very difficult to control revisions when we are dealing with macro economic aggregates like consumers expenditure, GNP, etc. This is because the estimates are often built up bit by bit from information obtained from different statistical inquiries, the results of which are generally published independently by Departments. A revision for example, to capital expenditure by the iron and steel industry may be important in relation to the capital expenditure by that industry, but in relation to total capital expenditure by all industries and services it may be tiny and in relation to the GNP trivial. But the revision has to be made. Another example, where it is difficult to control revisions, is when the estimate is obtained as a residual (e.g. personal saving). On the other hand, there are sometimes small revisions made which, while they may improve slightly the accuracy of individual estimates, may be considered too trivial to be included in say, the Blue Book. We are now considering the introduction of some form of *de minimis* rule under which revisions of past figures below a certain amount would not be made.

A single estimate of the gross domestic product

As has been pointed out above, the United Kingdom national income accounts contain two alternative estimates of the gross domestic product at current prices, and three different estimates of the GDP at constant prices. From the point of view of the user of statistics this is a serious limitation. It is not possible in practice to relate precisely changes in income, expenditure and output and to measure uniquely changes in output from one quarter to the next or indeed from one year to the next. However, all statistically advanced countries have problems of this kind.

Some countries avoid highlighting the statistical discrepancy in their national income accounts by the technical device of valuing expenditure on the gross domestic product only at market prices in the main tables so that direct comparisons cannot so readily be made with the estimates of income generated which by definition are at factor cost. Japan, United States, Australia and Sweden are among the countries that publish a statistical discrepancy between two independent estimates of the gross national product. On the other hand, Western Germany, Netherlands and France are among the countries that publish a unique estimate of the gross national product. Canada has a discrepancy in its national income accounts, but distributes it equally between the expenditure and income estimates. (Incidentally, most economists in Britain do not realise that only two or three countries in Europe compile and publish quarterly national income accounts.)

Our policy is to publish the best estimate of each of the various items of expenditure and income which enter into the gross national product. When all the estimates have been prepared, assembled and aggregated, there is inevitably a discrepancy (i.e. the residual error) between the two independent estimates of the gross domestic product. At this 'balancing' stage in compiling the national income accounts, all the various estimates are scrutinised carefully to see whether in the light of past experience any of them can be adjusted in such a way as to reduce the residual error. For the latest two or three years the estimates are not as reliable as those for earlier years so there is scope for adjustment. However, there are limits to which the figures can be adjusted and it is our practice to go to this limit before publishing the two independent estimates of national income and national expenditure. Allowances would be made for likely errors in the figures provided by Departments and, where appropriate adjustments would be made for, say, a dock strike to allow for differences in timing between the recording of exports and changes in stocks recorded by manufacturers. However, after a period of five years or so, estimates of individual series have become firmer and are probably more securley based on a recent benchmark census so that the scope for adjustment and for reducing the residual error in the national income accounts becomes correspondingly smaller.

The broad reasons for the statistical discrepancy in the national income accounts are reasonably well known and were pointed out as long ago as in the earliest quarterly national income articles published in *Economic Trends* in 1957 and in the first edition of *Sources and Methods* in 1956. The problem is essentially one of producing reliable series of income and expenditure statistics which are not only consistent over time but also consistent with one another. Because different sources of information are used for the different series, there are inevitably differences in coverage, valuation and timing. In addition, there are bound to be reporting and sampling errors.

Most of the estimates in the national income accounts are made up from many hundreds of thousands of individual transactions. Consumers' expenditure, for example, represents the sum total of transactions by tens of millions of consumers at over one million outlets. We cannot (and would not want to) count all these individual transactions in order to build up the national income accounts, so we have to resort to sampling. One problem is that many firms do not keep quarterly records of their activities. By and large, it is only the larger firms (but not all of them) that do so. A further problem is that many of the quarterly figures provided by firms are provisional estimates which may be revised when audited accounts become available after the end of the accounting year. It is particularly difficult to measure quarterly, for example, changes in the value of work in progress, capital expenditure and gross trading profits. Information obtained for items such as these in quarterly inquiries can only be provisional.

Because it is generally the larger firms that are approached in the quarterly inquiries, the sampling scheme will not be random and may not be representative. More representative figures, however, are collected when there is a follow-up annual inquiry. But in order to minimise the form filling burden on firms the smallest firms are either excluded from, or are only partly covered by, these annual inquiries.

It is sometimes suggested that an audit should be taken, from time to time, to check the national income accounts in order to pinpoint the errors in them. In fact something like this is done when a full scale census of distribution or a comprehensive census of production is taken. These provide firm figures for benchmark years which are used as a statistical basis for extrapolating the monthly, quarterly or annual statistics obtained from sample surveys. In some cases the figures in the National Income Blue Book are in fact based on precise accounting figures; examples are those taken from the accounts of the central and local government and public corporations. After several years have elapsed, the figures for financial years for these series are firm. But there remains the problem of how to allocate the figures over calendar quarters and this can lead to errors. The figures for profits and wages and salaries after some years have elapsed should also become firm as tax assessments are completed, but errors arise because statistics collected for administrative purposes are not always in the appropriate form for national income purposes.

People are sometimes surprised to learn of the large coverage which many of the sample investigations into the economic activities of the business sector have. The Inland Revenue, for example, carries out a quarterly inquiry into the gross trading profits of companies. Although only about 800 enterprises are approached, the figures account for about 7,000 companies and for about one half of total company profits. Similarly, the retail sales figures, based on a sample of about 10,000 organisations, cover not far short of one half of total retail sales, and the quarterly inquiries into capital expenditure and stock-building by manufacturing industry cover about two thirds of the totals for manufacturing industry.

However much we improve the various series, discrepancies are bound to remain, because of reporting and sampling errors, and because of differences in coverage, valuation and timing. The new system of industrial statistics (referred to below) will help us to provide more reliable estimates of industrial production, and of capital expenditure and stockbuilding by manufacturing industry, and the introduction of the Central Register of Businesses (also referred to below) will improve the frame from which samples are drawn and produce better statistics particularly for the distributive and service trades. But I do not believe that we will ever be able to get rid of the residual error in the national income accounts or of the discrepancy between the three estimates of GDP at constant prices.

This is unfortunate from the user (and public relations) point of view, but we will have to continue to live with the discrepancies and recognise the limitations of the statistics. I think it would be quite wrong for the compilers of the national income statistics to 'massage' the various estimates so as to eliminate the discrepancies completely. Series which may be considered accurate today may later turn out to be in error. For example, who would have forecast several years ago that the merchandise export figures were understated by 2 per cent? Who can tell what revisions to consumers' expenditure are likely to be needed when the results of the Census of Distribution for 1971 become available in two years time? Who would have anticipated the substantial revision to the estimates of changes in wholesalers' stocks which came to light following the Annual Inquiry for 1969?

However, we are not sitting back despondently and doing nothing. As has been pointed out already, series are continually being developed and improved. Also, we are conducting for the first time, a small follow-up inquiry to the Census of Production for 1970, to be carried out by personal interview. The aim is to discuss with firms ways of minimising the burden of future inquiries, discover whether the questions asked have really been understood, and whether the information requested is readily available in the firm's records. This kind of survey has been carried out as a matter of course following a census of population, but never before on the business statistics side. Surveys such as these, together with the long-standing practice of having continuing discussions with representative organisations of industry, will help to improve our statistics by tackling the problem at the 'grass roots'.

The possible introduction of a value added tax could lead to an important new source of information. It is possible that statistics of turnover derived from the administration of this tax could vastly improve the statistics available for the distributive and service industries and to better estimates of the output of these industries and consumers' expenditure on them.

Before concluding this section, I should point out that my remarks about the impossibility of completely reconciling the two largely independent estimates of gross domestic product based on income and expenditure data apply with equal force to the problem of reconciling the three independent estimates of real output based on income, expenditure and output statistics. It is true that the *Financial Statement and Budget Report* does contain a so-called 'compromise estimate' of the gross domestic product. This is an estimate which is produced so as to provide a single appreciation of recent developments, but it is purely subjective. On the basis of later and more complete information, the authors of the estimate would more than likely produce an alternative compromise estimate. Also, different authors would have produced different estimates. It is perfectly legitimate to do this, but in my view it is for the user and not the producer of the national income statistics to manipulate the figures in this way. Probably, the best the producer of the national accounts can do is to produce an arithmetic average of the three alternative estimates of GDP at constant prices, and this is what is now done. To go further and incorporate even this average estimate fully in the national income accounts by estimating a current price equivalent and including this in the main summary tables would in my view complicate them immensely and be of no real help to the users of the Blue Book.

Personal saving

Mention has been made of the large difference between the estimates of personal saving obtained by aggregating transactions in assets and liabilities, and the estimates obtained as the residual item in the personal income and expenditure account. This difference appears as 'unidentified items' in the financial transactions account of the personal sector. It has been pointed out in articles in *Economic Trends* (e.g. Berman, 1969) that a part of this represents errors in the estimates of transactions by the personal sector (recorded in the personal income and expenditure, capital and financial transactions accounts) and a part represents loans and credit of one sort or another advanced by industrial and commercial companies to the personal sector. Statistics of trade credit are now being collected from companies, and it is hoped that this will make it possible to make at least a rough estimate of quarterly changes in this item.

The Crowther Report on Consumer Credit (Cmnd. 4596) has pointed out that 'statistics of consumer credit are patchy and defective, suffering from many divergencies in definition and from eccentricities of inclusion and exclusion' (paragraph 2.2.4). Efforts will no doubt be made to remedy this situation, and this should lead to improvements in the direct estimates of personal saving and to reductions in the 'unidentified items'.

Input–output statistics

Input–output statistics provide an essential link between macro and micro economic statistics, and developments in them can usefully be considered at this point.

By any standard there has been a considerable improvement in the availability of input–output statistics in recent years. Until late 1969, the most up to date tables were a set of firmly based 45×45 tables for 1954, and a set of provisional updated 28×28 tables for 1963. Today, firmly based detailed tables for 1963 and provisional updated tables for 1968 are available.

The detailed tables for 1963 were completed towards the end of 1969 and the full input–output analysis was published as a Study in Official Statistics early in 1970. The analysis extended over 22 tables and distinguished 70 separate industry and commodity groups and included detailed make, absorption and imports matrices, industry× industry and commodity×commodity tables and a full analysis of final demand. They are the most detailed and complex tables ever published for the U.K.

In order to meet the criticism that input–output tables are always out of date we decided to start work on producing a set of detailed updated tables for the year 1968 as soon as the Study for 1963 had been completed. The updated tables are based partly on the provisional results of the census of production for that year and on national accounts data, and partly by applying a matrix updating procedure to the firmly based tables for 1963. Summary results of this updating exercise were published in the January 1971 issue of *Economic Trends,* and gave details of the transactions of 35 separate industry groups. However, these results represent an aggregation of a rather more detailed analysis for 70 industry and commodity groups, which corresponds very closely to the tables included in the comprehensive and firmly based study for 1963. Sets of the 70×70 tables either as printed tables, or in the form of computer readable input, were available from the CSO from February 1971.

I am not sure whether we achieved a record amongst at least the Western countries in producing a detailed input–output table so speedily. We were faced with the usual statistician's problem of deciding how much importance we should attach to reliability and how much to timeliness and to detail. We decided to go for timeliness, and in doing so we recognise that the tables we have produced are not as reliable as we would have liked them to be, but the tables are the best that could have been produced with the data available at the end of 1970. Work is now in hand on producing the next firmly based set of input–output tables, which will also relate to the year 1968. If the Business Statistics Office keeps to its programme for processing the census of production for 1968, the firmly based tables for 1968 will be completed about the end of 1972. These tables will be very similar in form to those published for 1963 but somewhat more detailed. We plan to distinguish 92 separate industry and commodity groups, of which 75 are within manufacturing industry compared with 57 in the 1963 Study. Details are given in an article published in *Statistical News*, February 1971.

Input–output tables are a powerful tool in model building exercises, and are also useful as an instrument of co-ordination in the field of national income statistics. For these reasons, we have plans to produce detailed firmly based tables at least once every five years and updated tables, distinguishing at least 35 industry groups, annually. We plan to experiment with producing constant price tables and to use them as a means of providing a check on the Index of Industrial Production and on the estimates of real product. Input–output tables should also help to provide a check on the estimates of gross domestic product at current prices. There is a great deal of research and development work to be done in this area, but the amount we will do will depend on the resources available to us.

Published macro-economic forecasts

Before turning to recent improvements in micro-economic statistics, I should mention the publication of the government's short-term economic forecasts in the annual *Financial Statement and Budget*

Report. These appeared for the first time in the *Financial Statement* for 1968–69 published in March 1968. This represents an important improvement in economic statistics, but not one for which statisticians can claim a large part of the credit.

Macro-economic data bank

As well as producing macro-economic statistics, it is the job of the Government Statistical Service to make them available in the most appropriate form. Until recently this was always the printed page, but it is now not the most appropriate form in all cases. There is now a need for data in a computer readable form and this, together with the need for computerising the statistical work of the CSO, has led to the development of the CSO experimental macro-economic data bank project.

The CSO now has its own small computer (ICL 190IS) which was installed in January 1970. Programs have been written to enable it to hold and manipulate a data bank of key economic series. These include the components of the Index of Industrial Production, national income statistics, balance of payments statistics and statistics of employment, prices and so on. The object is to hold those statistics which are most used by the CSO and other government departments for further processing or analysis. With the greater use now being made of computers in analytical and forecasting work, there is a demand for having statistical series available in the form of computer readable input. This will avoid the necessity of users having to take published series and punching them on to paper tape or cards before they can be used and will have the additional advantage of minimising clerical transposition errors. Experience in Canada and the United States suggests that there should be a demand for this kind of information from outside organisations as well as from within the government service. The input–output tables for 1963 and 1968 are available in the form of punched cards or paper tape, and have been made available to outside users in this form. (These outside users include stockbrokers, universities, market research agencies as well as several private large firms.) The resources being put into this project are pretty small at present as it is of an experimental nature. It will be interesting to see how big a demand there will be for statistical information in this form. Fortunately, because the information will not consist of primary data collected from individual firms but aggregated data, there will be no problems of confidentiality. The macro-economic data bank is now becoming operational.

III. Micro-Economic Statistics

There has been a considerable improvement in micro-economic statistics in the past few years and more are on the way. Many of these followed from the Report from the Estimates Committee on the Government Statistical Services, which emphasised the desirability of having more up to date and detailed statistics analysed where appropriate by area, industry, occupation and commodity, and in the form which would permit the detailed micro analysis which industrial economists and planners are seeking to make.

Business statistics

Much has been written, especially in *Statistical News* (e.g. Stafford, 1968) about the new system of industrial statistics which is gradually being introduced to replace the present system of detailed quinquennial censuses of production and the various short-term inquiries into production and deliveries. The detailed censuses of production have been criticised because the published results are always out of date and hence of no use to industry. The short-period statistics have been criticised because they are not comprehensive, not co-ordinated, and, in some cases it is alleged, not relevant. By introducing the new system of industrial statistics we aim to remedy this situation and produce information that satisfies the needs of both industry and the government.

The collection of statistics from manufacturing industry is now being put on a more systematic basis. Firms are being asked to continue to provide summary figures of total output or total sales for the monthly Index of Industrial Production. But, in addition, they are being asked to provide for each of their establishments (that is a factory or sometimes a group of related factories) quarterly details of the value of the deliveries of their products (or groups of products) and, where it is useful, quantity figures as well. The product groups for which information will be required are being worked out in detail in consultation with the representatives of the relevant industries. The programme, which involves introducing 170 different quarterly inquiries covering manufacturing industry, should be completed by the end of 1972.

These quarterly inquiries are being supplemented by annual inquiries which collect information on total sales and total purchases, changes in stocks and work in progress, fixed capital expenditure, wages and salaries and certain other data necessary to compile census net output and gross output. The first of these annual inquiries has taken place in respect of the year 1970. The quarterly inquiries are designed to provide up to date figures of sales by different industry groups which, when combined with information obtained from the annual censuses, will provide the kind of information which up till now has been obtained only in a full and detailed census of production. Under these new arrangements the detailed results will become available very much more quickly than hitherto. They will also make possible the calculation of indices of commodity output, as well as of industrial output, for use in input–output models. In addition to this regular information, it is intended to collect from industry at periodic intervals, possibly every five years starting with 1974, detailed information about goods and services purchased.

The quarterly inquiries will meet a good deal of the needs of industry for reliable, detailed and up to date statistics of deliveries. Prior to the start of the re-organisation of industrial statistics, quarterly and monthly statistics of deliveries or production were available for something like 2,000 products or product groups. When the re-organisation has been completed this total will almost certainly top the 5,000 mark.

The annual censuses of production will provide valuable information to both industry and government. For example, they will provide detailed figures of capital expenditure and employment for small areas and industry groups and will enable estimates of net output and net output per head for different industries and regions to be compiled. This kind of information has not been available hitherto on an up to date year by year basis.

There are at present no immediate plans to improve the statistics for the distributive and service industries. These are very patchy at present. The problem here is to obtain an up to date and comprehensive list of names and addresses of businesses to use as a sampling frame. Until the Central Register of Businesses is developed (see below) there is little prospect of any real improvement in this area.

Employment statistics

The present counts of the national insurance contribution cards exchanged provide the main basis for the principal regular series of statistics on employees compiled by the Department of Employment. The previous government planned to abolish the national insurance cards in 1972 when an earnings related social security scheme was to be introduced. Because of this, the Finance Act 1969 included a clause enabling the Inland Revenue to pass to the Department of Employment and the BSO lists of all PAYE points—that is, the names and addresses from which businesses in the United Kingdom operate PAYE schemes. This list provided the Department of Employment with a comprehensive register on which to base a census of employment. A full-scale trial census to test the feasibility of collecting statistics by this method was held in June 1970 and showed that it was practicable. Each PAYE point address was asked to list the names and addresses of each establishment for which it held pay records, the description of the business carried on at the address and information about the numbers employed analysed by sex distinguishing part-time and full-time workers. The census provides comprehensive statistics of jobs (a person with more than one job being counted more than once). The new census provides very much better figures of employment than we previously had. In particular it provides reliable figures of employment in small areas down to the local office areas (there are about 1,000 such areas in Great Britain). At present employment figures are available for such small areas but they are subject to very severe limitations and in practice are not sufficiently reliable for measuring year to year changes in employment at the local office area. The introduction of an annual census of employment should go a long way towards providing the detailed area figures of employment which planners are particularly interested in.

Incomes

The most important development in statistics of incomes in recent years has been the introduction of the Department of Employment's

New Earnings Surveys. This followed from a suggestion put forward by the National Board for Prices and Incomes. These surveys provide for the first time up to date and comprehensive information about the distribution of earnings within industries and occupations and about the detailed relationships between basic wage rates and total earnings. The survey is carried out by selecting a sample of employees who are in employment and whose national insurance numbers end in a certain combination of digits. This is a completely impersonal method of selection and in view of the way in which national insurance numbers are allocated, it provides an almost perfect random sample of all the employees in the working population. In contrast to earlier surveys which were brought out piecemeal industry by industry and which often omitted particular groups of industries, the new survey covers in principle all industries, all occupations and all sizes of establishments. The results of this survey show the proportion of employees whose earnings fall in each income range, the incidence of low earnings, the extent of the variation between the more highly and lowly paid employees within each occupation, age group and region and so on. Following a small pilot survey carried out in September 1967, a full scale survey based on just under a one half per cent sample was carried out in September 1968. Starting in 1970, surveys are now based on a one per cent sample carried out every April. Because of the success of this new inquiry changes have been made to the existing inquiries into wages and salary earnings. From 1970 the wage earnings inquiry, previously held in April and October, will only be held in October; and the salary earnings inquiry, which previously took place every October, has been dropped.

Another development is that the Inland Revenue now publish detailed figures of incomes analysed by type (e.g. wages and salaries, pensions and family allowances, etc.) and by family circumstances for different ranges of income and also for different regions.

From the administration of the graduated pension scheme, information has become available in the records of the Department of Health and Social Security about the gross earnings of persons of different ages covered by PAYE schemes through which the graduated contributions are collected. This information has been used to produce a series of analyses showing the average earnings of men and all women spinsters classified by age group for each standard region. The analysis is based on a sample equivalent to one half of one per cent of the total numbers registered for national insurance. The area analysis in these statistics is based on place of residence whereas the Inland Revenue analysis is based on place of work.

Regional data

There has been a considerable improvement in the availability of regional statistics in recent years. The first Abstract of Regional Statistics was published in 1965 and now appears annually; the latest issue for 1970 contains twice as many tables as the first. The Abstract brings together and makes readily accessible a good deal of information which was available elsewhere, but much of it is new. In particular, the Inland Revenue's surveys of personal income provide valuable information about the distribution of income in different regions. There is also the regional analysis of public sector capital expenditure and of industrial building and the regional income summaries derived from the New Earnings Survey and from the social security statistics already referred to.

A new development which is worthy of mention is that each shop enumerated in the Census of Distribution for 1971 will be allocated a grid reference locating it to within a 100 metre square of the National Grid. By using this co-ordinate reference it will be possible to produce statistics for any non-standard area in terms of the 100 metres square. This means that area analyses of data in the census of distribution need not be tied to local authority areas as in the past, which may change from census to census, but fixed in terms of points related to the National Grid. The National Grid is also being used as a basis for classification in the Census of Population for 1971.

So far the CSO has not concerned itself with making regional estimates of 'national' income and expenditure and of input–output tables. Some work in these areas is being undertaken in academic institutions, generally financed by the Social Science Research Council, and in the case of a study for Wales by the Welsh Office. The Scottish Office and the Northern Ireland Government are also working on estimates for their countries. A description of these various studies is given by A. J. Brown in a review article in the *Economic Journal* (1969). More recently Woodward (1970) has prepared detailed regional estimates of expenditure and income. A good deal of detailed regional information is now available (e.g. from the income surveys, the census of production and the Family Expenditure

Survey) on which to base these studies. But as usual the data are not quite in the right form for regional accounting purposes (e.g. income data relate to place of work and expenditure data to residential area). In one important respect the basic data are deteriorating. Many large and important enterprises with factories in different parts of the country, because of their centralised accounting arrangements, are unable to provide separate figures of total sales and total purchases and hence of net output for their individual factories. (See Fessey and Browning, *Statistical News*, May, 1971.)

The CSO is not at present planning to enter the field of regional national income accounting. If more resources become available for national income work, it would probably be more sensible to devote them first to improving the national aggregates, where there is a definite and continuing need, rather than to provide a regional dimension to them, where the needs are less obvious.

The Central Register of Businesses

One of the most ambitious projects the Government Statistical Service is working on, and to which the Estimates Committee attached considerable importance, is the creation and maintenance of a Central Register of Businesses. The Central Register can be described as a list of businesses classified by industrial activity, location, size and so on and held on a computer. The Business Statistics Office has been given the responsibility (in collaboration with the CSO and other Departments) for setting up and maintaining it.

The main objectives for having a Central Register are to provide an up-to-date list of names and addresses of statistical reporting units and other business units from which business statistics can be sought, and to achieve consistency and avoid duplication between different statistical inquiries. It has not so far been possible to maintain up-to-date and comprehensive registers of statistical inquiries directed at the distributive and service trades; instead it has been necessary to build up registers on an *ad hoc* basis for censuses and then to allow them to lapse. As a result, the short period statistics for these industries are not satisfactory. Another aim of the Central Register is to enable statistics on different subjects, which are often collected from different types of reporting units, to be properly related to form an integrated system of business statistics. For example, statistics on new orders and on capital expenditure are generally collected from head offices, or from financial centres, and may cover a number of factories. On the other hand, statistics of employment are generally available and collected for separate places of employment.

Achieving these aims will take quite a long time and will be expensive. However, there are some developments on which I can report progress. First of all, the registers of manufacturing establishments held by the Business Statistics Office and the Department of Employment have been largely reconciled. This agreed register will be used by the BSO and the Department of Employment in their statistical inquiries and is being made available to all Departments who wish to conduct statistical surveys directed at manufacturing industry.

A second development is that the Census of Employment has provided a comprehensive list of names and addresses of local units of businesses (that is, places of work) and when this has been investigated it is likely that it will provide a basis for a large part of the Central Register. However, there are two important snags to the list. First, it excludes businesses where all employees have earnings below the PAYE tax limit and all businesses without employees (mainly one-man businesses). Under existing legislation the Inland Revenue is not allowed to pass over to the Business Statistics Office, or the Department of Employment, the names and addresses of one-man businesses. The second snag is that the local unit, although it is the ideal reporting unit in an employment census, is not necessarily the appropriate unit in a production census. A factory, for example, may have a separate transport department, or packing department, and in a census of employment separate returns may be made for these departments. But in a production census separate accounting records may not be kept for these departments, so that a reporting unit in a production inquiry will differ from that in an employment inquiry. This leads to problems of reconciling reporting units in different registers which can be a very expensive operation. So far these problems have not been tackled for industries other than manufacturing.

Household surveys

In recent years there have been two important developments in the field of household surveys. First, from January 1967 the sample of households in the Family Expenditure Survey (FES) was doubled in size and completely redesigned. Over the course of each year an approach is now made to approximately 10,000 households selected from the electoral registers. About 70 per cent of these generally agree to co-operate. The results of the improved FES are now used more effectively, *inter alia*, in providing more securely based estimates of certain components of consumers' expenditure. A second important development was the introduction in October 1970 of a General Household Survey. This is normally considered a development in the field of social statistics, but it has very important implications for economic statistics. Questions are being asked on a wide range of topics, including housing, demography, employment status (past and present), education and income. About 15,000 households are being covered by the Survey, but this number will probably be increased as time goes on. The Household Survey will make it possible to keep up to date annually information previously obtained only from a census of poulation, to link information on a wide range of topics and to try out questions for possible inclusion in future censuses.

IV. Organisation

Any account of recent developments in official economic statistics cannot be complete without at least a passing reference to the important changes which are taking place in the organisation of the Government Statistical Service. The main features have been the establishment of two new statistical agencies—the Business Statistics Office and the Office of Population Censuses and Surveys—and the strengthening of the co-ordinating role of the Central Statistical Office. The Business Statistics Office was set up at the beginning of 1969 and will gradually become the agency for the collection of most business statistics from firms. The Office of Population Censuses and Surveys was established in 1970 by merging the General Register Office and the Government Social Survey Department to become the main Government agency for the compilation of statistics about individuals and households.

From the point of view of this paper, which is concerned solely with economic statistics, the establishment of the BSO is of particular importance. The gradual centralisation of the collection of economic statistics will take advantage of the many economies which a large computer and organisation can offer; it will enable the Office to make use of the best techniques for carrying out statistical inquiries; and it will ensure that different statistical inquiries are, as far as possible, properly co-ordinated and related to one another. The latter aim will be greatly advanced by the creation of the Central Register of Businesses at the BSO. A full account of these important organisational changes is given by Professor C. A. Moser in a paper read to the Manchester Statistical Society in March, 1971.

V. Conclusions

This paper has reviewed some of the important developments in economic statistics in recent years. It has shown that there have been considerable improvements, especially in the availability of micro-economic statistics. Evidence presented to the Estimates Committee in 1966 demonstrated that enormous improvements had been made to economic statistics during the post (1939–45) war period. The developments in recent years have reinforced and added to these improvements. At the beginning of this paper, I said that the criterion by which government economic statistics needs to be judged is their reliability as a basis for assessing economic developments and for decision making purposes. H.M. Treasury in its evidence to the Estimates Committee (page 36) stated that in the field of national income forecasting 'a major error of interpretation or forecasting is unlikely to be caused by defects in the statistics. There is still, however, a great deal of room for improvement and in view of the importance of the relevant decisions, it is very desirable that the improvement of the last few years should be maintained'. I think it is fair to say that this paper has shown that the rate of improvement has been maintained.

For the reasons I have given I believe that we will never be able to eliminate the residual error in the national income accounts, or the differences between the three independent estimates of the real product. The best we can hope for is to reduce discrepancies by steadily improving the basic data and the estimates of the various component series. Unfortunately, sometimes these improvements make the discrepancies worse. This work should also lead to a reduction in the difference between the two independent estimates of personal saving in the national income accounts.

Throughout the post war period, official economic statistics have been criticised for not being sufficiently up to date or sufficiently reliable. Although steps have been taken to meet these criticisms, the published statistics are still not as good as many users would like them to be. This is because the demands made on them are increasing in parallel. Fortunately, the decision maker does not (or should not) need to rely on only one or two series in isolation. To get the best picture of the situation he needs to look at a battery of statistics and test their validity by comparing them with one another. But this procedure can break down when econometric relationships based on past experiences (e.g. the relationship between changes in wage rates and unemployment) suddenly change. He may blame the statistics but sometimes it is the theories that are at fault.

A major problem is that decision makers (rightly or wrongly) are interested in relatively small changes, which are generally well within the margin of error of the series being considered. Decision makers must learn to recognise and respect the limitations of the statistics they are dealing with and not expect too much from them. Statisticians are always saying that too much attention should not be paid to month to month variations in economic indicators (after allowance for seasonal variations), and that particular series should be interpreted with caution. Nevertheless, another month's figures is an extra piece of information and must not be discarded. But it takes a clever man (and also a lucky man) to pick out turning points and changes in rates of growth at an early stage. In this connection, we might benefit by copying the Americans by developing leading indicators such as those published in the *Business Conditions Digest*.

The pioneering work of setting up the basic economic accounts has now ended. It was an exciting time establishing the main framework of the Blue Book, the quarterly national income accounts, the financial accounts and the input–output tables. The main task now is to continue to improve the existing statistics, for example, by extending the coverage and, where necessary, the frequency of surveys, improving the sampling frame, filling in the information gaps (especially for the distributive and service trades) and by improving the quality of the information provided by firms. In doing so it is important to minimise both the cost to the Government of collecting and processing the statistical data and the form-filling burden on the firms providing the basic data—it is not a simple matter getting the cost/benefit relationship right. The other side of the work is to develop better statistical techniques and to make better use of computers for producing earlier estimates. In these various ways, official economic statistics will continue to be improved to match, as far as possible, the increasing demands made on them. But in my view, it would be a mistake to assume that these demands will ever be satisfied completely.

References

BERMAN, L. S. (1969). Role of the personal sector in the flow of funds in the United Kingdom. *Economic Trends* November 1969. H.M. Stationery Office.

—— (1971). Further developments in input–output statistics. *Statistical News* No. 12. H.M. Stationery Office.

BROWN, A. J. (1969). Surveys of applied economics: regional economics, with special reference to the United Kingdom. *Economic Journal*, December 1969.

CENTRAL STATISTICAL OFFICE (annual). *National Income and Expenditure*. H.M. Stationery Office.

—— (annual). *United Kingdom Balance of Payments*. H.M. Stationery Office.

—— (annual). *Abstract of Regional Statistics*. H.M. Stationery Office.

—— (monthly). *Financial Statistics*. H.M. Stationery Office.

—— (monthly). *Economic Trends*. H.M. Stationery Office.

—— (1970). Input–output tables for the United Kingdom, 1963. *Studies in Official Statistics*. No. 16. H.M. Stationery Office.

CMD. 6527 (1944). *Employment Policy*. H.M. Stationery Office.

CMD. 6687 (1945). *Report of the Census of Production Committee*. H.M. Stationery Office.

CMD. 6764 (1946). *Report of the Census of Distribution Committee*. H.M. Stationery Office.

CMD. 9276 (1954). *Report of the Committee on the Censuses of Production and Distribution*. H.M. Stationery Office.

CMND. 827 (1959). *Report of the Committee on the Working of the Monetary System*. H.M. Stationery Office.

CMND. 4596 (1971). *Consumer Credit. Report of the Committee*. Chairman Lord Crowther. (Vol. 1. Report.) H.M. Stationery Office.

ESTIMATES COMMITTEE (1966). Fourth Report from the Estimates Committee on the Government Statistical Services. H.M. Stationery Office.

FINANCIAL STATEMENT AND BUDGET REPORT (annual). H.M. Stationery Office.

FESSEY, M. C. and BROWNING, H. E. (1971). The statistical unit in business inquiries. *Statistical News*, No. 13. H.M. Stationery Office.

MOSER, C. A. (1971). The Statistician in Government: a challenge for the 1970's. *Transactions of the Manchester Statistical Society*, March 1971.

STAFFORD, J. (1968). The development of industrial statistics. *Statistical News*, No. 1. H.M. Stationery Office.

WOODWARD, V. H. (1970). *Regional Social Accounts for the U.K.* N.I.E.S.R. Regional Paper 1. Cambridge University Press.

Appendix to Chapter 4

Major landmarks in official economic statistics, 1940–1970

1941 Central Statistical Office established
First National Income White Paper (Cmd. 6261)
The accounts are 'designed to measure in money terms the main elements in the national income, expenditure and savings and the net amount of funds available for government purposes from private sources'.

1944 Employment Policy White Paper (Cmd. 6527)
This laid down the broad lines along which official economic statistics should be developed in the post-war years. It listed the principal classes of statistics which must be obtained for the efficient operation of an employment policy. The list included regular statistics on employment, unemployment, savings, capital expenditure, production, balance of payments and national income.

1945 Report of the Census of Production Committee (The 'Nelson Committee') (Cmd. 6687).

1946 Report of the Census of Distribution Committee (The 'Hopkins Committee') (Cmd. 6764)
First issue of *Monthly Digest of Statistics*
'The aim is to publish in summary form statistics which show the changing pattern of the economic activity of the country.'

1947 Statistics of Trade Act
This reflected the recommendations of the White Paper on Employment Policy and the Reports of the Committees on the Censuses of Production and Distribution. It provided the general legal basis for collecting official statistics and for obtaining 'the information necessary for the appreciation of economic trends and the provision of a statistical service for industry and for the discharge of government departments of their functions'.
Interim Report of the Cost of Living Advisory Committee (Cmd. 7077).

1948 First full and detailed post-war census of production
First Standard Industrial Classification published
First official monthly Index of Industrial Production published
First Balance of Payments White Paper.

1950 First Census of Distribution and Other Services.

1952 First National Income Blue Book published in September
The annual National Income White Paper was reduced in size and contained only summary and provisional figures.

1954 Report of the Committee on the censuses of production and distribution (Cmd. 9276) (The 'Verdon-Smith Committee')

Its recommendations aimed at reducing the burden of the censuses on the business community whilst improving their effectiveness. One conclusion was that the detailed census of production was of little direct use to firms in industry and commerce.

1956 Mr. Macmillan's Budget speech in which he said that 'some official statistics were too late to be as useful as they ought to be and that we were always as it were looking up the train in last year's Bradshaw'. This was followed by a further statement by Mr. Macmillan in August in which he again emphasised the need for having up-to-date economic statistics. 'The Government do not need this information only for their own use. The business community and the public need it just as much.' He indicated the general lines of a new programme to improve the short-period economic indicators.

1957 First official quarterly estimates of national income published

The estimates were based solely on expenditure data. Corresponding estimates of factor incomes were added in 1958; estimates of expenditure at constant prices in 1959; seasonally adjusted figures of expenditure and income in 1960 and quarterly estimates of real output not until 1966.

Family Expenditure Survey began.

1959 Report of the Committee on the Working of the Monetary System (Cmnd. 827) (The 'Radcliffe Committee')

This emphasised the need for financial and monetary statistics and in particular the need for having statistics about the stock and transactions of financial assets and liabilities for the different sectors of the economy.

1962 First issue of *Financial Statistics*

White Paper on Incomes Policy: The Next Step (Cmnd. 1626)

This noted that up-to-date and regular information on wage rates and other relevant factors affecting the economic situation should be made available to arbitrators and negotiators in a convenient form and led to the publication of *Statistics on Incomes, Prices, Employment and Productivity*.

1963 First annual Balance of Payments Pink Book published.

1964 Publication of annual and quarterly financial accounts as an integral part of the national income accounting system.

1965 First Abstract of Regional Statistics.

1966 Report from the Estimates Committee on the Government Statistical Services

This was concerned with the organisation of the Government Statistical Service and in particular, with the co-ordinating role of the Central Statistical Office, the use of computers, and the need for having detailed statistics by area, industry, occupation and by commodity.

1968 First issue of *Statistical News*

This particular issue contains an article by Professor C. A. Moser (Director of the Central Statistical Office) which describes the future role of the CSO in the light of the criticisms made by the Estimates Committee's Report. The issue also contains an article by Mr. J. Stafford (Director of Statistics, Board of Trade) which describes the new system of industrial statistics to be introduced to meet the needs of both government and industry.

1968 Short-term economic forecasts included in *Financial Statement*.

1969 Business Statistics Office established

This Office took over the functions of the former Board of Trade Census Office and will become eventually the main data collection agency of statistics from business firms and be responsible for creating and maintaining the Central Register of Businesses.

1970 First census of employment.

5

Wage Determination with Bilateral Monopoly*

J. Johnston†

THIS PROBLEM has recently been re-considered by Hieser,[1] whose analysis is in the tradition of Hicks[2] and Shackle.[3] His treatment improves on theirs to the extent that he gives an explicit discussion of the main gains and losses of the participants to the wage bargain but, as will be argued below, the analysis of the forces determining the level of that bargain is still obscure and unsatisfactory. This is essentially because:

(i) the analysis is non-probabilistic in character, thus failing to deal adequately with expectations,

(ii) it does not explicitly deal with the *sequential* nature of the bargaining process in which a wage claim is formulated by the union, a counter offer made by the employer, negotiations take place with the possibility of breakdowns, strikes, revised offers and so forth, and

(iii) it does not examine the possibility of second guessing or bluffing by either party. Unfortunately general theories of bargaining, which Hieser ignores but of which Coddington[4] gives a very useful summary and critique, do not afford an adequate treatment of the wage bargain, mainly because they are very general and do not incorporate the crucial and specific elements that Hieser has delineated.

The plan of this paper is as follows. Section I discusses the Hieser analysis. Section II develops a simple model (Model A) which

* I am indebted to my colleagues D. J. Coppock and E. V. Morgan for comments on an earlier draft of this paper.

† Professor of Econometrics, University of Manchester.

[1] R. O. Hieser, 'Wage Determination with Bilateral Monopoly in the Labour Market: A Theoretical Treatment', *Economic Record*, March 1970, pp. 55–72.

[2] J. R. Hicks, *The Theory of Wages*, second edition, Macmillan, London, 1963.

[3] G. L. S. Shackle, 'The Nature of the Bargaining Process', chapter 19 in *The Theory of Wage Determination*, ed. J. Dunlop, Macmillan, London, 1964.

[4] A. Coddington, *Theories of the Bargaining Process*, Allen and Unwin, London, 1968.

attempts to incorporate the three main points made above. Section III then develops a more complicated model (Model B) and Section IV contains conclusions and some comments on the possible implications of the model for current discussions of wage inflation.

I. The Hieser Analysis

Hieser postulates a monopolist producer faced by the market demand curve, DD′, for his product as in Figure 1. The technical production function is given and the prime cost curve per unit of output is assumed to be horizontal. The monopolist is assumed to be fully integrated, producing his own raw materials, so that the only prime cost is labour. The *initial* prime cost curve is shown by CC′ in Figure 1 and is determined by the opportunity wage, OC, at which 'free' labour would offer itself. With labour being the only prime cost a suitable definition of units means that employment and output can both be measured by the same number Q on the horizontal axis in Figure 1.

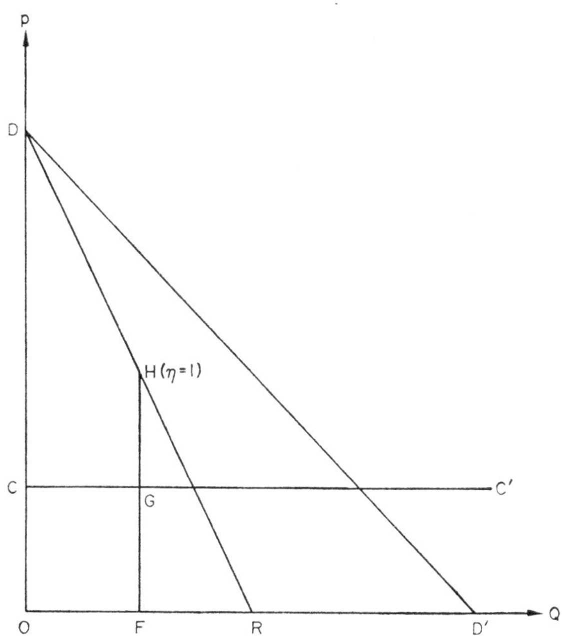

Fig. 1

In addition to the above assumptions Hieser now postulates the existence of a trade union with a closed shop. The union will bargain for a money wage rate in excess of OC and the union's objective is assumed to be to raise the money wage rate (w) until the money wage bill (wQ) is maximised. DR is the marginal revenue curve in Figure 1 and is also the monopolist's demand curve for labour. The elasticities of DD′ and DR are defined respectively as

$$\text{elasticity of DD}' = \varepsilon = -\frac{dQ}{dp} \cdot \frac{p}{Q}$$

$$\text{elasticity of DR} = \eta = -\frac{dQ}{dw} \cdot \frac{w}{Q}$$

The wage bill is maximised at $\eta = 1$, that is at the point H in Figure 1, and so the union would desire to push the money wage up from FG to an upper limit of FH. In doing so employment will be continuously reduced but the money wage bill will be increased. Further increases in the money wage above FH would, however, reduce the wage bill.

It can be shown that for any output Q

$$\eta = \tfrac{1}{2}(\varepsilon - 1) \quad \ldots\ldots\ldots\ldots (1)$$

and the familiar relation between average and marginal revenue gives

$$w = p\left(1 - \frac{1}{\varepsilon}\right) \quad \ldots\ldots\ldots\ldots (2)$$

or

$$\frac{w}{p} = \frac{\varepsilon - 1}{\varepsilon}$$

At point H, $\eta = 1$, so $\varepsilon = 3$ and at that point $w/p = \frac{2}{3}$. Thus the *maximum wage bill* that the union might possibly extract from the employer is *two-thirds of value added.*

So far so good. Hieser's main concern is to analyse the relative bargaining power of the two parties 'in terms of the balancing of gains and losses by both sides in the stances of resistance or concession'. This is done by formulating gains and losses as *functions of the duration of strikes*. Thus all bargaining in the absence of strikes is excluded from consideration. *The implicit assumption is that any disagreement, however small, leads automatically to a strike.* Moreover, *there is no formulation in the model of a union claim or the monopolist's response so that the extent of any disagreement does not appear explicitly in the model.*

The cost of strike action to the workers is defined to be

$$L = sQw + Q.U(s, w) \qquad (3)$$

where

s = Duration of strike (in wage periods)
w = Prevailing wage rate
Q = Prevailing employment
$U(s, w)$ = Supplementary function, 'representing the increasing marginal utility of that money loss (sQw), and thus likely to increase sharply for high values of s

and

sQw = Gross wages lost during the strike.

Net gain per period from a wage increase is defined by

$$G' = Q.\Delta w - w\Delta Q \quad (\text{ignoring } \Delta w.\Delta Q)$$
$$= Q.\Delta w(1-\eta)$$

Discounting this stream over time

$$\text{Total gain} = G = Q.\Delta w(1-\eta)V_m(j) \qquad (4)$$

where $V_m(j)$ is the sum of unity over m periods discounted at rate j. Equating (3) and (4) would give a series of break-even points for labour in terms of pairs of s, Δw values at which gain equals loss. The resultant equation is

$$\Delta w = \frac{sw + U(s, w)}{(1-\eta)V_m(j)} \qquad (5)$$

Since $\eta = \frac{1}{2}(\varepsilon - 1)$ this can be rewritten as

$$\Delta w = \frac{sw + U(s, w)}{\frac{1}{2}(3-\varepsilon).V_m(j)} \qquad (6)$$

This break-even function for labour may be expected to have the form shown by curve OU in Figure 2.

The intriguing and vital question is what if anything this function tells us about the behaviour to expect from the union. Hieser's analysis implies that the union should, of course, select a policy in which gain will exceed loss. It might be plausible to go further and say that the union should select the policy with the *maximum net gain.*

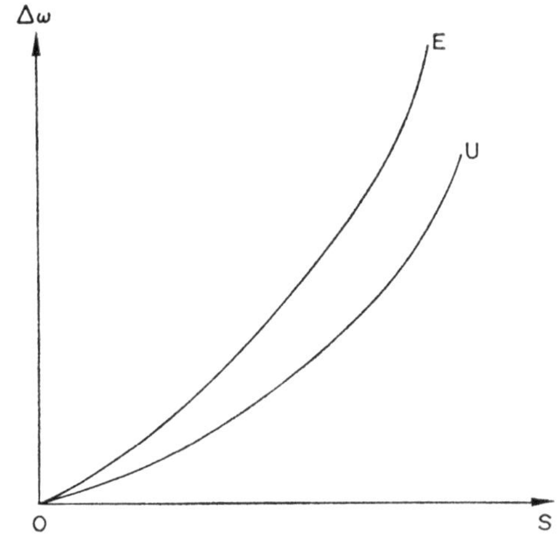

Fig. 2

Hieser is silent on these points. To consider these issues in more detail return to the formulations of gain and loss in equations (3) and (4). At any given initial situation the gain, G, is simply proportional to Δw and the loss, L, is an increasing function of the duration of the strike, s. If the employers' initial offer is Δw_1, giving a gain of G_1, the net gain (G−L) is shown by OG_1 in Figure 3. Should the union accept or not? Clearly it all depends on what is likely to happen if they do not accept. The net gain after a strike will only exceed OG_1 if the strike forces the employer to raise his offer to a level giving G_2, where $G_2 - G_1$ exceeds the loss suffered by the workers during the strike. In terms of Figure 3 the union should only strike if the offer G_2 is going to be forthcoming before the strike has lasted s_1 periods, where $s_1 L_1 = G_1 G_2$. If the offer G_2 is made some time between s_1 and s_2 the union is now in a worse position than if it had accepted G_1 initially without a strike. Nonetheless, its best course may be to accept the offer now made. Indeed the employer's revised offer may well be less than G_1, the union's net gain negative and yet it may be best for the union to acquiesce. The Hieser analysis is silent on these points and it is clear that equations (3), (4), (5) and (6), *of themselves*, cannot say what union behaviour ought to be or will be. The reason has probably become clear from this paragraph. It is basically that the analysis takes no explicit account of uncertainty and is essentially non-probabilistic in form. But the 'best' action for

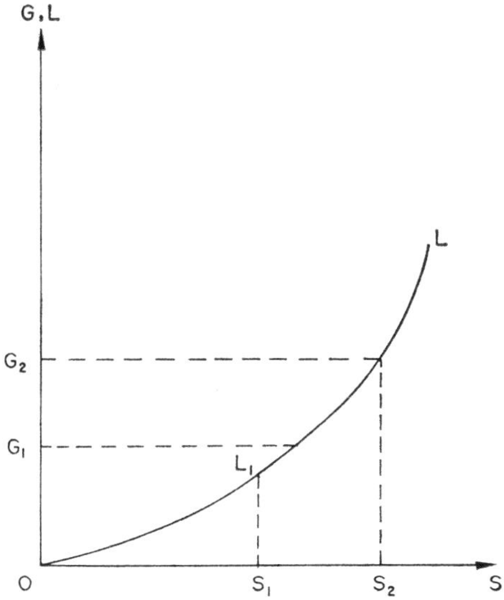

Fig. 3

union or employer is conditional on their expectations about an uncertain future and about the uncertain reaction of the other party to the disagreement. It is difficult to see how any progress can be made with a non-probabilistic treatment of this problem.

Turning now to the second basic element in the Hieser analysis, the loss of profits to the employer as a result of the strike is given by

$$L_1 = \frac{sQ.w}{\varepsilon - 1} + Q.F(s, w) \quad \dots\dots\dots\dots\dots\dots (7)$$

where $F(s, w)$ is the employer's supplementary function, measuring loss of goodwill and financial stress which again is likely to increase sharply with s. In addition to profits lost during the strike the loss of profits from the wage increase is[5]

$$L_2 = Q.\Delta w.V_n(i) \dots\dots\dots\dots\dots\dots\dots (8)$$

where $V_n(i)$ is the present value of a stream of unit payments over n periods discounted at the rate i.

Hieser then equates L_1 and L_2 to give what he terms the employer's break-even function, namely,

[5] This ignores a term in $\Delta w.\ \Delta Q$.

$$\Delta w = \frac{1}{V_n(i)}\left(\frac{sw}{\varepsilon - 1} + F(s, w)\right) \quad \ldots\ldots\ldots\ldots\ldots (9)$$

A possible shape for this function is shown by curve OE in Figure 2. We may note in passing that this is a peculiar use of the term 'break-even'. It is not a balancing of gain and loss. Both constituent elements are losses, one being the loss from the strike and the other the loss from the wage increase. No connection is postulated by Hieser between the length of strike and the size of wage increase that the employer might get away with. The function given by (9) will increase monotonically in the Δw, s plane and merely shows the locus of Δw, s values at which the loss from a strike of duration s is equal to the loss from a wage increase of Δw.

If we set $U(s, w) = F(s, w) = 0$ and also assume $V_m(j) = V_n(i) = V$, equations (6) and (9) reduce to

$$w = \frac{sw}{\frac{1}{2}(3 - \varepsilon)V} \quad \ldots\ldots\ldots\ldots\ldots\ldots (6')$$

$$w = \frac{sw}{(\varepsilon - 1)V} \quad \ldots\ldots\ldots\ldots\ldots\ldots (9')$$

These are simplified versions of the two 'break-even' functions and Hieser's use of them is illustrated in Figure 4, where it has been

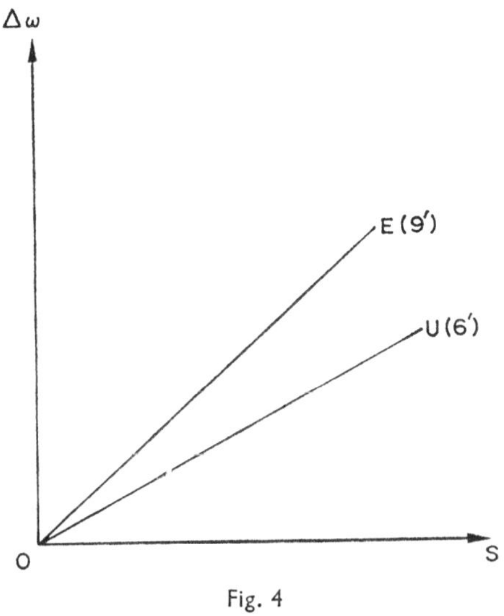

Fig. 4

assumed that the elasticity of demand (ε) has a value such that the slope of the employer's break-even line OE exceeds that of the union line OU. Hieser then asserts:

(i) 'as long as OU lies to the right of OE, the union will always outlast the employer', and

(ii) 'pressure and counter-pressure from both sides will cease when OU coincides with OE'.

These two statements are puzzling, both with respect to their meaning and their derivation from what has gone before. The derivation is not given in any explicit fashion. As we have already seen the OU curve does not really say anything about likely union behaviour. Still less does the OE line say anything about employer behaviour. For instance a strike of s weeks will have cost the employer a certain sum L_1; there is some wage increase, Δw, whose cost to the employer will be equal to L_1, but so what? The employer is presumably more interested in knowing what wage increase might settle the strike now and what increases might be required at various future dates if the strike is not settled now. Hieser's analysis discusses none of these issues and it does not seem to me that anything can be deduced from it about the length of strike that will ensue nor the settlement that will emerge. His first proposition might be interpreted to mean that the union claim must be granted in full at the end of the strike, which seems helpful until one remembers that the union claim does not appear explicitly in the model. The meaning of the second proposition is even more obscure. If OU and OE coincide throughout their length what values of s and $\mathrm{T}w$ will emerge? A strike of infinite duration and an infinitely large wage increase would appear to be feasible, as are no strike with no wage increase or any intermediate combination. If the shape of the curves is such that they meet at just a single point of tangency there still seems nothing in the logic of the article to ensure that the tangent point represents a solution to the conflict.

II. A Suggested Solution—Model 'A'

The following is an attempted solution to the Hieser problem, using a probabilistic model with hopefully plausible assumptions about union–employer behaviour. The process starts with the submission of a union claim for a wage increase of amount Δw^c. In the circumstances the maximum increase that the union should actually achieve is indicated by GH in Figure 1. The claim should probably be greater than this but for the moment we will not discuss how the size of the claim should be decided by the union. We will discuss first of all the optimal reaction by the employer to the claim.

The employer will consider making an offer in the range 0 to Δw^c.[6] For any offer that he makes there exists the possibility that even prolonged and skilful negotiation will not secure its acceptance by the union and that a strike will follow the breakdown of negotiations. The probability (π) of such a strike must clearly depend, among other things, on the size of the offer in relation to the claim. One would expect the probability to decline monotonically with the size of the offer. The simplest linear hypothesis then suggests

$$\pi = 1 - \beta . \Delta w \qquad (10)$$

where Δw denotes the wage increase offered and

$$\beta = 1/\Delta w^c \qquad (11)$$

The function (10) is shown in Figure 5(a), where for an offer Δw the distance $(1-\pi)$ indicates the probability of acceptance and the distance π the probability of a strike. A strike is certain if the employer refuses to make a positive offer, and on the other hand, has zero probability if the claim is granted in full. It should be stressed that (10) is the employer's subjective estimate of strike probabilities at the time he frames his initial offer.

If a strike takes place there are four main possible outcomes:

(i) The strike is settled on the employer's initial offer. This presumes that the financial power of the employer in relation to the losses sustained is sufficiently great, or is thought to be so, in comparison with the relative financial power of the union and its members for the former to be able to outlast the latter.

(ii) The strike is settled on the union's initial claim.

(iii) The strike is settled on the basis of a revised offer from the employer.

(iv) The dispute goes to arbitration.

In the course of selecting his initial offer in response to the claim, Δw^c, the employer must evaluate these alternatives. We will omit

[6] There is nothing in the assumptions of this problem to rule out the possibility of a *negative* offer, that is the offer of a *wage cut* in response to the demand for a wage increase. However, rather implausible parameter values would be required to yield an optimal offer in the negative range.

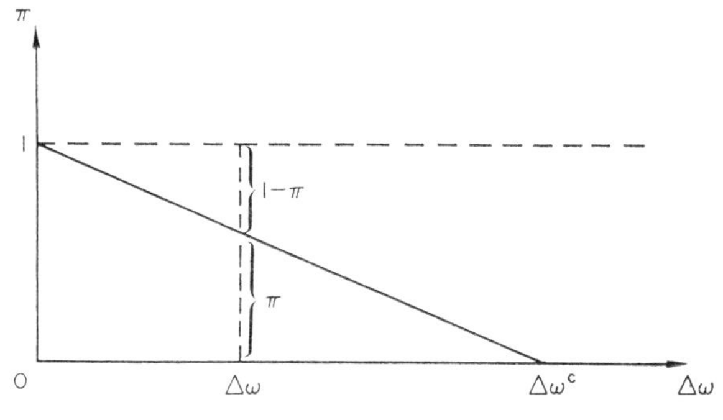

Fig. 5a

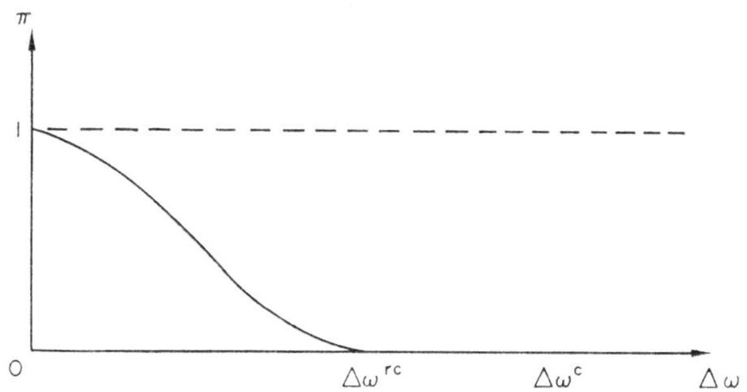

Fig. 5b

arbitration as we have nothing useful to say about it in the framework of our assumptions. We further confine attention in this section to the first two outcomes leaving the third to be dealt with in Section III. The evaluation of the first alternative is only feasible if some relationship exists between the length of strike and the wage increase that is accepted at the end of it. A possible relationship is indicated in Figure 6. This shows that a strike has to last s_1 periods before the union agrees to accept the employer's initial offer Δw_1, or s_2 periods to accept an initial offer of Δw_2 and so forth. A zero offer would eventually be accepted after s_0 periods, which probably approaches the maximum length of strike that the union could possibly endure, while a zero strike length follows from an offer which meets the claim in full. Again it must be emphasised that Figure 6 represents the employer's subjective estimate of the $s(\Delta w)$ function at the time he frames his initial offer.

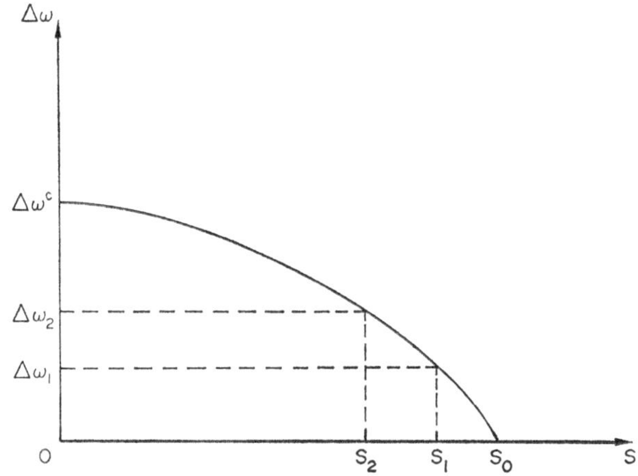

Fig. 6

The $s(\Delta w)$ function depends on both financial and psychological factors. First there is the financial ability of the union and its members to sustain a strike, which depends on the size of reserves, savings and borrowing power in relation to the cost per period of the strike. Second there is the intensity of the union's strength of will or determination to carry out the strike, and there is a presumption that this will be related to the extent to which their expectations have been disappointed or their sense of 'justice' outraged. In the face of an unchanged offer from the employer union expectations have to be painfully revised downwards. The rate of downward revision might be expected to be inversely related to the levels of the financial and psychological 'stocks' and, for given 'stocks', the time required to achieve an adjustment will be positively related to the size of the adjustment.

These factors may be elucidated with the help of Figure 7. From equation (4) the gain (G) to the union from a wage increase is proportional to the size of the increase. Thus in the figure G^c is the gain corresponding to the union claim, Δw^c, and G_1 that corresponding to an employer's offer of Δw_1. The OL curve shows the cost of the strike to the union as a function of the duration of the strike. The strike has begun because the union has refused a gain of OG_1. Rational behaviour on their part would imply that they are expecting a gain greater than OG_1 and, indeed, one which is sufficiently greater than OG_1 to at least compensate for the strike cost involved in securing the

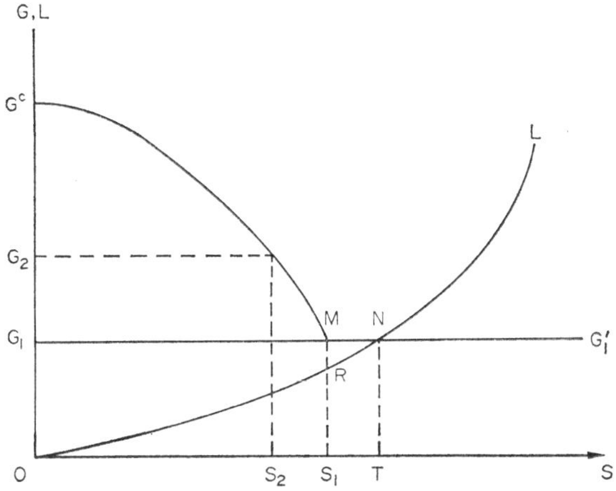

Fig. 7

incremental gain. At the commencement of the strike we take the union's target gain to be OG^c. The crucial question is how this target or expected gain is adjusted by the union as the strike proceeds and the employer refuses any further increase. A possible path is shown by the curve G^cM, where expectations remain fairly high in the early days of the strike but then decline rapidly in the face of the employer's unchanged position, giving a strike of length Os_1 before the wage increase of Δw_1 is accepted. Other things being equal, a greater initial offer, Δw_2, corresponding to a gain of G_2 would have produced a smaller disappointment of expectations, which would in turn require a shorter period of time to be eliminated.

The $s(\Delta w)$ function of Figure 6 is thus drawn with a negative slope, which agrees with Hicks' 'resistance curve.'[7] The OU function of Figures 2 and 4, also in the $s\Delta w$ plane, has a positive slope, which corresponds to Shackle's 'inducement curve'.[8] Shackle's criticisms of the negative slope of Hicks' curve would seem misplaced. The truth would appear to be that both curves are valid and correct! They measure different things and both have a place in a complete theory, though the $s(\Delta w)$ function is the more fundamental. Referring again to Figure 7, the path of the union expected gain curve has met G_1G_1'

[7] See J. R. Hicks *loc. cit.*, p. 143.

[8] See G. L. S. Shackle *loc. cit.*, p. 302, and also pp. 299–305 for his comments on the Hicks' construction.

in the point M to the left of the OL curve. Thus the *net* gain to the union, MR, is positive. It is, however, less than the net gain, OG_1, that was available to them at the start of the strike. Their initial expectations have been disappointed and have had to be painfully revised downwards, as is true of all cases implied by the $s(\Delta w)$ function of Figure 6. The union expectations curve may, more plausibly, move in discontinuous jumps and indeed it may meet G_1G_1' to the right of OL, thus giving a net loss to the union. The OL curve is a simple accounting relation indicating the wage increase (and corresponding G) at which the cost of the strike has just been balanced. *Ex post* the union may be found to have made a smaller net gain than it otherwise might; but behaviour is determined by uncertain expectations, not by *ex post* arithmetic, and these expectations are embodied in the $s(\Delta w)$ function. However, there is a sense in which the OL curve may influence the shape and position of the $s(\Delta w)$ curve, in that the union, in adjusting its expectations during the course of the strike, probably does so with an eye on the position of its OL curve. For example, if the union had recently financed a strike so that its strike fund and members' savings were low the supplementary function would be much greater than usual and hence the OL curve much higher than usual. This could be expected to accelerate the downward adjustment of expectations.

If the employer's own financial reserves would not sustain strikes of the durations pictured in Figure 6 he must either make an initial offer very close to or equal to the claim to keep the chance of a strike as low as possible, which is outcome (ii), or, if a strike does occur, work to settle it through an improved offer fairly quickly.

Returning to outcome (i) let us write a linear hypothesis for Figure 5 as

$$s=\delta(\Delta w^c-\Delta w)=\delta\left(\frac{1}{\beta}-\Delta w\right) \quad \ldots\ldots\ldots\ldots(12)$$

This gives a strike of zero duration if the offer equals the claim and a strike of duration $s_0=\delta\,.\,\Delta w^c$ if a zero offer is made. The single parameter, δ, may thus be taken as an expression of the union's propensity to endure a strike for it determines the maximum length of strike, given the claim, and also indicates the reduction in length of strike associated with a unit increase in the wage offer.

Under outcome (i) the *expected cost* to the employer of an offer, Δw, is thus

$$E(C) = \pi(L_1 + L_2) + (1 - \pi)L_2$$
$$= \pi L_1 + L_2$$

which on substitution from (7) and (8) gives

$$E(C) = \pi\left[\frac{sQw}{\varepsilon - 1} + Q.F(s, w)\right] + Q.\Delta w.V_n(i) \quad \ldots\ldots (13)$$

Since equations (10) and (12) specify π and s as functions of the offer Δw the expected cost, for any given claim, reduces to a function of the single variable, Δw, that is,

$$E(C|\Delta w^c) = f(\Delta w)$$

If the employer's utility is taken to be linearly related to the monetary sums involved his optimal decision is then to choose Δw to minimise $E(C|\Delta w^c)$.

The expected cost function (13) may be re-written as

$$E(C) = \alpha_1 \pi s + \alpha_2 \pi F(s, w) + \alpha_3 \Delta w \quad \ldots\ldots (14)$$

where

$$\alpha_1 = \frac{Qw}{\varepsilon - 1} \qquad \alpha_2 = Q \quad \text{and} \quad \alpha_3 = Q.V_n(i)$$

In the first instance let the supplementary function $F(s, w)$ be zero, so that

$$E(C) = \alpha_1 \pi s + \alpha_3 \Delta w \quad \ldots\ldots (15)$$

Substituting from (10) and (12)

$$E(C) = \frac{\alpha_1 \delta}{\beta} - (2\alpha_1\delta - \alpha_3)\Delta w + \alpha_1 \beta\delta(\Delta w)^2 \quad \ldots\ldots (16)$$

On these assumptions the expected cost function is a quadratic in Δw and the squared term has a positive coefficient. Thus there is a unique offer, Δw^*, which will minimise expected costs, namely,

$$\Delta w^* = \frac{1}{\beta} - \frac{\alpha_3}{2\alpha_1\beta\delta}$$
$$= \Delta w^c\left[1 - \frac{\alpha_3}{2\alpha_1\delta}\right] \quad \ldots\ldots (17)$$

Since the various equations have been written so that all parameters are positive it follows that

$$\Delta w^* < \Delta w^c$$

that is, the cost-minimising offer will be less than the claim. The extent to which it is less depends on the relative sizes of the parameters in (17). Rewriting them in terms of the original quantities gives

$$\Delta w^* = \Delta w^c \left[1 - \frac{V_n(i).(\varepsilon - 1)}{2w\delta} \right] \quad \ldots\ldots\ldots\ldots (18)$$

Thus, for a given claim, the cost-minimising offer should be smaller

—the greater is $V_n(i)$, that is, the longer is the time span over which the employer discounts and/or the lower is the rate of discount he uses

—the greater is the elasticity of demand for the monopolist's product

—the smaller is the current wage rate (w)

—the smaller is the union strike propensity, δ.

Our functions (10) and (12) have only been defined for the range $0 \leqslant \Delta w \leqslant \Delta w^c$. However, there is nothing *a priori* to restrict the term $\alpha_3/2\alpha_1\delta$ in (17) to be less than unity. If it exceeds unity the optimal offer would be a wage reduction and, if the rules of the game do not allow this, we would in this case set

$$\Delta w^* = 0$$

The nature of the cost-minimising offer is shown in Figure 8, which pictures the E(C) function of (15). This is the sum of $\alpha_1 \pi s$, which is a quadratic in Δw with minimum (zero) value at $\Delta w = \Delta w^c$, and a linear term $\alpha_3 \Delta w$. The positive slope of the latter ensures that the cost-minimising offer is less than the claim. The figure shows Δw^* lying in the range 0 to Δw^c, but clearly a strengthening of the α_3 factor, which is the estimated cost of the wage increase, relative to the factors measuring the expected cost of the strike could tip the E(C) function upwards at the right until its minimum in the range $O \leqslant \Delta w \leqslant \Delta w^c$ occurs at $\Delta w = 0$.

The derivation of the cost-minimising offer in (18) has rested on the two assumptions that the supplementary function F(s, w) is set at zero and that the linear approximations of (10) and (12) adequately represent the probability of a strike and its likely duration. The removal of the linearity assumption is unlikely to upset our conclusions. Both the $\pi(\Delta w)$ and the $s(\Delta w)$ functions are almost certain to decrease monotonically and both should have zero value when the offer is equal to the claim. Thus the $\alpha_1 \pi s$ term in E(C) will decrease

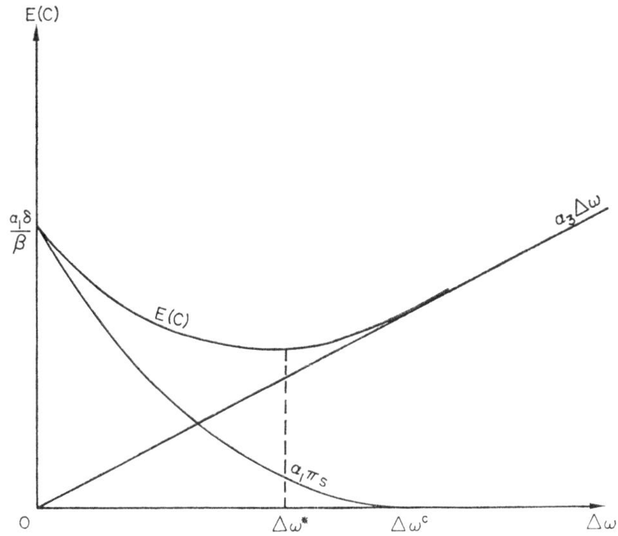

Fig. 8

monotonically with increases in Δw reaching zero at Δw^c, so that the cost-minimising offer will be less than the claim as before. The supplementary function may be expected to be non-linear in s. Let us for simplicity ignore the wage variable and write the supplementary function as

$$F(s) = bs^2 \qquad (19)$$

Referring back to the definition of the expected cost function in (14) and using again the $\pi(\Delta w)$ function in (10), the $\alpha_2 \pi F(s, w)$ term in E(C) becomes

$$\alpha_2 \pi F(s, w) = \alpha_4 (1 - \beta \Delta w)^3 \qquad (20)$$

where

$$\alpha_4 = \alpha_2 b \delta^2 / \beta^2$$

Equation (20) defines a cubic which declines monotonically from a value α_4, when $\Delta w = 0$ to zero when $\Delta w = \Delta w^c$. It has a point of inflexion at zero when the offer equals the claim; it is convex to the origin over the range $0 \leqslant \Delta w \leqslant \Delta w^c$ as is the $\alpha_1 \pi s$ term in E(C). The addition of this extra term to E(C) will obviously raise the cost-minimising offer above the level indicated by (18) and we can add an additional condition to those listed after (18) namely,

—the cost-minimising offer should be greater (less) the more (less) importance is attached to the supplementary function.

Returning to the definition of the cost-minimising offer in (18) it is seen that the two elements in it over which the union can exercise control are the size of the claim, Δw^c, and the employer's estimate of their strike propensity, δ. The latter will have been influenced by their previous dealings with the employer and can possibly be substantially influenced by current threats in so far as the employer takes them seriously. It would appear, however, that apart from this all the union has to do to secure any offer it desires is to make a large enough claim. This is clearly unrealistic and can be dealt with by an appropriate modification of the $\pi(\Delta w)$ and $s(\Delta w)$ functions. The difficulty has arisen because we have assumed a non-zero strike probability even for offers close to the claim. However, the employer will normally 'discount' part of the claim. His estimate of the strike probability will more realistically have the form shown in Figure 5(b) rather than 5(a). It reaches zero at Δw^{rc}, which we may define as the employer's estimate of the 'real claim'. Thus the employer is convinced that an offer in the range Δw^{rc} to Δw^c will be accepted by the union without a strike, though possibly only after discussion and negotiation, while an offer below Δw^{rc} runs a real danger of provoking a strike. A corresponding modification of the $s(\Delta w)$ function means that formula (18) is modified by replacing Δw^c by Δw^{rc}. Thus movements in Δw^c will only affect the initial offer if they lead the employer to change his estimate of Δw^{rc}. This and the strike propensity, δ, are the crucial parameters on which the union must work if they are to get as good an offer as possible out of the employer.

So far we have paid little attention to negotiation as compared with strikes. It has been assumed that once the employer is armed with estimates of the $\pi(\Delta w)$ and $s(\Delta w)$ functions he calculates the cost minimising Δw^*, makes that offer, tries to have it accepted without a strike but if unsuccessful, sweats out the strike until the union finally accepts. It is, perhaps, more plausible to make the following revised assumption. From his estimates of the $\pi(\Delta w)$ and $s(\Delta w)$ functions the employer makes his calculation of Δw^* as before. However, his initial offer to the union is some figure *less than* Δw^* and the range from this figure up to Δw^* is the one over which he is prepared to negotiate, with Δw^* kept in reserve as the final figure at which he will 'stick', letting a strike ensue if agreement cannot be reached on Δw^*. Thus the employer has a negotiating range, of which Δw^* is the upper limit. This upper limit is not revealed to the union. The lower limit is stated and serves as the commencing point for negotiation. As negotiations proceed the employer's offer may be revised upwards depending on the relative bargaining powers of himself and the union. The definition of the negotiating range implies that a serious union strike threat at a level short of Δw^* can force the employer to revise his offer upwards to a level nearer to or equal to Δw^*. Thus the probability, π, of the previous analysis must now be redefined to mean the probability of negotiations reaching the employer's upper limit, Δw^*, and breaking down at that point. The probability $(1-\pi)$ is then the probability of a negotiated settlement at some level *less than or equal to* Δw^*. In so far as there is any non-zero probability of negotiated settlements being reached at less than the employer's sticking point the E(C) function is no longer a simple curve, but is rather a broad line or band in the E(C), Δw plane. One would expect the band to be narrower the greater is the power and skill of the union bargainers in relation to the employer, and vice versa. The shape of the E(C) function, however, is still governed by the same considerations as before and subject to this qualification about its 'thickness' the previous analysis carries through. It is also possible that during the course of the first round of negotiations the employer revises his estimates of the $\pi(\Delta w)$ and $s(\Delta w)$ functions on the basis of his latest assessment of union attitudes. Thus he may revise his estimate of Δw^* before the negotiations have reached agreement or broken down. This is a possible additional source of 'revised' initial offers, but in practice it would be impossible to distinguish between revisions due to recalculations and revisions which were part of the initial negotiating plan.

III. Some Complications—Model 'B'

A major simplification of the previous section has been the assumption that, if a strike occurs, it is allowed to continue until the union is prepared to accept the initial offer, Δw^*. Let us now postulate the existence of two offers, namely an initial offer, Δw_1, which may be accepted with probability $(1-\pi)$ or rejected with probability π, and a revised offer, Δw_2, which only comes into play after a strike has taken place and which is sufficient to settle the strike after s_2 periods. This situation may be depicted as follows:

Accepted with probability $(1-\pi)$ —Cost $=\alpha_3\Delta w_1$

Initial Offer Δw_1

Rejected with probability π —Settled at Δw_2 after s_2 periods with Cost $=\alpha_1 s_2+\alpha_2 F(s_2)+\alpha_3\Delta w_2$

Under these circumstances the expected cost, *before any initial offer has been made*, is now

$$E(C)=(1-\pi)\alpha_3 . \Delta w_1+\pi[\alpha_1 s_2+\alpha_2 F(s_2)+\alpha_3 . \Delta w_2]$$

which, on using (10), becomes

$$E(C)=\alpha_3\beta(\Delta w_1)^2+(1-\beta\Delta w_1)[\alpha_1 s_2+\alpha_2 F(s_2)+\alpha_3 . \Delta w_2] \ldots (21)$$

The choice of an optimal initial offer is now more complicated in that the possible second-stage offer, Δw_2, must be considered as well. The solution is to consider the second-stage first of all and to derive the $\Delta w_2{}^*$ and the associated $s_2{}^*$ which constitute a minimum-cost settlement to the strike. Then letting

$$\alpha_5=\alpha_1 s_2{}^*+\alpha_2 F(s_2{}^*)+\alpha_3\Delta w_2{}^* \ldots\ldots\ldots\ldots (22)$$

it is seen that α_5 is some given constant, which on substitution in (21) gives

$$E(C)=\alpha_3\beta(\Delta w_1)^2+\alpha_5(1-\beta . \Delta w_1) \ldots\ldots\ldots\ldots (23)$$

which can now be minimised with respect to Δw_1, thus yielding the optimal initial offer.

Once a strike has actually commenced the costs to the employer will be L_1+L_2 where

$$L_1=\alpha_1 s+\alpha_2 F(s) \quad \text{and} \quad L_2=\alpha_3 . \Delta w$$

The cost-minimising strike length can then be determined from

$$\frac{dL_1}{ds}=-\frac{dL_2}{ds}$$

Assuming, as before, that the supplementary function can be represented by $F(s)=bs^2$ this last condition gives

$$s_2{}^*=\frac{\alpha_3-\alpha_1\delta}{2\alpha_2 b\delta} \ldots\ldots\ldots\ldots\ldots\ldots (24)$$

The corresponding cost-minimising wage increase can then be determined from relation (12), namely, $s=(1-\beta.\Delta w)\delta/\beta$ as

$$\Delta w_2{}^* = \frac{1}{\beta} - \frac{s}{\delta}$$

$$= \Delta w^c - \frac{\alpha_3 - \alpha_1\delta}{2\alpha_2 b\delta^2} \quad \ldots\ldots\ldots\ldots\ldots\ldots (25)$$

The significance of these results can be illustrated with reference to Figure 9.

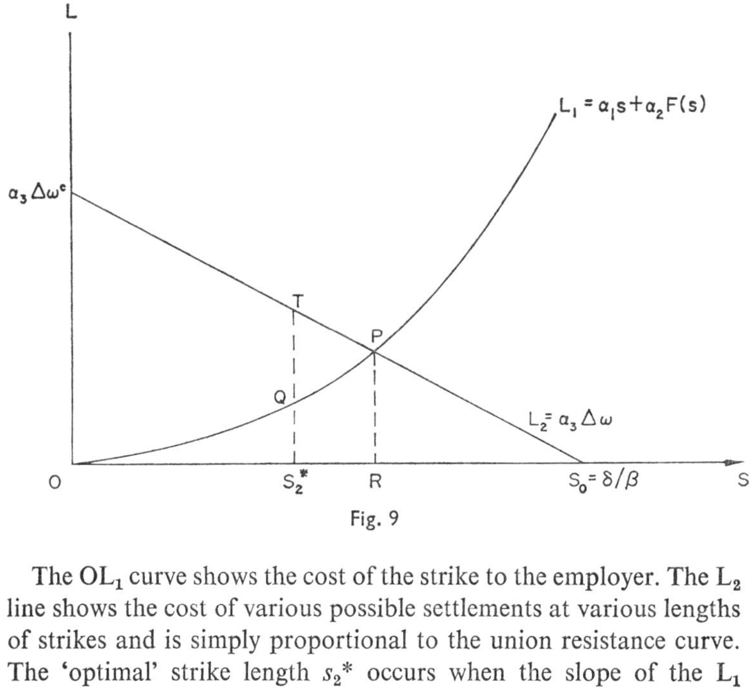

Fig. 9

The OL_1 curve shows the cost of the strike to the employer. The L_2 line shows the cost of various possible settlements at various lengths of strikes and is simply proportional to the union resistance curve. The 'optimal' strike length $s_2{}^*$ occurs when the slope of the L_1 function is numerically equal to that of the L_2 function, that is where the marginal strike cost is just offset by the marginal reduction in the settlement cost. If both L_1 and L_2 were linear, the optimal strike length would be either zero or the maximum possible, $s_0=\delta/\beta$, that is, the optimal strike-settling offer would be either the full claim, Δw^c or else zero, depending on whether the slope of the L_2 line was numerically smaller or greater than that of the L_1 line. With L_2 linear and L_1 convex from below it is still theoretically possible that the minimum value of $L_1 + L_2$ occurs at one of the boundary points. It is probable, however, that the minimum occurs at an interior point so that we would expect

$$s_2^* < \delta/\beta$$

and

$$\Delta w_2^* < \Delta w^c$$

Rewriting (25) in terms of the original parameters gives

$$\Delta w_2^* = \Delta w^c - \frac{V_n(i) - w\delta/(\varepsilon - 1)}{2b\delta^2} \quad \ldots\ldots\ldots\ldots (26)$$

This gives the same qualitative conditions on Δw_2^* as those obtained in Model A for Δw^*, namely, the cost-minimising settlement for a given claim will be positively related to the rate of time discounting used by the employer, the current wage rate, the union strike parameter (δ) and the supplementary cost parameter (b), and negatively related to the time span over which the employer discounts and the elasticity of demand.

Minimising (23) with respect to Δw_1, and using (22), yields the optimal initial offer as

$$\Delta w_1^* = \frac{\alpha_1 s_2^* + \alpha_2 F(s_2^*) + \alpha_3 \Delta w_2^*}{2\alpha_3}$$

$$= \tfrac{1}{2}\Delta w_2^* \left(\frac{L_1^*}{L_2^*} + 1\right) \quad \ldots\ldots\ldots\ldots\ldots\ldots (27)$$

where L_1^* and L_2^* are shown by the points Q and T in Figure 9 and are the strike costs and settlement costs corresponding to the optimal s_2^*, Δw_2^* values derived above. If the optimal strike length, s_2^*, had turned out to be equal to the distance OR in Figure 9, then

$$L_1^* = L_2^* = PR$$

and from (27) $\Delta w_1^* = \Delta w_2^*$. This clearly is a special case. When L_1^* and L_2^* are equal we have a point on Hieser's 'break-even' function for the employer and then the optimal strike-settling offer, Δw_2^*, would turn out to be identical with the optimal initial offer, Δw_1^*, and the model of the previous section is optimal. For the case illustrated in Figure 9, L_1^* is less than L_2^* and the optimal initial offer will be less than the optimal strike-settling offer. This will be true for all s_2^* which lie to the left of the point R in Figure 9, while for points to the right of R the optimal strike-settling offer would be less than the optimal initial offer.

This last conclusion immediately highlights an important assumption that has been implicit in the development of this section, namely, that the $s(\Delta w)$ function is invariant to any offers that have already been made. If on the other hand it is to be expected that a revised offer which is less than the initial offer, whose refusal had initiated the strike, would so incense the union that a much longer strike would be required to achieve their consent to that offer than would have been the case for an *initial* offer of the same amount, then effectively there would be a *kink* in the $s(\Delta w)$ function at Δw_1^* and revised offers below the initial offer would in practice be ruled out of consideration. We would now have $\Delta w_1^* \leqslant \Delta w_2^* \leqslant \Delta w^c$, that is, the optimal initial offer is very likely to be less than the claim but it is not certain to be, as was the case with Model A.

It should be stressed that the only purpose of introducing s_2^* and Δw_2^* into the analysis has been to improve the decision-making on the initial offer Δw_1^* and we have seen that the optimal initial offer, as determined in (27), will in general be different from the one derived under the simpler assumptions of the previous section. The remarks made there about a negotiating range *up to* the optimal offer should also be applied to the model of this section. Should the initial offer fail and a strike take place any revised offer actually forthcoming from an employer may well differ from the Δw_2^* that he had already derived in the process of determining Δw_1^*. The reason is that the negotiations leading up to the strike and the initial conduct of the strike may well lead him to revise his estimate of the underlying $s(\Delta w)$ function, which he must now use in his calculation of the cost-minimising strike settlement.

Even his new estimate of the position of the $s(\Delta w)$ curve may be in error. If he has over-estimated the strength of union resistance his offer will be needlessly high and the union pleasantly surprised. They will probably adopt the conventional postures of resistance, but are in no danger of not accepting. If the employer has underestimated the position of the curve, the continuation of the strike is a real possibility. The employer is then likely to revise his estimate of the $s(\Delta w)$ function upwards and produce a higher offer. It is also possible that the union moves some way to meet him, if the information they obtained during the discussion of the Δw_2^* offer leads to a moderation of their attitudes.

The analysis of this paper was substantially complete before I came across the study by Ashenfelter and Johnson.[9] Their main concern was the analysis of strike activity and while this has implications for wage change they do not derive any specific results on wages. Apart from that, their analysis differs from that given here in two major respects. Firstly, they assume that a strike is inevitable if the employer does not concede the full claim. 'The firm . . . has the choice of agreeing to y_0 and avoiding a strike or of rejecting y_0 and incurring a strike which will result in a lower wage increase.'[10] In their model y_0 is the minimum wage increase acceptable to the union rank and file at the point of contract expiration. Thus there is no $\pi(\Delta w)$ function in their model nor any very explicit role for negotiation to secure acceptance of an offer less than the claim. Secondly, there is no treatment of, nor indeed on their assumptions any reason for, revised offers in their model.

IV. Conclusions

The two contributions of the Hieser analysis are the explicit derivation of the upper limit to union bargaining and the elucidation of the various costs and benefits to employer and union. The outcome of the bargaining process in his analysis, however, remains obscure. By the use of probabilistic considerations and the development of an expected cost function for the employer it is shown that there is, in general, a unique cost-minimising initial offer and, if this fails, a unique cost-minimising strike-settling offer. The levels of these offers and the connection between them are seen to depend on a few basic parameters of the relevant cost and probability functions. Under plausible assumptions the actual wage change will be less than the claim and in certain cases might be zero (if not negative). While the latter case cannot be ruled out on *a priori* grounds, a sufficient increase in the union's strike propensity could shift the optimal employer offer above zero.

It might be thought that an implication of the above analysis is that at each negotiation the union should extract as much as possible from the employer without ever putting a strike threat into effect.

[9] O. Ashenfelter and G. Johnson, 'Bargaining Theory, Trade Unions and Industrial Strike Activity.' *American Economic Review*, March 1969, pp. 35–49.
[10] Ashenfelter and Johnson *loc. cit.*, p. 38.

Thus the union should make claims, get some fraction of the claim each time and proceed towards its ultimate goal without incurring the losses and hardships of strikes. This, however, is a false conclusion. The employer's estimates of the $\pi(\Delta w)$ and $s(\Delta w)$ functions will not remain unchanged over time. They are affected by all his experience and knowledge, including that gained from past negotiations and strikes as well as from the current situation. Downward revisions by the employer of his estimate of the union's strike propensity, δ, automatically reduce his optimal offer and could, in fact, reduce it to zero. The actual occurrence of strikes is thus an essential condition for the continuing rise of the money wage bill in this model. As time passes and the power of the union to sustain a strike is built up again one would expect subsequent claims, which in turn would be partially successful, and the union would over time approach the maximum possible share for wage income. The sequence of events after unionisation is thus rising money wage rates, rising money wage bill, rising product price accompanied by falling output and reducing employment for the union's members. In so far as reduced employment opportunities are a constraint on the union's activity one would expect it to moderate their pursuit of increased wage rates.

The assumptions of the Hieser problem are essentially static—no change in technology, no change in the monopolist's demand function and no general inflation or deflation. In a general inflation a proportionate marking up of all prices and wage rates will keep real wage rates approximately constant. Any bargaining for money increases beyond that level will put us back in the framework of the Hieser problem and will be influenced by the specific factors already analysed and specified in equations (18), (26) and (27), namely the time span over which the employer discounts, the rate of discounting he uses, the elasticity of the demand function for his product, the current wage rate, the union strike propensity and the employer's supplementary cost parameter. Variations in general economic conditions as reflected, say, in the general unemployment rate, might be expected to have some marginal influence on these specific variables, but it is only through such mediation that they will affect the settlements reached. Thus in sectors of the economy where the institutional arrangements correspond approximately to the Hieser assumptions rational economic calculation on the part of employers can lead to wage increases in response to union demands even though there has been no change, or even an adverse change, in the level of excess demand that a conventional Phillips curve analysis regards as an essential pre-requisite for a wage increase.

Appendix: Mathematical Derivations

Equation (17)

$$E(C)=\frac{\alpha_1\delta}{\beta}-(2\alpha_1\delta-\alpha_3)\Delta w+\alpha_1\beta\delta(\Delta w)^2 \quad\ldots\ldots\ldots(16)$$

$$\frac{dE(C)}{d(\Delta w)}=-(2\alpha_1\delta-\alpha_3)+2\alpha_1\beta\delta.\Delta w$$

$$\frac{d^2E(C)}{d(\Delta w)^2}=2\alpha_1\beta\delta>0$$

Equating the first derivative to zero.

$$\Delta w^*=\frac{2\alpha_1\delta-\alpha_3}{2\alpha_1\beta\delta}$$

$$=\frac{1}{\beta}-\frac{\alpha_3}{2\alpha_1\beta\delta}$$

$$=\frac{1}{\beta}\left[1-\frac{\alpha_3}{2\alpha_1\delta}\right]$$

$$=\Delta w^c\left[1-\frac{\alpha_3}{2\alpha_1\delta}\right] \quad \text{since } \beta.\Delta w^c=1. \quad \text{from (11)}$$

Equation (24)

$$L_1=\alpha_1 s+\alpha_2 bs^2$$
$$L_2=\alpha_3\Delta w$$

and

$$s=\frac{\delta}{\beta}(1-\beta.\Delta w)$$

Thus

$$\Delta w=\frac{1}{\beta}-\frac{s}{\delta}$$

and

$$L_2=\alpha_3\left(\frac{1}{\beta}-\frac{s}{\delta}\right)$$

$$\frac{dL_1}{ds}=-\frac{dL_2}{ds}$$

then gives

$$\alpha_1 + 2\alpha_2 bs = \alpha_3/\delta$$

which gives

$$s^* = \frac{\alpha_3 - \alpha_1\delta}{2\alpha_2 b\delta}$$

and (25) then follows from substitution in

$$\Delta w = \frac{1}{\beta} - \frac{s}{\delta}$$

Equation (27)

$$\Delta w_1{}^* = \frac{\alpha_1 s_2{}^* + \alpha_2 F(s_2{}^*) + \alpha_3 \Delta w_2{}^*}{2\alpha_3}$$

$$= \frac{L_1{}^*}{2\alpha_3} + \frac{\Delta w_2{}^*}{2}$$

$$= \frac{\Delta w_2{}^*}{2} \cdot \frac{L_1{}^*}{L_2{}^*} + \frac{\Delta w_2{}^*}{2} \quad \text{since} \quad L_2{}^* = \alpha_3 . \Delta w_2{}^*$$

$$= \frac{\Delta w_2{}^*}{2}\left(\frac{L_1{}^*}{L_2{}^*} + 1\right)$$

6

A Trade Union View of Economics

Giles Radice†

I OUGHT TO begin by presenting my credentials—or lack of them. Though even my best friends (or worst enemies) would not call me a professional economist, I have received some training in economics. So, while the world of elegant equations and impressive econometric constructs is not my natural habitat, I am enough of an economist to be able to express a view on the utility of economics to trade union problems. A warning at the start. Trade unions exist to serve their members. So naturally they tend to look at economists and their work from the point of view of whether or not it is useful to them. There is nothing strange in that—so do businessmen and governments.

Traditionally, British trade unionists have tended to have little time for 'main-stream' economics. Partly, their aversion has been an ideological one. To trade unionists whose formative years were in the 1920s and 1930s, the work of professional economists seemed to be merely justification of a system which they detested. The era of mass unemployment with all that it meant in individual, social and organisational terms was not, perhaps, the best background against which to develop an appreciation of the finer points of neo-classical economics. To recapture the flavour of the period, one has only to read the bitter exchanges which took place on the Macmillan Committee on Finance and Industry between one of the members of the Committee, Ernest Bevin, who was then General Secretary of the Transport and General Workers' Union and an instinctive Keynesian, and a key witness, Montagu Norman, Governor of the Bank of England and self-appointed guardian of the classical system. To all Bevin's ideas, Norman responded with what Bevin's biographer describes as 'the bleak negatives of . . . cold self-satisfaction'.

† Head of the Research Department of the General and Municipal Workers' Union.

It is true that, since the war, trade unionists have come to accept (more or less grudgingly) the existence of the 'mixed economy'. However, much of the old distrust of economics has remained. The trade unionist's experience is that he usually hears about economics in a highly normative context—and they are not his norms. It is a common occurrence for an employer to tell us during negotiations that our wage claim shows a total disregard for 'elementary economic facts'. Leaving aside for a moment the professional competence of union wage claims, imagine the feelings of a trade union negotiator. He knows perfectly well that most employers whom he meets know as much—or as little—about theoretical economics as he does himself. He is also well aware that the employer's own use of 'elementary economic facts' can be highly dubious. The 'facts' may not turn out to be 'facts' at all. Even if they are as correct as it is possible for facts about human activities to be, they are often presented in a selective way and out of context. 'Economics' becomes a weapon in the bargaining process and, to trade unionists, at any rate, its reputation as an 'objective' science inevitably suffers.

On the macro level, trade union attitudes have been more ambivalent. Until recently, older trade unionists were at least thankful that governments seemed to have discovered how to deal with mass unemployment. However, by the 1960's, the sluggish performance of the British economy, increasing familiarity with stop-go, and the persistence of inflation caused trade unionists, amongst others, to question not only the effectiveness of economic policy, but also of economists and economics. In the early days of the Labour Government, trade unionists were prepared to participate in various forms of incomes policy as a means of breaking out of the vicious circle of economic weaknesses into a virtuous circle of export-led growth. They were not prepared, however, to be put into the dock as the villains of the piece, as, with the failure of successive governments' economic policies they increasingly became. With the advent of the present administration, the devotees of the Phillips curve, already influential under Labour, seemed to be in the ascendant. Whatever the economic merits of the Phillips theory (I shall deal with this later), as a fully fledged economic policy it is socially repugnant. Influential trade unionists blame economists as much as governments for what they consider to be a concerted attack on organised labour—and, given the marginalists' view of trade unions as an unwelcome blot on the perfection of their model, who is to say that they are entirely wrong?

Now, I have not come here to drag classical theory through the mud. Nobody who has any sort of training as an economist can fail to admire the beauty, the complexity and the comprehensive nature of the inter-locking concepts of traditional economics. Of course, they provide us with some insights about wage-determination.

The difficulty about the classical theory is that it does not begin to be a sufficient explanation of what happens in the real world. This is, of course, generally recognised by labour economists. Professor Alexander in his introduction to B. J. McCormick's book on *Wages* (Penguin 1969) says 'Wage theory has for long been a particularly unsatisfactory area in economics. There are the usual 'difficulties of avoiding a circular explanation of the supply side . . . and on the demand side, of disentangling the contributions to total product of the various factors of production. To these difficulties must be added the social and political complications arising from the differential spread of wealth and power in society and in the labour market.'

Take the position of unions, for example. In classical equilibrium theory, unions are either superfluous or creators of unemployment. The intersection of the demand curve for labour (derived from the demand for the product) and supply curve for labour determines the equilibrium wage. Either the wage lies at the equilibrium level—in which case the union might as well not have bothered—or it forces the wage above the equilibrium—in which case the quantity of labour demanded is less than the quantity supplied and unemployment results. So much for trade union efforts.

Determined labour economists like Dunlop have tried to place trade unions within the marginalist framework. Adapting what was essentially the traditional 'theory of the firm', Dunlop developed an 'economic' model of a trade union. This model views the union as an economic decision-making unit having as its primary objective the maximization of wages in relation to employment. I have no wish to enter the Ross/Dunlop controversy in detail but I cannot resist quoting Ross's comment that 'the volume of employment associated with a given wage rate is unpredictable before the fact and the effect of a given rate upon employment is undecipherable after the fact'. (A. M. Ross: Trade Union Wage Policy, University of California 1948 p. 14.) Certainly the Ross and other models which give weight to power and political factors in predicting the behaviour and success of trade unions in the furtherance of their objectives are far more convincing to a trade unionist than Dunlop's narrowly economic model.

When a trade union goes to the bargaining table, objectives are not purely economic. A crucial part of its job (perhaps the most important) is the democratic one of restricting one-sided management decision-making by making an increasing number of issues the subject of joint decision-making. Even on wage issues, it does not operate in the way Dunlop imagines. The kind of issues that are traditionally prominent in a wage claim include general increases in the cost of living (a macro-economic variable), increases in rates in other industries (a social justice argument), and the firm or industry's 'ability to pay' (which usually centres around productivity and profit records). Behind these considerations lie the pressures of membership expectations, of inter-union rivalry, and of organisational imperatives of one sort and another. On the other side of the bargaining table, the employers tend to talk in similar language—though, obviously, interpreting the figures in a way that suits their use. The outcome of the negotiating process will depend on a number of factors, including the militancy of union members, the organisational effectiveness of the union, and the company's ability to resist strikes.

Obviously embedded in all this may be demand and supply factors. I fully recognise that a trade union which operates in a firm or industry in which there exist no available substitutes for labour, in which labour costs are a low percentage of total costs, and in which the demand for the product is inelastic will tend to be in a stronger position than a union which operates in a firm or industry in which none of these conditions hold—the more so if, under the influence of technology, the industry is expanding fast. But the ability to cash in on these conditions will depend on the organisational effectiveness of the union. Similarly, a well organised union, in a less obviously agreeable economic climate, may be able to achieve good results for its members. Organisational factors are reinforced by use of the 'comparability' argument. A settlement which takes into account wage movements in other industries may have justification in classical economic terms only as a labour retention device. In bargaining however, it has an independent force which cannot be discounted. Professor Jan Pen, commenting on this use of union power, says 'the conclusion of practically all students of the British wage pattern is that this (*the inter-industry wage differential*) has remained fairly stable over a longish period. There is nothing to be seen of a considerable lead by the rapidly growing branches of industry nor of a pronounced lag by others.'[1] Now it may be that there are economic

[1] *Income Distribution* by Jan Pen, Penguin, 1971, p. 109.

forces at work which also explain this surprising stability of the horizontal wage structure (see the study by H. A. Turner and D. A. S. Jackson[2]), but union negotiating policies are part of the explanation. Union pressure for greater equality has also been a major force behind the tendency for differentials between skilled and unskilled manual workers and some white collar workers and manual workers to narrow.

The importance of social norms—of what different groups consider to be a 'fair' remuneration—is particularly striking in the civil service (where it is the official method of determining pay) and in high managerial positions. Top managers usually fix their own pay. Indeed, trade unions find it very irritating that managers who put such stress on the primacy of economic forces in the discussion of union wage claims should decide their own salaries by criteria which owe far more to a desire for status and an all too human greed than to managerial productivity.

The inadequacy of marginalist theory as a guide to what happens in the real world has also been shown up by recent studies of local labour markets. 'All the evidence suggests that there are factors operating within individual plants which effectively isolate it partially from the external economic forces operating in the local labour market. Conditions in the internal labour market (*the individual plant*) can apparently lead to relatively high wages, or in other situations create conditions in which rather low wages exist without undue difficulty in recruitment or retention. There are forces (*within the individual plant*) emanating from workers, trade unions and management. Regarding these as institutional forces, though they may express themselves through informal groups, then often they may seem more powerful than straight economic forces.'[3] Those who wish to hang on at all costs to their theory can lay stress on the existence of market imperfections, on the workers' and employers' inadequate knowledge of wage rates and on the non-wage advantages of the low-wage plant. Others may feel as I do, that traditional theory does not provide a sufficiently satisfactory explanation of what actually happens in labour markets.

[2] *On the Stability of Wage Differences and Productivity-Based Wage Policies: An International Analysis*. British Journal of Industrial Relations, March 1969.
[3] *Local Labour Markets and Wage Structures*, ed. Robinson, Gower Press, 1970, p. 65.

Turning from micro- to macro-economics, a trade unionist is conscious of entering a world which, in some respects, is less artificial. Trade Unions, unlike economic theoreticians, have always been aware of the influence of macro-economic variables on collective bargaining—the effect, for example, of the general level of prices on money wages. Since Keynes, macro-economics has tended to be more relevant to our problems. The Keynesian equations were not only beautiful, they also brought macro-economics into line with the real world of mass-unemployment, under-consumption and under-investment. For trade unions, the Keynesian revolution has a special importance. This was because the central position of national income and expenditure in the Keynesian system enabled trade unionists to refute the charge of the classical school that their wage increases were the cause of mass unemployment. The insight that greater income led to greater consumption and thus more employment was a liberating one for trade unions. At last, there was a theory in which we could play a constructive role.

It was natural that, in the years since 1945, much work in Britain should have been done on inflation. With our deplorable growth record, inflation has assumed an importance that it does not have in other, faster growing economies. We have, however, been disturbed by two very different theoretical explanations which are influential not only in academic but also in government circles. The monetary theory of Milton Friedman and the Chicago School has the merit of simplicity. No bother about inflationary spirals, employment, trade unions and all the other familiar and complicated relationships. All governments have to do to stop inflation is to control the expansion of the money supply. Well, it is a very nice theory but in practice pretty ineffective. This is because, except in a Weimar Republic situation of galloping inflation, the velocity of circulation of money adjusts to wages and prices rather than the other way round.

Professor Phillips's attempt at applying econometrically economic theories relating changes in the wage rate to the percentage of unemployment has also worried us. Mr. Worswick's Presidential address makes the point, which is worth repeating, that professional economists cannot be absolved from responsibility for the idea taken up in recent years by civil servants and politicians that some relatively small (though, in human terms, catastrophic enough) increase in unemployment would be sufficient to check inflation. After all, the present situation when the highest percentage of unemployment since the war goes hand-in-hand with the highest rate of price increases is not the first direct refutation of the Phillips curve theory. We know that, despite high levels of unemployment between 1932 to 1939, wage rates rose. And, if you examine the figures for the 1950's, they also suggest that the simple relationship between the level of unemployment and increases in prices does not hold for this period. As Professor Lipsey has said about the 1950 figures, 'Increased union power may mean that, for any given level of demand for labour, wages are now pushed up faster than previously.'[4]

In practical terms, the result of Professor Phillips's theory is that the government turned down the TUC's advice to reflate the economy in the months following the Conservative election victory. We argued that the most effective background against which to tackle prices was one in which firms would be allowed to run their plants at full capacity. We said that economic expansion would not only provide more jobs but could actually bring down unit costs. The government apparently hoped that if they followed Professor Phillips and allowed the army of the unemployed to grow, the capacity of unions to negotiate high wage settlements would be affected. The experience of the last fifteen months has refuted Professor Phillips—but it is a pity that we should have wasted such a vital period in a tragically futile testing of a hypothesis which, in the extravagantly simple form put forward by Phillips, was already untenable.

Professor Lipsey himself is much to blame for the fashionable rejection of incomes policy since he and Parkin argued on the basis of complex but misguided econometrics, the use of the wrong data, and an over-determinist model dividing years simply into policy on and policy off, that Incomes Policy had *increased* inflation when it was operating (by the norm becoming the floor).

I do not have the time to look in detail at income distribution. Until recently, economic theory had not made much of a contribution to our knowledge of what happens in the real world. Hugh Dalton pointed out as long ago as 1920 that the emphasis of economists on the functional distribution of incomes in effect largely relegates the personal distribution of incomes 'a problem of more direct and obvious interest' to the status of a residual to be studied if at all 'by plodding statistical investigations, which professors of economic

[4] See Professor R. G. Lipsey, 'Can there be a Valid Theory of Wages?' *The Labour Market*, edited by B. J. McCormick and E. Owen Smith, Penguin Modern Economics, 1968.

theory were content to leave to lesser men.'[5] In fact, in the developed economies, labour's share fluctuates and tends to rise. Of course, if one leaves out white collar workers (the fastest growing section of the labour force) and forgets about government employees (the government's contribution to national income is between 20% and 25%), one might be able to get away with the view that labour's share is constant. But, to argue in these terms is to evade the issue, unless, of course, one believes that the real problem of labour's share is in the words of R. Solow, 'how to be constant though variable'. The work of Solow is, in fact, extremely valuable in that it gives a satisfying theoretical explanation of how increasing capital accumulation can actually lead to an increasing labour share. One can even fit the effort of the unions into the theory.

Of much more practical value to trade unionists, however, is the work of the human capital school. Although, of course, there are other factors involved in the inequalities of income, the work of Becker and Mincer reminds us of the critical importance of education and training to earnings distribution. Over the next twenty years, we shall, as a community, need to pay more attention to training and education if we wish to create a less inegalitarian society.

Much of what I have said about economics may sound carping. I hasten to say that this is not because I am against the idea of economic theory.

On the contrary, theory is vitally important provided, of course, that it can provide a satisfactory explanation of real-life as well as stylised facts and make predictions. The trouble about the state of labour economic theory is that, though in many directions, it is patently unsatisfactory, it is still the best we have. As Albert Rees said this year when addressing a Conference of Canadian labour economists 'It is one of the truisms of the history of economic doctrine that ultimately one can only defeat a theory with another theory.'[6]

I do not necessarily believe in the idea of one simple theory. But we need labour economic theoreticians who are prepared to face up to the difficulties that the existence of social power and institutional variables raises for wages theory. I do not pretend to know how this

[5] *Some Aspects of the inequality of incomes in modern communities*, by Hugh Dalton, G. Routledge & Sons, 1920.

[6] *The Current State of Labour Economics*, by Albert Rees, Industrial Relations Centre Queen's University at Kingston, Ontario 1971, Report series 16, p. 3.

can be done, but I am comforted that both in this country and America there are already labour economists constructing models which, in particular, have relevance to problems confronting trade unionists. The integration of the theory of games approach to wage bargaining (which explains how economic factors set targets and resistance points to negotiate and tactical manoeuvring to reach one's opponent's maximum point of settlement) into economic theory can be useful.

I would re-echo the President's call for more involvement by economists in matters which have direct policy implications. Of course, economists will find themselves bumping up against sociologists and industrial relations experts. So much the better. I would add that it would be extremely useful for the trade union movement if economists could devote more attention to problems that concern us. I have already mentioned the work of the human capital school. Valuable work has also been done (though mainly in the United States) on the structure and duration of unemployment. We need to develop models which will provide us with the framework of an effective labour market policy. We need far more study on the causes and structure of low pay and differentials generally. We need more detailed analysis of the problems involved in the drive for equal pay and opportunities for women. Work on the structure of product markets is, of course, very relevant to collective bargaining.

On a more general level, we need far more work on the facts and causes of income distribution—on the distribution between earned and unearned income and the distribution according to age, size of family, occupation and so on. We need detailed and realistic advice on the way to combine economic expansion with relatively stable prices and a healthy balance of payments. I do not promise that the trade unions will always wish to accept your advice or your findings. But more knowledge about problems which are, at best, rather cloudy, will, in the long run, be to everybody's advantage.

Finally, I would put in a personal plea for more economists to come and work for the trade unions. It is not enough for us to criticise economics (as I have been doing). We have to make our own contribution. This is not a Utopian objective. In Sweden, some of the best economists in the country work for the Swedish trade union movement. I am also encouraged by a number of developments in the British trade union movement. In recent years, the TUC, through its Economic Review, has been playing an increasing role in public debate on economic policy. If successive governments had listened a little more closely to their arguments, our economy might be in a more healthy position today. In collective bargaining, individual unions have co-operated with academic economists. The Ford and ICI wage claims showed the kind of contribution that a professional economist can make to the preparation of wage claims. In my own union, we already have a first class economist and, at the beginning of this month, we will be taking on a business economist to help us answer the perennial employer's question in negotiations 'Where is the money coming from?' I am not arguing that trade union research departments can be serviced by economists alone. We need industrial relations experts, sociologists, and statisticians as well. But the judicious employment of economists could give trade union arguments at all levels a bite they sometimes lack.

7

Economics, Economists and Industry

T. M. Rybczynski†

ECONOMICS is now passing through a stage of rapidly increasing self-questioning and self-criticism. Its role, function, contribution and value as well as its development are subjected to intense scrutiny which has come not only from within but also from outside the profession. Some signs of this critical attitude can be discerned in the address of Sir Alec Cairncross, the present President of the Association. David Worswick's presidential address to Section F was wholly devoted to the problem of progress in economics, the essence of his paper being, to use his own words, that 'too much of what goes on in economics and econometric theory is of little or no relevance to serious economic science'. Professor Phelps Brown, delivering his presidential address to the Royal Economic Society earlier this year, concerned himself with the same issue finding, to quote him, the 'divergence between economics and practical problems increasingly a cause of disappointment and disquiet not only to those who have to tackle those problems, but also to those concerned with the advancement of economics as a science'.

These doubts and anxieties have not been confined to the profession in the U.K. They have also been voiced in other western countries and in a subdued way have also been expressed in the planned economies. Delivering his presidential address to the American Economic Association at the end of last year, entitled 'Theoretical Associations and Nonobserved Facts', Professor Leontieff discussed the same issue of the relevance and irrelevance of the practical problems to which economists address their efforts and the adequacy of the scientific means with which to try to solve them.

The spread of economics as a separate discipline in the continental countries is causing Europeans to re-think its place and role while the

† Head of the Economic Research Department, Lazard Bros.; Visiting Professor in the University of Surrey.

Marxist economics, as thought and practised behind the Iron and Bamboo Curtains, is likewise increasingly subject to re-examination.

In many ways the doubts and apprehensions now expressed resemble those of the two earlier important transition periods, that of the late twenties and early thirties, which brought into being that classic contribution from Professor L. Robbins 'On the Nature and Significance of Economic Science' and was followed by the Keynesian Revolution, and earlier of the 1870s and 1880s when under Marshall modern economics was emerging from its formative stage.

The reasons for the present doubts and uncertainties are many and have been discussed in the papers I mentioned as well as directly and indirectly in many other contributions. As mentioned by Leontieff and others they partly reflect the phenomenal success of and expansion in the body of economic knowledge and associated with it a very rapid increase in specialisation beginning to resemble very closely that existing in natural sciences where different branches also find it difficult to understand each other.

But to me the present doubts and anxieties can also be attributed to a large degree to the inadequate effort made by the profession to extend its efforts to learn more about and understand the functioning of industry, commerce and finance and the changes which are taking place in these fields and which in brief encompass the micro rather than macro subjects of the body of knowledge. Indeed it is my view that our understanding and ability to influence efficaciously some of the broader trends—the demand management, rate of growth, the pressure on costs and prices—could be improved if our knowledge of industrial developments were put on a better and sounder footing.

One of the remarkable features of the development of economic science during the last one hundred years or so has been its ability to address itself to the pressing and urgent problems of the day while at the same time building up a corpus of knowledge of increasingly wide application influencing and guiding policy-makers. These problems in the past have been predominantly of the aggregative type with the result that the emphasis of economics—both as regards the development of theory and empirical work—has tended to be on these particular aspects.

The emphasis on the aggregative problems—reflecting the preoccupation with trade cycle and depression—had also found its reflection until the early fifties in the employment of economists. The bulk of non-academic economists until 20 years or so ago—and their numbers were very small indeed—had worked almost entirely for the government, central bank and other official agencies, mainly in the capacity of administrators possessing specialised knowledge. Of course, their presence in the administrative and also advisory post has been of unquestioned value. By using their professional training and equipment to bear on the immediate policy issues they made it possible to approach them in a rational and competent manner. Moreover, they were able to generate the provision of new statistics and new information that has become of wider use and by maintaining a close contact with the academic world keep the latter well informed and indeed involved in the problems faced in these days.

This pattern of development has served economics and the profession very well. By enabling society to solve the problems of unemployment and leading to the universal acceptance of the long-term aims of economic policy—as stated, for example, in the 1944 White Paper on *Employment Policy*—it has provided a conclusive proof of the value of economic science as such and of the members of the profession.

While the aggregative or macro problems are still with us and will remain for many years to come, their nature has changed in a way that requires much improved knowledge and understanding of the micro-aspects. Among the five most pressing problems facing economics at present Professor Phelps Brown includes three which in my view must draw upon a better understanding of how individual firms work. These are 'fostering growth in poor countries and improving the performance of the industrialised economies', 'checking cost inflation while maintaining full employment' and 'checking the adverse effects on the environment and the quality of life of industrialism, population growth and urbanism'. (The other two are 'adjusting the balance of payments' and 'deciding the scope of the free market and government intervention'.) In surveying the present position of economics and its prospects Leontieff likewise calls for a shift from what he describes as 'casual empiricism to systematic large-scale factual analysis' necessary to achieve 'true advance in which improved theoretical formulation raises new empirical questions and the answers to these questions, in their turn, lead to new theoretical insights'.

There thus appears to be emerging a growing consensus among the members of the profession that, if economics is to continue to advance and to fulfil a useful and valuable role in the affairs of mankind, it must try to deepen its knowledge and understanding of the functioning and actions of the individual units making up the economy, among which industry and the consumer are most important. If this view is accepted, as it is beginning to be among the leaders and academic brethren, it raises the important issue of economics, economist and industry.

While the new attitudes have been spreading only very slowly industry has been increasingly drawing on economics in one way or another, realising that it can be of immediate and often great assistance and value. Indeed the very rapid growth of the business economist profession—there are now some 2,000 business economists in the U.K., about 8,000 in the U.S.A. and a small but growing number on the Continent of Europe—and its success are a living testimony to this development. It is certainly no exaggeration to say that the growth of the profession as a whole has benefited in no small measure from this development and from the use of economics by the employment of economists in business. Moreover, not an inconsiderable number of the advances that have been made in the body of knowledge can be traced to work done at least initially in business. Examples of the latter include work in the financial field, analysis of risk, investment, expectations, etc., some of which have had a not unimportant bearing on theory—and indeed have been incorporated in it—as well as having become now a part of the standard approach to the formulation of policy by the authorities and individual firms.

Since the growth of the business economist and of business economics has, in my view, formed such an important part of the development of the last twenty years or so it is worth while devoting some time to this subject because of the light the past and likely future developments in this particular sphere can throw on the kind of advance which would be of greatest value to the whole body of economics including all the different branches in the academic and non-academic field.

During the last twenty-five years which have elapsed since the end of World War II and which may well be called the golden age for the economist of every description, not only the business economist, one can distinguish two periods. During the first, which came to an end in the U.K. around the middle sixties or so, the business economist's principal pre-occupation was the analysis and assessment of the environment and the development of quantitative methods designed to help individual decisions, e.g. investment, sales, etc.

This 'partial' rather than 'general' approach involved essentially the development and application of forecasting to the needs of business. The forecasting of external environment—which only in recent years has become accepted in academic circles—did not in those days imply the full translation of the repercussions of the prospective changes for the purposes of short-term and long-term policy decisions. Neither was the development of the quantitative approach to individual decisions integrated with business as a whole. The introduction of systematic forecasting and quantitative analysis, also accompanied by analysis of risk, though generated by the economist in business, above all in the U.S.A., was carried on increasingly in conjunction with the universities, which likewise co-operated very closely, especially as far as environmental forecasting is concerned, with the economists in government and special research institutes. Although these two functions (environmental and specific forecasting) were primarily within the province of the business economist, co-operation with other professionals within business and outside began to grow, including mathematicians, econometricians, operations research teams, etc. The functions discharged in performance of these tasks were essentially advisory rather than executive and involved applying economics as received and absorbed at university to analysis relating to the various operations of the firm, e.g. sales, purchases, etc.

During the second phase, which started in the second half of the sixties, the emphasis began to shift toward a 'general' approach and above all strategic and planning functions relating them to the efficiency of existing operations. While making the business economist an integral part of the firm this change altered the nature and application of environmental analysis as well as of the methods used and specific tools required for individual decisions. The essence of the planning and strategic function as now undertaken by the business economist is to relate the firm to the external environment, to see the relationship of the various operating units to each other and to help directly in formulating policies bringing these two elements together, that is to say developing a strategy whose principal aim is the future path of advance utilising the company's strengths and resources in the most favourable combinations to achieve certain objectives rather than the concern about the existing operational characteristics and the efficiency of the current operations.

Before discussing the bearing these developments have on academic economics and the whole body of economics, two points deserve mention. First, that many of the business economists, as those in the Civil Service in the past, tend at a certain stage of their career to move into management and become fully-fledged executives and administrators, while others prefer to continue along their professional career path. This development is certainly welcome; it is in line with that in many other professions but poses certain problems of what is the best way of achieving such a transition. I have discussed these problems at greater length elsewhere. Sufficient is to say for the moment that these problems, important though they are, do not appear to have attracted enough attention.

Secondly, it is also worth while looking ahead to see what problems the business economist can be expected to face in the future in the light of the already known trends. There are three areas which in my view are likely to assume greater significance and which can be expected to occupy more of his energy and time. In the first place there is a large number of important issues arising from the growing integration of the world economy and the internationalisation of business. For the business economist they raise the problem of environmental forecasting in the widest sense of this word, i.e. the questions of the future economic and political groupings, the policies they will pursue and the bearing they will have on strategic investment, finance, sales and other decisions as well as tactical questions in these and other areas. Secondly, and this is the natural result of the first factor, there appears to be a marked extension in the horizon of individual firms, both as regards time and geographical area of operation. This trend requires firms to re-assess their present and future competitive position in the light of competitive developments in the whole world. Finally, the steadily growing concern of the authorities with environment and an increasing degree of intervention by governments with emphasis on social costs and benefits is bringing the business economist into the field of the possible consequences of business decisions in the wider framework.

One of the outstanding developments of our time in business and in other areas is an attempt on the part of firms to take a much longer and comprehensive view and a much greater uncertainty as regards the developments in the near future and the certainty that the pace of change will accelerate with uncertainty of what such changes will be. The business economist has now well adapted the new conventional tools such as those of macro-forecasting, technological forecasting, input–output and other methods—and financial forecasting with the help of the flow-of-funds analysis. He has also tried to use such advances as have been made in other branches of social sciences—such as politics, sociology, etc.

These developments are increasingly calling for intelligent integration of rational analytical approaches that will enable companies to assess their future and take such decisions as they must take now paying due regard to the risk and rewards evaluated in quantitative terms from various angles.

The implication of the present and the future developments in business economics—to revert to the question I put earlier on, i.e. the bearing the growth in business economics has for the whole body of knowledge—is that business needs economics and will require it even more in the future in a not dissimilar way that business requires and depends on progress in natural sciences in the institutions of higher learning. What is and will be in demand will be reliable methods and analytical tools capable of quantifying various elements and risk relating to individual decisions in a closely interdependent world. There will also be a need for the weapons to deal with the selection of alternative strategies and their implications. Such tools will have to extend much further than at present and embrace new fields as well as being able to bring together various disciplines. To be of use they will have to be backed by impressive, ever-widening and reliable statistical information provided to a large degree—in one way or another—by the industry itself. This ever-increasing demand for tools and materials provides one challenge to those concerned with academic economics. Possessing now enormous computing and analytical power they are in the position to devote some of their time and energy to both the low glamour questions of standardising and making comparable existing statistics, helping to generate new information and building constantly up-dated data banks as the source of raw and partially processed raw material, without which the maintenance of advance as I understand it would not only be difficult but also impossible. They must also try to integrate their efforts with those of other social and also some of the natural sciences.

Equipped in this way they can address themselves to a much greater degree than hitherto to specific company questions and industrial problems.

Such a redirection of effort would certainly receive wholehearted support from industry leading to more fruitful co-operation between the three branches while also strengthening the traditional role of economics as a science concerned with the allocation of scarce resources in an expanding and changing world.

This course, by adding to the understanding of the working of the industrial world and its complexities, can be expected to enable the measurement of the changing constants and parameters as well as variables necessary for the testing of hypotheses and the building of realistic models.

The task of extending and strengthening the co-operation between industrial and academic economists is both important and urgent but not at all easy in view of the rift that has been developing between the two branches, itself due to a certain loss of sense of direction referred to at the beginning of my paper. To overcome that loss of sense of direction and to establish a new course is perhaps the most significant challenge facing all members of the profession. If the challenge is not met successfully it may well lead to economics following the fate of the mediaeval scholastic system which, although gaining in elegance and sophistication, perished because of loss of relevance to the problems of the real world.

To meet the challenge will require a concerted effort to re-channel a lot of work now done, patience and perseverance, and active collaboration with those on the other side of the fence. I am glad to say that awareness of the need to do so has been spreading and that some bridges have already been built. But perhaps I can conclude by some personal views about what industrial economists may require and offer in more specific terms to their other colleagues as a very modest contribution to the discussion now taking place.

The point from which I would like to start is that only a relatively small proportion of those graduating in economics, between 15 and 20% out of the present total of over 2,500, take up employment as economists, defined very widely, in industry, excluding government, and that their numbers diminish still further as some of them take up the management career. So numerically the business section of the economist profession is likely to remain small and probably grow more slowly than in the past. However, their professional competence will have to be of the very highest order. The present system of education they have can be briefly described as formal training at university or college plus apprenticeship. The problem of the formal education of the economist has been very much in the limelight and all I will try to do is to offer a few brief remarks. First, those who wish to take up economics in industry or for that matter in government should receive somewhat more specialised training than those who wish to follow other avenues. This may be given as a part of the third year course or perhaps as a first post-graduate degree. Such a specialisation should cover not only a very good command of analysis but also of various forecasting techniques (of the environmental and specific type) as well as some knowledge of the importance of other social sciences. Secondly, there should be updating and refresher courses for those who remain active members of the profession but find it difficult, as some academic members do, to keep up with the new developments and distinguishing between those which are important and those which are not.

Thirdly, it is my strong conviction that universities and colleges offering specialised courses of the type I mentioned could benefit by framing their syllabuses in consultation with industrial practitioners or their associations, such as for example the Society of Business Economists.

Another area which deserves attention in my view is that of the expansion of specialisation in various industries which has been long adopted in the U.S.A. and Germany but is only beginning to spread here. We have The National Institute for Economic and Social Research, The Trade Policy Research Centre, The Centre for European Studies at the University of Sussex and a few others. The creation of new centres would help to bring together various specialists from all walks of life and provide them with the assistance and stimulus and facilities they may require.

As the body of knowledge expands industry is likely to find (as it already has) that the division of labour is worth while and that some of its problems can be solved quicker in co-operation with specialists in academic and similar institutions and that collaboration on a continuous basis is an attractive proposition, because of the advantages it offers which, in turn, would provide non-industrial economists with what is needed.

There are many other ways of bringing together various branches of the practitioners of economic science. I will not dwell on them, especially as the Royal Economic Society is now actively pursuing this course, except to say that their successful implementation requires a will to do so. This now appears to be growing and I hope that the meeting of Section F will contribute to this, helping economics to make further real progress benefiting not only members of the profession but, as in the past, society as a whole.

8

The Economic Consequences of the Severn Bridge*

E. J. Cleary†

ECONOMIC links between South Wales and what is now the South-West Region, especially Bristol, are of long standing. In pre-railway days the Severn estuary was not a very exceptional or unusual barrier; coastal shipping was at least a fairly prevalent transport mode. The short crossing high up the estuary was not easy; Thomas Telford saw the English Stones, the location in his day of the ferry, as 'One of the most forbidding places at which an important ferry was ever established—a succession of violent cataracts formed in a rocky channel exposed to the rapid rush of a tide which has scarcely an equal on any other coast'. At Nash Point the estuary is 8 miles wide; 12 miles further up, at the English Stones, it is only 1 mile wide. This helps to account for the tides that impressed Telford and also the attraction of the area to bridge builders.

South Wales and the South West shared the benefits conferred by the coming of the railways, a little late perhaps, with the bridge at Sharpness, opened in 1879, and more powerfully with the tunnel, opened in 1886. However movements between the two regions had little chance to accommodate to the influence of the motor vehicle (except for a car ferry which was opened in 1926) until distinctly late in the day, with the opening of the Severn Bridge in 1966. It is not my purpose to review the tangled history of why there was not an earlier bridge, but it is important to bear in mind that economic contacts between the two areas were insulated from the changes that the growth of road transport was producing elsewhere, including the contacts between these two areas and other parts of the country.

* This paper is based on parts of a research project carried out at the University of Bath School of Management, Newport and Monmouthshire College of Technology and the University College of Swansea under the joint direction of Professor R. E. Thomas and Mr. E. J. Cleary and financed by the Department of Economic Affairs.

† Senior Lecturer, University College of Swansea.

Before the Bridge opened, Chepstow to Bristol was 12 miles as the crow flies or, as the car goes *via* Gloucester, 55 miles.

It is fair comment that at least in the inter-war years the transport demands of South Wales, at least in respect of its dominant coal and metal producing industries, were well met by the railways. On the other hand Bristol, with its wide variety of industries, many of them consumer oriented, could have put a road bridge across the Severn to good use. Had such a bridge been built before the last war, its benefits, at least as far as producers were concerned, would have been somewhat lop-sided in favour of the South West. The emergence of a more varied industrial structure in post-war South Wales somewhat alters that crude judgement. Indeed had a bridge been built in the late 1940s, as post-war plans firmly envisaged, the restructuring of industry in South Wales might have proceeded more easily.

Something of the immediate impact of the opening of the Severn Bridge can be seen from brief details of two traffic surveys; the first in August 1966, a few weeks before the Bridge opened, the second a year later. Both represent one weekday's traffic. At the first survey 22½ thousand light vehicles (cars and light vans), crossed a screen across the main routes into South Wales[1] and 7½ thousand heavy vehicles—the distinction between the two classes being at 30 cwts unladen weight. A year later on a similar day there were just over 32 thousand light and 8½ thousand heavy vehicles. This increase in traffic was not all due to the Bridge. Each year there is a modest—some would say excessive—increase in traffic anyway and there were some special local factors at work. Making allowances for these factors about half the 14½ thousand light vehicles crossing the Bridge and about a quarter of the five thousand heavy vehicles were on journeys which would not have been made if the Bridge had not been there; they were generated traffic. The growth of traffic was not, of course, the same on all routes. Some, such as London–South Wales, were less affected, in the sense of smaller reductions in journey time and distance than others, such as Cardiff–Bristol, where the distance was cut by more than half. To take a few examples. On an August weekday in 1966 there were 329 light vehicles moving between Cardiff and Bristol; a year later the number was 1466. The corresponding figures for Somerset to Monmouthshire (excluding Newport) were 77 and 425. To take the same routes in respect of heavy vehicles, for Bristol–Cardiff the rise was from 176 to 389, and for Monmouthshire–

[1] Including the car ferry in 1966 and the Severn Bridge in 1967.

Somerset 20 to 43. The response of traffic to the new opportunities created was substantial, and predictably light vehicles were responding more rapidly than heavy vehicles. The decision to go across the Severn on a family outing is very much less complex than one to send a 10 ton lorry on an extra trip, which must be preceded by finding the extra traffic which will justify that trip. Indeed the varying speed of response of different decision taking groups was a theme that recurred in the data collected.

For the picture of the general growth of traffic in the first few years I refer you to Table 1. For comparative purposes figures are given of

Table 1

Traffic Crossing the Severn Bridge

Thousands/Percentages

	Motor Cycles	Cars and Vans	Lorries	Buses	Total
1966 (9th Sept.–31st Dec.)					1,551·3
1967 Calendar Year	31·8	4,701·9	996·8	90·3	5,820·8
1968 Calendar Year	26·2	5,099·9	1,245·4	81·5	6,453·0
1969 Calendar Year	24·4	5,337·0	1,384·5	70·0	6,815·9
1970 Calendar Year	22·4	5,662·4	1,551·2	70·4	7,306·4
1968 as percentage of 1967					
(i) Crossing Bridge	82·4	108·5	124·9	90·3	110·9
(ii) Vehicle miles nationally on rural trunk and classified roads	93·7	109·4	106·0	106·3	108·6
1969 as percentage of 1968					
(i) Crossing Bridge	93·1	104·6	111·2	85·9	105·6
(ii) Vehicle miles nationally on rural trunk and classified roads	88·9	102·5	100·0	101·1	102·0
1970 as percentage of 1969					
(i) Crossing Bridge	91·8	106·1	111·7	100·7	107·1

traffic on rural trunk and classified roads nationally, as these seem the most appropriate of those available. The constantly changing mileage of motorway open inhibits the obvious comparison with motorway traffic nationally. The Road Research Laboratory did report an increase of 14% in 1968 compared with 1967 in motorway vehicle miles travelled as reflected at the 11 recording sites common to the two years.[2]

Motorcycles are a proportionately unimportant component of total traffic and show a greater decline at the Bridge than nationally. For buses the decline in numbers crossing the Bridge is atypical of the national picture. However the comparison is affected by the large novelty coach trip traffic to the Bridge especially in the Summer of 1967 and to a lesser extent of 1968. These movements provide a reasonable explanation of the pattern of decline of coaches. Cars and light vans increase at the bridge roughly in line with national figures, though as with coaches, making 1967 the initial base of comparison, a year with high Bridge sightseeing traffic, means that the table underestimates the growth of what might be called bread and butter traffic. The most significant difference between the national and the Bridge figures is in the case of lorries. Uninfluenced by a sightseeing element in 1967, lorries show an increase of one quarter in 1968 compared with 1967, and 1969 and 1970 show further increases of 11 per cent over the previous year, well in excess of the change nationally. The strong growth of lorry traffic has continued into 1971; the January–April returns show a further increase of 18 per cent on the same period for 1970. The comparable increase for cars and vans was 9 per cent. Thus while the initial impact of the opening of the Bridge was smaller in the case of lorries than of cars, the later response of lorry traffic has been consistently stronger. However it is still the case the lorries form a smaller proportion of total traffic at the Bridge than on motorways nationally. At least they did in 1968, the one point at which comparable data are available. Lorries were 23 per cent of total vehicles at the Bridge in February 1968 and 12 per cent in August compared with 28 per cent in February and 17 per cent in August on motorways nationally.

I turn now to the purposes for which the light vehicle journeys are being made. Table 2 gives an estimated breakdown—based on a series of traffic surveys—of the purposes of the 5 million car journeys across the Severn Bridge in 1968. You can see that journeys on firm's business, that is, roughly speaking, journeys at the employer's expense, and journeys to visit friends and relations are the two largest categories; each is responsible for about one quarter of the total journeys made. Holiday journeys are the next largest class and

[2] J. B. Dunn, 50-Point traffic census results for 1968 (RRL Report CR 302) Crowthorne, 1970, p. 5.

Table 2

Purpose of Light Vehicles Crossing the Severn Bridge, 1968

Purpose	Whole Year No.	%	Total Monday-Friday No.	%	Total Saturdays No.	%	Total Sundays No.	%
	Thousands							
Firm's Business	1,420	28	1,336	41	59	7	25	3
Collection and Delivery	100	2	91	3	9	1	—	—
Service and Maintenance	36	1	34	1	2	—	—	—
Work	394	8	342	11	32	4	20	2
Shopping	213	4	140	4	73	9	—	—
Holidays	706	14	381	12	223	26	102	10
Visiting	1,256	25	464	15	250	29	542	54
Sightseeing	513	10	225	7	76	9	212	21
Paid Entertainment	166	3	74	2	65	8	27	3
Other and Multiple	272	5	140	4	60	7	72	7
Total	5,076		3,227		849		1,000	

while such journeys are most frequent in the summer months they are quite substantial from March or April onwards depending on the date of the Easter holiday. Journeys to and from work are 8 per cent of the total with Bristol and Monmouthshire contributing most of the journeys. There is a commuting group of 4 or 5 hundred people on average. The number varies since some of them are groups of contractors' men who will be commuters during the course of a contract. Sightseeing accounts for one tenth of the total and, excluding the residual, other and multiple purpose, category, the remaining purposes, shopping, journeys to places of entertainment, collection and delivery of goods and service and maintenance account collectively for the remaining 10% of journeys. These minor purposes are of particular interest since they represent a group of activities (with the exception of the other and multiple purpose category) where the new opportunities opened by the Bridge in respect of urban services, created the possibility of substantial changes in behaviour patterns. Bristol as the largest urban centre, and Cardiff as the second largest, could now provide services to a much larger area and there was the possibility of heightened competition between these two centres. The data show that while people were taking some advantage of these new opportunities, this group of purposes as a whole covered under 10% of total traffic, so that, at least in the early years, there was no revolution in the pattern of these services. In the case of shopping in particular the Table may well overstate the facts, since the winter week-end traffic estimate is heavily dependent on a late November Saturday survey when Christmas was already stimulating trade.

While newly generated traffic was about half of total traffic this traffic generation did not affect all purposes equally. At a survey in August 1967, nearly a year after the Bridge opened, covering both weekday and weekend traffic, questions were asked to enable journeys to be classified as diverted—that is the journey from the point of origin to destination would have been made whether the Bridge was there or not—or generated. The results showed that generated traffic was smallest for business travel and holidays. It was less than one quarter of the total (22 and 24 per cent to be exact) for each of those purposes. Generated traffic accounted for 39% of visiting journeys. For all other purposes generated traffic accounted for over half of the total, the relevant percentages being, in ascending order—Collection, Delivery, Service and Maintenance, 57; Work, 66; Shopping, 76; Paid Entertainment, 76 and Sightseeing, 83. For some journeys seeing the Bridge itself constituted the main reason for the journey or the choice of route. This category of facility-created traffic was 12% of total journeys and accounted for one third of all sightseeing trips.

The extent of generated traffic was, as expected, much greater between points close to the Bridge, where the saving in time and distance was greatest, than on longer routes. Taking the area Bristol, Somerset and East Gloucestershire on the one side of the estuary and Cardiff, Monmouthshire, including Newport, and West Gloucestershire on the other, journeys within this area constituted 62% of all generated journeys compared with 37% of all diverted journeys.

From the economic point of view it is of importance to know not only the purpose of a journey but also where that purpose is accomplished. A cafe owner may be pleased that the Bridge is being used for sightseeing but will be much more pleased if those sightseeing journeys have as their destination places near his cafe. From traffic survey data estimates were made for the year 1968 of the home origins and places of accomplishment of the traffic for each purpose. Time does not allow a detailed consideration of these matrices but I will say a little about the general direction of traffic for each purpose. I will use, inaccurately, the national labels Wales and England for destinations west and east of the estuary respectively. This must not be taken as a Welsh claim to West Gloucestershire and Herefordshire, both important areas to the west of the Bridge, still less to the West Midlands and the North West, traffic from both of which use the Bridge route to avoid congestion in Gloucester city on their way to the South West.

For sightseeing roughly 7 journeys were into Wales for every 3 into England. Monmouthshire, excluding Newport, gains much from this traffic, being the destination for some 80,000 trips and the origin for about 5,000. Bristol is the home origin for about 85,000 trips and is also the destination for a substantial number, 32,000.

Where the purpose of the trip is admission to some place of entertainment—theatres, zoos, ice rinks and so on—the modest traffic is very much in the opposite direction to that of sightseeing. Something like 8 trips out of every ten are directed into England, in most cases Bristol, which is the destination of 60,000 such trips but the point of origin for only 10,000.

With shopping, remembering that this is not a very important purpose overall, the direction of traffic is similar to that of paid entertainment. Three trips out of four are directed into England with the Bristol area as the main destination. The most important single area of origin is Monmouthshire, outside Newport, with 26,000 journeys. However allowing for its smaller population West Gloucestershire is still more important. In the case of West Gloucestershire the Bridge is particularly important, bringing areas such as Lydney and Chepstow very much nearer to Bristol than was previously the case with a corresponding realignment of urban services. A household survey in 1968 showed that 72% of Chepstow households had made at least one shopping trip to Bristol in the previous year. That survey enabled more detailed questions about reasons for making journeys to be asked than is possible in traffic surveys and showed that the emphasis was laid on greater range of choice, not on price or any other factor, as the reason for shopping trips to Bristol. Clothing was by far the most important item purchased—consumer durables were rarely mentioned.

Journeys where visiting friends and relations was the purpose were nearly equally balanced between trips into England and into Wales. The other feature of this traffic was that it was much less concentrated in particular areas and the average length of journey was higher than for the purposes already discussed.

For holiday journeys there were four such trips into England for every three into Wales. However, as mentioned earlier the Bridge had relatively little influence here. Holidays were among the purposes where traffic generation was relatively low.

Traffic on journeys to work was again fairly evenly balanced with six journeys into Wales for every five journeys into England. This is perhaps a little surprising given the relative levels of unemployment on the two sides of the estuary.

Turning to travel on business, the pattern is again unbalanced with eight journeys into Wales for every five into England. However in the case of business travel it is less easy to infer economic advantage than with most other purposes. Flows of money cannot so readily be inferred from flows of people; it turns on whether the object of the trip is buying or selling or, as in many cases, neither of these but a consultation, say, between branch staff and regional or head office. Also much turns on the industrial structure of an area—a smaller number of personnel movements is required to organise the sale of intermediate products in bulk to manufacturers than to sell final output to a range of retail outlets. An industrial survey showed considerable personal travel within firms. While the overall ratio was eight trips for business purposes into Wales for every five into England, the ratio varied a good deal between areas. The unbalance was very high in respect of the London area with two and a half business trips from London into Wales for every one in the opposite direction. Among areas to the west of the Bridge Newport was the nearest to balance, with 128,000 business journeys from England and 97,000 to England. Three quarters of firms engaged in manufacturing in South Wales and the South West were using the Bridge for staff travel and almost 60% of firms in distribution. Among manufacturers the balance of movement was into England and among distributors into Wales.

For all purposes the vast majority of journeys were either generated or would have been made by car where they were diverted. There was however some diversion to car travel from other modes of transport. At a survey in August 1967 an attempt was made to find the extent to which traffic was diverted from the railways. The results showed that 5·2% of total vehicles were in that category. While this is a modest contribution to total Bridge traffic it may look different from the railway's view point. In terms of people rather than vehicles it means that about 1,500 travellers were lost to the railways on an

August weekday. The only purpose for which more than 10% of journeys would have been made by rail had the Bridge not existed was firm's business. This in part reflects the low volume of generated traffic for that purpose. Most of these rail-diverted journeys were between Bristol, Cardiff, Newport and Swansea. These routes accounted for three quarters of the total. In the first year after the Bridge was opened British Rail publicised a faster and more frequent service between Bristol, Cardiff and Newport in an effort to retain this traffic. The effort was not successful and the frequency of service (though not its speed) was later reduced.

Another carrier to suffer from the opening of the Bridge—apart of course from the Aust–Beachley car ferry which ceased operations with the opening—was the cross estuary pleasure steamer company. Competition from the Bridge has led to the withdrawal by the company of its service between Cardiff and Weston-super-Mare. Lower down the estuary, where the relative importance of the decrease in distance was less, the company continues to operate between Swansea, Porthcawl and Ilfracombe.

I have been talking largely in terms of the pattern of light vehicle traffic in 1968 but of course the pattern is not static. With the passage of time the relative and absolute importance of traffic on various routes changes. One feature has been the relative decline of traffic between areas close to the Bridge. Taking again the area Bristol, East Gloucestershire and Somerset to the east and Monmouthshire including Newport, West Gloucestershire and Cardiff to the west, cross Bridge journeys within this area were 52% of all cross Bridge journeys at a survey a little before Easter in 1967; a year later this figure had fallen to 49% and a further year later, in 1969, to 43%. The same pattern applied to summer traffic with a fall from 40% in August 1967 to 31% a year later. In part this pattern is explained, especially in August, by the decline in novelty traffic—where the Bridge becomes the object of sightseeing trips—and such trips are in the majority of cases, short distance. However the pattern of decline also reflects the fact that those close to the Bridge are quickest to see the opportunities it creates. It takes time for those at a greater distance, whose contacts with the other side were more limited in pre-Bridge days, to make some use of the Bridge and in doing so appreciate the possibilities for further use that are opened up. Growth of traffic over time has been stronger than average for a number of areas at some distance from the Bridge such as Wiltshire and the area between Oxford, Southampton and London to the east side of the Bridge and West Wales, Swansea, Hereford and Brecon to the west. There is a narrower range of differences between the rates of growth of traffic for areas to the west than for areas to the east.

The overall picture that emerges is that the Bridge has generated substantial new traffic for both commercial and leisure purposes. While five million cars crossing the Bridge in 1968—two and a half million round trips—is a formidable total, averaged over the population in the areas between which the Bridge has substantially reduced distances, it is less striking. About half of total traffic is between areas within about 30 miles of the Bridge. A further one and a half million journeys have one trip end in this area, giving roughly a further third of a million round trips originating in the area near the Bridge. Allowing an average of 3 people per car, this would mean that on average each person in that area made 3 cross Bridge trips in a year. In this area, as the household survey shows, a high proportion, about three quarters, of all households made some use of the Bridge. However a cross Bridge trip 3 times a year scarcely constitutes a dramatic change in the pattern of life, and of course most people make less than 3 such trips. About one in fifteen households average one trip per head per month—which no doubt implies a higher frequency for at least some members of the household—so that for this not insignificant group the Bridge implies a sharper change. About 1% of households in that area average a trip per week and for this group the Bridge implies a considerable change in patterns of life. In Chepstow for example, about 4% of households fall into this category. Further the size of these groups, where the Bridge has had a real impact, is growing over time, with the growth of traffic.

Let us return to the question of the diversion of traffic from the railways, this time in terms of goods traffic. The large increase in lorry traffic since 1966 on what are now cross Bridge routes, suggests some significant changes in traffic modes. Of course not all of the increase was at the expense of the railways. While the years since the Bridge was opened have not been years of rapid growth in national product there has been some growth and this means some increase in lorry traffic on these routes. Again without growth in national product the opening of the Bridge could lead *via* industrial re-organisation to an increase of trade between the two regions at the expense of trade within each region separately or at the expense of some third region. There is evidence of both sorts of change from industrial surveys to which I will return. As far as the railways are concerned some evidence emerges from an analysis made, with the generous help of British Rail, of all dispatches from South Wales for the month of March in 1966, before the Bridge was opened, and in 1967 and in 1968. Table 3 gives the results in respect of dispatches to Bristol and the South West and to London. As Table 3 shows, the changes are

Table 3

Freight traffic, other than coal, measured in tons, from the Cardiff Division of British Rail

	Destination					
Origin	Bristol and South-West			London		
By District	March 1966	March 1967	March 1968	March 1966	March 1967	March 1968
Newport	9,462	7,469	6,538	11,207	21,801	16,708
Cardiff	14,791	8,175	10,217	10,138	7,575	6,549
Swansea	9,849	9,377	15,822	7,029	7,135	5,991
Total	34,102	25,021	32,577	28,374	36,511	19,248

not smooth, indeed the 'lumpiness' of rail traffic rapidly emerged in the analysis, where a single large contract, such as that for conveying oil, can upset the picture considerably.

However the table does show some consistencies. As far as the region most likely to be affected is concerned, that is Bristol and the South West, there is a continuous decline in traffic from Newport and an overall decline from Cardiff, with Swansea as the exception. At least there is the expected direction of change as one moves farther from the immediate area of the Bridge. With regard to London, Newport is the exception; here there is an example of the lumpiness of traffic. There was a fall of over 7,000 tons in Newport–London traffic in the two categories, slag, cinders and ash and other earths and stone between 1967 and 1968 with the completion of a large sewerage works contract. Table 4 carries the story a stage further with a product analysis for Newport to Bristol and West of England. The fall in traffic is largely accounted for in the product groups given. As far as can be discovered the 1967 animal feeding stuff figure is a freak figure (one explanation offered was that it was a consignment that lost its way!); the main traffic in this commodity is in fact into Wales from the Bristol mills. It is notable that the four products are

Table 4

Fall in traffic Newport to Bristol and South-West of England (tons)

Product Group	March 1966	March 1967	March 1968	Change 67/68
Animal Feeding Stuffs	18	1,839	Nil	−1,839
Creosote, Pitch & Tar	1,904	1,368	Nil	−1,368
Timber (other than Pit Props)	436	290	73	− 217
Other Miscellaneous Metal	20	159	Nil	− 159

all bulky. In the cases of Creosote and Timber there is evidence of a very clear change of mode.

The industrial surveys threw some further light on the question of traffic modes. A survey early in 1969 of manufacturers and distributors in South Wales and South West North (roughly Gloucestershire, North Wiltshire and Somerset) showed that some 15% of large manufacturers (those employing more than 100 people), 10% of small manufacturers (employing 20–99 people) and 13% of distributors had made a change from rail to road in their dispatches in respect of the other side of the estuary. The survey also showed that such changes were proceeding in respect of dispatches to other areas, so that the change is only partly the result of the opening of the Bridge. In the case of the South West changes from rail to road were as frequent for dispatches to London and the South East Region as they were in the case of Wales. That a substantial number of large manufacturers expected to increase road dispatches as against rail, nearly one quarter in fact, and had not by 1968 achieved that result, may help to explain the continuing rise in lorry traffic across the Bridge.

It is time I said something about the effect of the Bridge on industry generally and about economic ties between the two regions. The opening of the Bridge could be expected to influence manufacturers in a number of ways. The first possibility is that new organisational links might be set up, particularly where firms are parts of wider groups having interests on both sides of the estuary. Where such links are established a second series of events might follow. It might now be possible to rationalise activities by concentrating production on one side or by specialisation of function, possibly with some balancing of outputs between plants on both sides. Another consequence might be changes in administrative arrangements or a pooling of inventories. There was a great deal of organisational change in progress flowing from sources other than the Bridge. The late 1960s were a period of high activity in industrial 'take overs' and South Wales and, especially, the South West were not immune. In fact nearly a quarter of the large manufacturers were involved in one way and another in take-overs. A survey of large manufacturers showed that, before the Bridge opened, of 462 manufacturers in South East Wales and South West North, 117 had some unit of the same organisation on the other side of the estuary; this included other manufacturing plants and depots. Thus 25% of large manufacturers had a cross estuarial link. Two years later a second survey showed that there had been few changes in these links. In all 5 plants had been closed, all in South East Wales, 5 plants had been opened in South Wales and 3 plants opened in the South West. These changes represent just over 2% of large manufacturers opening plants and just over 1% closing plants—the 1968 population of large firms surveyed being a little smaller than 2 years earlier. Clearly the Bridge had little influence on matters of industrial location. Given the short time span and the less than buoyant national economic climate, no very substantial change could be expected.

A second possible change would be in the input of factors of production. This has three aspects. Clearly there is the possibility of new sources of raw materials or of changes in such sources as a result of rationalisation by suppliers on the lines noted above. Then there is the switching of supplies, larger intakes now coming from across the estuary and less from other sources. Lastly there is the possibility of new sources of labour.

Regarding new cross estuarial sources of supply drawn on for the first time, the second survey in late 1968 and early 1969 in South Wales and the South West found that 5·9% of large manufacturers and 2·9% of small manufacturers were in this category. Newport was the area with the largest proportion of firms drawing on new sources for supplies. Among industries, the South Wales clothing and footwear industry was the most prominent case with 6 firms out of 25 making a change. This was however a forced change due to rationalisation by a supplier outside both regions resulting in a concentration of activity in the South West; the Bridge could of course have been a factor in that rationalisation. Overall while there were some cases of supplies drawn from new cross estuarial sources, they were proportionately not very important.

When we turn to the possibility of the increased use of existing cross estuarial sources of supply there is a picture of greater change. Among the group of large manufacturers 10% reported such a change and among the small manufacturers 15%. The Bristol–Severnside area figured prominently with 9% of large firms and 19% of small firms. Above average percentages of firms were also found in Cardiff, Bridgend, Swansea and Port Talbot, North Wiltshire, the Forest of Dean and the Wellington–Westbury area. Among industries in South Wales the following were prominent—Bricks, Timber and Furniture, Clothing and Footwear, Engineering and Metal Manufactures. Prominent South West industries were Mining and Quarrying, Timber and Furniture, Engineering, Food, Drink and Tobacco and Other Metal Goods. These increases in cross estuarial supplies were no doubt partly at the expense of other regions and 10% of large manufacturers and 9% of small manufacturers reported reductions in supplies from other regions.

The reasons given by the large manufacturers for these changes were—in rank order—(1) Savings in transport cost; (2) Improved service; (3) Supplier had transferred depot across the estuary; (4) Better terms; and (5) Sub-contracting within the group.

Improved service is important not only where it leads to a new source of supply or an increase in supplies from existing sources; it is a useful means of holding existing markets. It is of some interest that a large number of manufacturers saw their cross estuarial suppliers as having improved their service after the opening of the Bridge—though of course not necessarily because of that opening. Of those firms drawing supplies from across the estuary 40% reported an improvement, the figure being slightly higher for firms in West South Wales and the Wellington–Westbury area than in the areas closer to the Bridge. An analysis of the industries concerned shows something of a pattern, with the highest proportion of firms tending to be in those industries where existing strengths in one region (e.g. Mining and Quarrying in South Wales and Paper in the South West) have become available to firms in the other region.

The same feature can be viewed from the other side of the counter; that is, we ask which manufacturers see themselves as being able to offer improved service to their customers after the opening of the Bridge. Respondents may not be wholly objective here! However the pattern is not dissimilar to that set out above, but with a rather higher percentage of firms seeing themselves as being able to give a better service; just under 50% as against the 40% noted earlier.

A further and important aspect of manufacturing industry is the extent to which firms have increased their output for dispatch across the estuary. The industrial survey at the end of 1968 showed that 77 of the large manufacturers had done so, 31 in South Wales and 46 in the South West. The industries with the largest proportions of firms increasing output were, in descending order, Bricks, Pottery, Cement and Glass, Food, Drink and Tobacco, Mining and Quarrying, Timber and Furniture, Vehicles and Engineering. In all these industries more than 10% of firms reported increased output for despatch across the estuary. Among small manufacturers a smaller proportion of firms increased output for despatch across the estuary, 11·5% of the total compared with 13·3% for large manufacturers.

Of course changes such as the opening of the Severn Bridge do not only concern manufacturing; distribution channels are also affected. In general the picture of change in distribution is not dissimilar from that I have outlined for manufacturing. There was a distinct strengthening of distributional links between the two regions after 1966, but with a rather greater degree of structural change than in manufacturing.

I would like to end with a particular example, taken from the service and distribution field, to illustrate the old principle that while technical or environmental change can alter the opportunities open to people, in the end it is individuals (or in these days I should perhaps say organisations) that have to exploit the opportunities.

In the belief that farmers were likely to be fairly sensitive to market opportunities a study was made, thanks to the good offices of the Ministry of Agriculture, of entries at certain fat stock markets. Records kept in connection with the Fatstock Price Guarantee Scheme enabled the home origin of animals sold to be identified. Three markets were studied, Thornbury (the nearest market to the Bridge, some 4 miles to the east), Winford (6 miles south of Bristol and 17 miles from the Bridge) and Chippenham (32 miles east of the Bridge). The area of origin of all cattle, sheep and pigs certified at these markets was analysed for a 3 week period at the start of each quarter for the 2 years from April 1966. The first two periods were before the Bridge was opened and the remaining six after.

All three markets were practically isolated from supplies from west of the Severn before the Bridge opened. Afterwards there were scarcely any movements to Winford market, but at Chippenham there is a modest movement that is of some relative importance in the case of sheep. There is no sustained pattern of growth at either market and at least some movements may well have been of an experimental nature. There is also the return load influence. Chippenham is a biggish market, especially for pigs and where a farmer takes a truck to bring back an intended purchase, he may well take a few animals to sell since he has effectively free transport to the market for them.

Details of movements from west of the Severn to Thornbury are given in Table 5 and here the picture is very different. From a situation of practically zero movements before September 1966, there is a

Table 5

West of Severn Movements to Thornbury market & their relative importance

Period	No. of animals from West of the Severn			Total certified at Thornbury in period and percentage from West of the Severn					
	Cattle	Sheep	Pigs	Cattle	%	Sheep	%	Pigs	%
1 (April 1966)	15	2	0	143	10	113	2	568	0
2 (July 1966)	0	0	0	137	0	521	0	338	0
3 (Oct. 1966)	40	280	0	167	24	779	36	606	0
4 (Jan. 1967)	147	487	16	334	42	809	60	453	3
5 (April 1967)	72	69	22	208	35	185	37	686	3
6 (July 1967)	37	250	51	141	26	702	40	362	14
7 (Oct. 1967)	129	1,162	17	246	52	1,235	94	641	3
8 (Jan. 1968)	254	632	99	408	62	723	87	837	12

substantial traffic after the Bridge opened. Two special factors influence the picture. First, in the early 1960s Thornbury was a declining market, but in 1963 a new auctioneer took over the market and it was growing before the Bridge opened. Second, after the market on October 7th, 1967 (the second week of the seventh three weekly period analysed) Chepstow market was closed, forcing some farmers to seek a new market and in some cases the, not wholly voluntary, choice would be Thornbury.

That there was the expectation of some advantage to farmers west of the Severn in selling through Thornbury is clear from the speed of the response to the opening of the Bridge; that that expectation was well founded is confirmed by later growth. That the advantage is fairly small can be inferred from the relatively narrow area west of the Severn from which animals are sent to Thornbury. The vast majority are from the Chepstow, Newport, Lydney and Usk areas with a few from Monmouth and Abergavenny and only $2\frac{1}{2}\%$ of the total animals from more distant areas.

It would be nice to trace all the changes consequent on the opening of the Bridge with the same precision as in the case of fatstock markets. In trying to summarise even parts of a larger body of work I have neglected to dot many geographical i's and cross many statistical t's. The overall picture of change is fairly much in line with what an economist would have expected, but in tracing some expected changes a sharp eye, but I hope not too much imagination, is needed, because the degree of change is small.

SYMPOSIUM ON TRAFFIC AND TOWNS

9

Introduction

K. M. Gwilliam†

THE SUBJECT of this symposium is of crucial importance in the protection and enrichment of the quality of life in our society. Some commentators have even gone so far as to suggest that the whole future of our economic and political system depends on the success with which it handles the problems of urban planning. Moreover, transport planning is seen at the heart of these problems for two main reasons;

(i) Firstly, it is already clear that the production of transport services can, of itself, do great environmental damage. Excesses of noise, fumes, visual intrusion and so on can make our towns increasingly unpleasant to live in from the point of view of general amenity.

(ii) Secondly, and of equal importance, there is a danger that developments in the transport sector may contribute to an undesirably increasing polarisation of urban society. Increasing affluence, giving the ability to afford private transport, puts increased pressure on the financial situation of public transport services. Decline in their quality and quantity in response to decreased demand not only accentuates the problems of urban poverty by adding another dimension to the deprivation of the poor but also creates new classes of underprivileged amongst those too young, too old, too infirm or just temperamentally unsuited to the private car.

Thus urban transport planning faces us not only with technical problems in the design and management of transport systems but also with very fundamental political and ethical questions in the determination of the social values which we shall adopt in our urbanised society.

Neither the problem, nor its recognition, is new. It was brought strikingly to public attention by Professor Buchanan nearly ten years

† Professor of Transport Economics, Centre for Transport Studies, University of Leeds.

ago with the publication of *Traffic in Towns*. But since then there have been a number of developments in the urban transport situation which have substantially altered either the public response to the problems or the institutional setting in which the problems have to be faced.

A number of such developments merit brief mention as background to the papers. Firstly, there has been a recognition that traffic congestion problems cannot be divorced from the more general transport problems of towns. Whereas our earlier studies, based very much on American experience, were essentially concerned with traffic congestion *per se*, we have more recently moved on to a wider appreciation of the role of public transport. To some extent this has been recognised and accompanied by statutory changes. For example, the 1968 Transport Act went some way towards providing a framework within which planners were less institutionally inhibited in looking for public transport solutions to the problems facing them.

A second important change has been the recognition that transport strategy and transport planning is but one aspect, albeit a very important one, in urban development. The requirement of structure plans under the 1968 Town and Country Planning Act ensures that urban transport planning shall be properly seen in this wider planning context. Whether we have yet adequately come to grips with the requirements of this change of perspective, either in our academic studies or our practical planning, is a matter for debate. But it is certainly the case that transport planning will eventually be substantially affected by it.

A third important area of change lies in the channels through which our social values are determined. Dissatisfaction with the traditional procedures for avoiding injustices in the planning process led the Planning Advisory Group to recommend a new procedure whereby public participation, or at least a check on public acceptability, is sought at the general strategic level as well as at the more detailed level at which it has previously been made effective. Again, whether the institutional measures provided really come to grips with the problem or not is a matter of debate. But it does seem likely that provision for a richer role for informed public opinion in the planning process means that transport planning will never quite be the same again. One might argue, with some justification I think, that a more series attention to environmental standards is an early result of this process.

From this brief glimpse of the background to our project we can see that it is one of immense complexity requiring the application of a wide range of skills. The purpose of holding a joint session of Sections F and G of the British Association is to demonstrate and examine this requirement. Our papers discuss the different contributions which can be made to solving—or at least ameliorating—the urban transport problem by different disciplines, and explore the relationship—and possibly conflict—between them.

The discussion divides into two parts, roughly corresponding with the economist's distinction between the short run and the long run. The first four papers discuss the management of the existing infrastructure assuming that only minimal investments, of short gestation periods, are possible.

Each of the first three contributors was invited to give his views about the objectives of management of the system as he sees them and to describe the types of management measures which his own discipline can contribute. This brief is, of course, somewhat restrictive in two ways. Firstly, engineers are not unaware of pricing devices, though their views on their merits may be very mixed; nor are economists totally ignorant of, or necessarily opposed to, essentially administrative devices of traffic management or restraint. The papers demonstrate a great deal of mutual awareness, tolerance, and indeed overlap in technique. The second dimension of restrictiveness is the brief related to the time period. While the economist happily makes the short run/long run distinction for expository purposes, it is clear that the engineer and town planner find it much less easy to categorise their analyses and policies in this way.

The consideration of the shorter term management problems, in so far as we can distinguish them sensibly, is completed by a paper which looks at these immediate problems from a public transport operator's viewpoint.

The second group of papers (corresponding to the afternoon session) consider some longer term planning problems. Professor Smeed considers the problem of selecting an appropriate general design for urban road networks. Mr. Wolley describes and discusses some of the problems of implementing such design when it involves inserting new roads into an existing urban fabric. Finally, Professor Beesley considers the interaction in the planning process between a wide range of objectives, criterion and decision procedures.

The presentation of each group of papers was followed by a long and wide ranging discussion of the problems raised. Limitations on space, and the essentially discursive nature of these discussions, make it impossible to reproduce them in full. The last paper therefore represents an attempt to synthesise from these discussions some conclusions on the more important aspects of the problem which the contributors considered in greatest detail.

10

Management: The Town Planner's Viewpoint

David Bayliss†

FIRST I would like to make it clear that I hestitate to put forward 'The Town Planner's Viewpoint'. A profession can only be said to have a viewpoint when there is established tradition of practice from which a viewpoint can be derived. Although some town planners are involved in urban transport management issues there is not, to my knowledge, a confirmed professional body of wisdom on this matter.

The concept of managing the passage of persons and vehicles through the streets of our towns is not new; some parts of Ancient Rome were restricted to vehicles, Old London Bridge was one-way, and the first traffic signals were introduced in London in the pre-electric era. Indeed some of the most effective means of management exist and are accepted today, perhaps the most notable of these being the confinement of vehicles travelling in opposite directions to different parts of the carriageway.

Traffic management started in earnest in this country about ten years ago and has been directed to increasing the speed, safety and capacity of the passage of general traffic. Many of the measures taken during this period were seen as temporary expedients awaiting the longer term provision of new highway capacity and as such often fell short of the standards required of more permanent additions to the urban scene. Typically many schemes introduced in this period paid insufficient attention to environmental sensitivity and the relative needs of different types of traffic.

The sixties were also an important period for public transport with increased congestion on the roads and increased ownership of private transport resulting in declining patronage in general and increased

† Group Planner, Studies Division of the Transportation Branch, Greater London Council.

The views expressed in this paper are those of the author and do not necessarily reflect the attitudes or policies of the Greater London Council.

operating costs for road based public transport. The result of this is that public transport, largely managed as a commercial enterprise but with some acknowledgement of its position as a publicly owned monopoly, has already become unable to finance new capital works and is now becoming unable to maintain existing service levels whilst achieving operational viability. This is not the case in this country alone but is a situation prevailing in almost all post-industrial urban areas.

It is useful to argue that management of movement in our towns will be necessary under two heads. Not because these inevitably require different methods but to make it clear that comprehensive management (as opposed to operational codes for individual bits of the transport system) is here to stay. The two heads are therefore:

(i) Management as a means of controlling the shorter run problems of urban transport (socio-economic growth pains).

(ii) Management as part of the design of future transport systems.

To take the second point first. In this country most of our existing urban areas were moulded before the Second World War. This was a period of slow change and low prosperity compared with today. Personal wealth, for example, has increased since 1950 more than in the entire first half of the century. Thus most of our present towns are designed to suit a low affluence/slow change society whereas they are being used by a high affluence/fast change society. The resultant stresses present a formidable challenge for urban management of all kinds. Nor is this problem going to diminish in the near future. We are renewing most of our towns at between 1% and 2% per annum, the larger more problematic towns renewing at the slowest rate, whereas urban car ownership is increasing at about 5% per annum, this being closely matched by the growth in the use of roads. At this rate, even with an increase in the size of our urban areas from the present 4½ million acres to 6 million acres by the end of the century the density of the urban car population will double from the present 3 cars/acre to 6 cars/acre by which time it will be six times as great as it was in 1950.

Over the past twenty years British towns have been living, to an excessive degree, off their traffic capacity and environmental 'fat' which is now getting rather thin, and, although it is unlikely that we will wake up one morning to find ourselves buried with cars, the variety, ubiquity and intensity of the urban traffic problem has been slowly increasing and becoming more menacing and looks like continuing to do so, unless measures are taken to mitigate it.

It is difficult to see how in the long term a reasonable strategy for dealing with this problem can be devised without including a large highway development programme. I do not intend to argue this; the traffic effectiveness of our urban road systems can probably be doubled by the end of the century by a substantial highway development programme and good highway system management. However if the pressure is to double also, even in the long term, the problem would be just as bad if nothing else were done; thus we would have doubled the quantity but effected no improvement in quality. There can be little doubt that present day society expects rather better than that.

Comprehensive management will be required in the long term therefore as a fundamental component of future urban transportation systems.

What sort of techniques are likely to be available over the next three decades and what are the sorts of tasks for which management measures will be required?

Techniques can be identified at three levels:-

(i) Internal operational procedures of different facilities.

(ii) Comprehensive transportation management techniques dealing with the roles and relationships of the different components of the transportation system.

(iii) Comprehensive urban management techniques dealing with the relationships of transportation with other urban activities and planning issues.

The first of these sets of measures are well known and widely practised. These include:

(i) Advanced bus and train scheduling and control.

(ii) Low cost running schemes for public transport (one/man buses, etc.).

(iii) On street parking and waiting regulation.

(iv) Conventional traffic management.

(v) Marginal cost related fares systems for public transport.

These will probably be referred to more fully and expertly by other speakers.

The second of these sets of measures are receiving most attention, at the moment from economists, engineers and town planners and these include:

(i) Public transport fares policies.

(ii) Area licensing schemes.

(iii) Road pricing.
(iv) Staggering of work hours (really level III).
(v) Comprehensive parking control.
(vi) Schemes for selective availability of road space (e.g., bus priorities).

The implementation of any of these schemes presents formidable problems and usually some undesirable side effects so that in the event of a mixed package is likely to be employed.

I. Public transport fares policies

I think it is useful to start considering problems to do with pricing with the premise that individuals should pay the full cost of goods and services they receive unless there are good reasons why they should not. This is not to take an ideological posture but to impose a discipline in examining the substance of non-market arguments. There are reasons why public transport fares could be legitimately varied from the full cost level:

(i) Congestion/traveller costs are lower on public transport and a switch to public transport could produce a better balance.

(ii) Environmental costs are lower on public transport and a switch could improve the situation in this respect.

(iii) Reasonable mobility, like decent housing and education, should be ensured by government for social reasons and thus the costs of this should, in part, be met by the community at large rather than by the individual consumer.

There are a number of reasons why this should be approached cautiously:

(i) The payment of fares is a valuable measure to Management of the demand for their product and a discipline for the consumer to avoid wasteful consumption.

(ii) Higher income groups travel most and although they have a bias to the private car they often consume more public transport than low income groups and thus we could end up with those best able to pay benefiting most.

(iii) Public transport is also environmentally intrusive and the private car is probably not as great an offender in some respects as it is sometimes assumed to be.

(iv) Monetary cost is only a partial component of the total disutility of using public transport (probably between $\frac{1}{4}$ and $\frac{1}{3}$) the greater part being time and effort expended in its use.

However it is likely that the already accepted principle of capital subsidies for public transport will be extended slowly to service related operational subsidies (service not used in the bus service sense), selective assistance from general funds enabling the retention of the market element where appropriate and reducing the possibility of some of the difficulties of crude subsidisation.

The development of policies of this kind inevitably takes us into a wider urban management field. Suppose, for example, all reasonable public transport fare systems effected an undesirable redistribution of income. It would be necessary to make compensatory adjustments, yet this would have to be done *via* some non-transportation mechanism. A further real difficulty is that most of the means of income redistribution are under the control of central government and yet the needs may well emerge at a local level. This strongly suggests a greater degree of local control of taxation.

II. Area licensing schemes

These usually involve the designation of an area within which only licensed vehicles can operate for part or all of the day. Licences would be issued by sale and/or status. Although such a scheme would reduce traffic selectively in specified areas it would have the following disadvantages:

(i) Inevitably a serious boundary problem will arise (parking, congestion, property values, activity changes, etc.).

(ii) Once licensed there is no disincentive to travel; in fact the reverse would be the case.

(iii) It is doubtful if a manageable licensing system could be sufficiently discriminatory.

(iv) It would be difficult to enforce.

(v) A sale system could have undesirable discriminatory effects between different income levels.

The main attraction of a system of this kind is that experimentation is fairly easy and I believe that we may see experiments in area licensing in 4–8 years.

III. Road Pricing

Road pricing is currently the most discussed and researched form of transport management and is based on the premise that road users should be charged directly for the use of road space (rather like the use of electricity or a taxi), this charge being related to the marginal social cost of their travel. Denys Munby will be talking about this system so I will simply raise some of the difficulties which will have to be considered from a planning point of view.

Effects on income distribution

One of the most serious objections to a system of road pricing is that it is potentially regressive in terms of income distribution. No one can be sure of the prices that would have to be set, but in large towns and cities they could well be between 1p and 10p per vehicle mile. At an average of 3p per vehicle mile the annual cost to a motorist would be £150 if he runs 5,000 miles per annum in the pricing area. At present a low income marginal motorist probably pays £50 per annum in 'motoring related' taxes whereas a high income motorist pays £100 per annum or more. Thus all urban motorists would pay more but the poorer motorist, on this basis, relatively more than the rich motorist. This assumes that all other motor taxes are abolished; a common assumption is, in fact, that purchase tax could be retained to reduce this imbalance. It is likely that prices would be higher in peak periods than in off-peak periods. Low income motorists travel proportionately more in the peak than do high income motorists.

It is likely that prices would be higher in the inner congested areas and around outer foci than in the outer lower density areas. Low income motorists tend to live and work in the congested inner areas to a degree and around outer foci. Thus there are a number of income distribution problems to be dealt with before road pricing can be completely accepted.

Effects on Public Transport

It is generally held that road pricing would produce a fairer competition between public and private transport and this is undoubtedly the case; contrary to popular belief, the results however may not be wholly beneficial for public transport. Two difficulties which can arise are those of temporal and physical peaking. High peak-hour road prices would mean greater transference to public transport during the peak than during the off-peak. Now one of the basic problems of public transport economics is high, and increasing, peaking factors. At present the marginal cost of extra peak hour capacity on buses in large cities is about seven times that of marginal off-peak extra capacity. The situation for rail is somewhat similar, with the added fact that there are cost thresholds of new track and terminal capacity on some parts of busy urban rail systems, if peak loading has to rise without further overcrowding and congestion.

Typically urban rail systems are radial and most congested in the inner area where network convergence takes place. Again transference would be greater in these inner areas where the marginal cost of increased capacity is at its highest.

Effects on the Environment

One objective of a good urban transportation management system should be to minimise environmental costs. Most traffic/environmental phenomena exhibit the qualities of a decreasing function, i.e., double traffic levels less than doubles the environmental nuisance. There are therefore economies of scale of concentration, provided serious congestion does not result. A road pricing system based on marginal traffic congestion costs would tend to work in the opposite direction to this by pricing traffic off the congested main roads to less busy residential streets. There are ways of minimising this; by environmental management, and by setting prices to reflect both traffic and environmental costs; but these are potentially very complex and as yet unproven.

Despite these disadvantages the appeal of road pricing is still great and it is likely that the Government will start the first field experiment in the next couple of years.

IV. Staggering of Work Hours

Part of the purpose of city life is spatial and temporal proximity for specialist activities. To a degree personal and institutional decisions as to working hours are irrational and create peak demands on the transport system to no purpose. To impose a staggering regime would necessarily be largely arbitrary without intimate knowledge of office practices and the effects of particular starting and finishing times on the transport system. However staggering, which has not been readily implemented in the past, could be promoted by a local taxation concession to 'off-peak firms' and it would then be up to the individual institutions to take a more thoughtful and responsible view of whether or not it was really in their interests to start some or all of their employees during peak periods.

V. Comprehensive parking control

This method is increasingly being adopted in British towns as a first stage management measure. The principle is to relate the capacity of parking space, by time of day, to the capacity of the road system associated with it both locally and remotely. There are a number of disadvantages to parking control:

(i) Insofar as there are controlled and uncontrolled areas or facilities there will be through traffic which is not affected.

(ii) Parking is indiscriminate in that it affects all traffic bound for the controlled area equally, irrespective of whether or not it is using congested parts of the system.

(iii) The availability of much parking space is, or is seen to be, under the control of private firms and individuals. This has changed markedly since the early 1960s but will have to change much further if this means of management is to be sufficiently effective.

(iv) Parking controls are difficult to enforce and a management regime will not be effective if it is continually flaunted.

These controls can be by price, physical capacity, timing or licensing. Although any of these on their own would be in some respects inadequate, a mixture of price, timing and physical capacity can usually be made to work reasonably well.

VI. Selective availability of road space

This differs from area licences in that priorities are related directly to particular parts of the road network rather than to an area which will have both congested and uncongested sections of the network within it. Typical of this type of scheme is the exclusive bus lane; here the bus is identified as a priority vehicle and given special rights where they are of particular advantage. The effect of such priorities is usually to make a small reduction in journey speeds with a marked increase in reliability through the priority section. Schemes of this kind are potentially beneficial where the priority traffic demand approaches the capacity of the priority facility and the introduction of priorities does not escalate the cost of using the network to non-priority traffic to unacceptable levels.

Unfortunately there are relatively few sites meeting these criteria in British towns, with their narrow and irregular road patterns, and so one prospect in the short term, is to adopt a wider category of priority traffic which produces a more balanced distribution of traffic between the priority and non-priority groups. This could be done by price or status or both.

From these brief examinations of individual means it is possible to draw two main conclusions. Firstly, the effects of many likely management measures spill outside the transportation sector and they must be seen as part of a wider urban management package. This wider package will almost certainly involve changing the relationship between central and local government in the direction of greater local discretion. Secondly, because the sorts of management measures likely to be offered and employed during the next two or three decades may well produce unwanted side effects, the urban administrations must establish a set of criteria to gauge them against. I suggest that such a set should include:

(i) The technology required must be in existence or imminent.

(ii) The system should not rely on substantially different administrative procedures than those in existence or being developed.

(iii) Redistributional effects (allowing for compensatory adjustment) should be in accord with a generally acceptable notion of equity.

(iv) The system must be readily enforceable.

(v) Environmental conditions and options should not deteriorate and should be improved if possible.

(vi) The efficiency of the system as a whole should be increased.

11

Management: The Engineer's Viewpoint

T. E. H. Williams†

THE TERMS OF reference for my contribution to this Symposium were limited to the 'relatively short-term management methods for traffic in towns, with minimal financial investment and short gestation periods'. Before I confine myself to those boundary conditions, I feel that I should stress the fact that the Civil Engineer considers his responsibilities in traffic management to be interlocked with his activities in the *planning* of the urban infrastructure, the *design* of the various facilities associated with traffic and their *construction*.

The requirements of traffic management procedures have to be borne in mind when the roads, bridges, access ways, lay-bys, intersections, on-street parking bays, and off-street car parks are being designed and constructed. Also, traffic management considerations have to be accommodated in the design of new towns, industrial estates, shopping centres, housing estates, city centre renewal projects and many other civil engineering activities in the urban field.

The civil engineer's approach to traffic management is a blend of scientific method through controlled experiments, together with the results of cumulative practical experience. The information gained from experiments under laboratory and field conditions enable the quantitative assessments of *functional efficiency, safety*, and *cost-effectiveness* of the measures in question. Relatively recent examples of this sequence of activities in this country are:

(i) the design of direction signs for motorways and major all purpose roads, which involved the form and size of letters and the combination of colours for the letters, arrows and sign background.

(ii) The development of mini-roundabouts for intersections.

(iii) The experiments with bus-priority lanes and routes in urban areas.

† Professor of Civil Engineering, University of Southampton.

(iv) 'Area traffic control' experiments, in London and Glasgow where computers are linked to a number of traffic signals in efforts to obtain *optimum* efficiency from a road network.

The 'feedback' to planning and design from these and many other experiments involving management techniques provide a basis for comparison of various proposals for dealing with traffic situations.

In more strategic terms, the comprehensive transportation studies which are nowadays linked with surveys of land use development include many basic traffic management indices—e.g. journey origins and destinations, travel habits, journey times, delays, interchange of mode of transport and parking.

The degree of enforcement which is required for traffic management procedures will be dictated by the standards of the road networks—from motorways, through primary and secondary routes to the local roads.

With the *urban motorway*, the amount of traffic management is minimal, because the general high standard of structural design involved with motorways produces a consistency in geometric characteristics which are reflected in their traffic capacities and safety records. The segregation of vehicles from pedestrians and the physical separation of conflicting streams of vehicles by means of multi-level interchanges and dual carriageways avoid the hazards of unexpected situations due to sudden changes of traffic or design conditions. The element of surprise for the driver is reduced to its practical minimum.

In contrast with the single-purpose motorways there are wide varieties of all-purpose roads. Their management characteristics include speed limits of various magnitudes, turning controls, parking restrictions intersections at-grade with signals and roundabouts. These measures represent the compromise in standards of design which are adopted to meet the needs of local and long-distance traffic; public and private transport; delivery trucks and vans; access ways to properties; cyclists and pedestrians. The effects are visible in the daily contest for road space between vehicles and pedestrians in towns and villages throughout the country. There are examples in abundance of situations where inconsistencies in road design lead to vehicle-pedestrian conflicts and hazards to safety; traffic management procedures without re-design and reconstruction cannot be expected to be very successful in such cases.

At the present instant in time, there is an excessive gap between the feasible standards of construction for motorways and those for all-purpose traffic routes in urban areas. There is an urgent need to physically establish the hierarchy of roads in urban areas to provide more logical and positive systems of traffic routes from the motorways through primary roads to other roads of a secondary and local character. The design of such systems would span the range of situations which require drivers of vehicles to be progressively conditioned to the radical changes from the absolute priority to vehicular movement which is available on motorways to the highest possible priority for pedestrians in residential areas.

The clash between traffic function and amenity is clearly evident in our towns. Environment suffers when the amount of traffic using a road exceeds that which is acceptable for the type of human activity in the area. It is imperative that efforts should be continued to channel industrial and heavy commercial vehicles on routes which adequately cater for their needs in areas of suitable environment. Traffic Management procedures will only be wholly effective if the appropriate road networks are available. This presents formidable problems in most of our older towns, where residential areas, commercial centres and industries are intermixed. That is one of the most significant components in a traffic–roads–environment triangle.

It is a truism in the case of traffic management in towns that the solution of a problem in one area often gives rise to new problems in adjacent areas. It happens with single intersections and also with entire town centres. The decanting of traffic from one point of major congestion to other points of less congestion, which in turn present their own problems, lead to the conclusion that the control of traffic on an area-wide scale is an obvious necessity. That brings us to technology and the ways in which its products and methods may be applied to systems of traffic control on an area-wide basis.

Experiments are under way in many countries throughout the world, which involve the coordination by computer of traffic control devices over major areas of cities. The pattern of future development in the control of urban traffic may well lie in that direction. Progress has been hampered in that field to date by the lack of finance, effort and political confidence in such methods at local authority and government levels. It is to be hoped that, when the results of the current experiments are available and provided they are satisfactory, rapid progress will be made in the integration of computer facilities with other methods of traffic control in towns and conurbations.

The capacities of road networks provide their own restraints on traffic, whether they be private cars, public transport, industrial articulated vehicles or commercial vans. The effects are to be seen only too often in the congestion on many town roads. The costs to industries of the delays to their vehicles on congested roads is a matter of the greatest importance in these days of increasing competition for markets for our goods.

Significant relief of congestion will only be a reality when satisfactory systems of public transport services are available to commuters. The efforts which are now being made in some of our towns and conurbations to provide a reasonable alternative to the private car as a mode of transport for the one-journey-per-day commuter, reflect the awareness which exists of that core issue of traffic management in towns.

Parking produces its own group of traffic management problems. The payment for the use of parking meters, ground level car parks and multi-storey garages is such a common feature of present urban life that it is difficult to appreciate the storms of protest which arose within the last decade when such facilities were first proposed.

Where these measures are correctly used, they can serve as a very effective management technique for the control of commuter traffic. We should, however, recognise that the private motorist is a very adaptable, and often unscrupulous, being. To beat the parking system is one of the hobbies of the urban dweller.

In considering *safety*, for drivers and pedestrians the objective should be to *segregate*, wherever possible, vehicles from pedestrians and the faster moving vehicles from the slower moving service vehicles. There are significant dangers involved in any compromise in this field, as is often proved by accident statistics. The increasing rate of introduction of pedestrian precincts in town centres is a step in the right direction.

The future should see the development of new methods of public transport of the Cabtrack type for urban areas, which would make use of air space and sub-surface areas. They should serve to attract the commuter away from his private car for his journey to work, and thus help to ease the problems of traffic management on our roads.

Certain types of central areas may well have to resort to road pricing measures, in addition to more stringent parking regulations, together with the control of traffic circulation by computer-based methods.

To Summarize: I see the Civil Engineer's roll in the field of Traffic and Towns as being one of accommodating *Continuity with Change.* He attempts to do this by the quantitative assessment and qualitative appreciation of the problems of *Access, Circulation and Parking* and aims to provide the *Networks* of *Roads* which will allow adequate provision for mobility and the means for development of areas of suitable environment for the residents and commuter-worker in our towns.

The fact that the civil engineer's activities in regard to urban traffic do not allow him the luxury of planning without the ultimate responsibility for construction and management places considerable demands on his professional skills. The success or failure of his efforts depend on the amount of blending of appropriate management procedures with design and construction.

12

Management: The Economist's Viewpoint

D. L. Munby†

I THOUGHT I would start by asking the question 'Why doesn't the market work in towns?' That is one way of introducing the economist's contribution. After all, in most spheres the market is recognised as a way of handling the conflicting demands of a whole mass of people. I don't want to go into too much detail, but I think you can find in the case of cities almost all the reasons for market failure acting together. You find joint costs (the roads provide facilities for all kinds of traffic); you find joint demand (the householder who buys a house, buys access with it). You find economies of scale, as has been pointed out. You find monopoly (every piece of land is effectively a monopoly site and no two pieces of land are the same). Therefore the ordinary competitive processes cannot work in the ordinary way. (Anyone who has ever tried to get an estate agent to value properties for him will know that the market just hardly exists.) Then there are the large range of non-marketable goods that are a very important aspect of urban life. For instance, there is the provision of public parks, and the question of environmental standards, noise, fumes and the like; in particular for transport there is the valuation of time and the loss of time. Thus we can see that cities provide a range of circumstances in which the market does not work well, or in which there is no price, or prices cannot be interpreted in the normal way. That is particularly true in relation to the use of road space. The simple fact is that, even if it were possible, we have not got an adequate pricing system for the use of road space.

It is perfectly clear that, if you provide any good at a price substantially less than cost, there will be a high level of demand (as compared with supply). There is, in this sense, nothing surprising about road congestion. If tomatoes were given away free, or at a very low price, then it is likely that there would be queues for tomatoes.

† Reader in the Economics of Transport, University of Oxford.

Equally, and I think this is not clearly recognised by many people, there is nothing necessarily wrong, from an economic point of view, with road congestion. After all, congestion is simply a situation in which the addition of extra vehicles on the road slows down traffic flow; the situation in which average costs are rising and marginal costs are rising even more rapidly. From an economic point of view it is not at all inconceivable, indeed it is quite likely, that the efficient use of road space will be at a point at which congestion occurs. It would of course be possible, if you are willing to suffer other adverse effects on the urban environment and to invest an enormous amount of resources, to provide for free flow in urban situations, just as it would be possible to provide free wine in public fountains (which would be more desirable in my view than free traffic flow). The limit in both cases is that of cost.

By looking at the situations in which the market does not work, and by looking at the solution which would occur if there were a proper market, we may get some indication of how to make improvements and what improvements to make. Now the economist is not solely concerned with costs and markets in a narrow sense; he is also concerned with alternatives, which means finding out what they are, and judging between them. I would like to bring to your attention in this connection a case about which I have just been reading, namely that of Thomas Cubitt, which shows that even 19th century profit-seeking business men used planning tools. Thomas Cubitt made very large sums out of the development of London and Brighton. He was responsible for the development of a large part of Belgravia, and of his 'Cubitt-town' in Pimlico. In his work as a developer he took a very long-run view. Because of this he was much concerned with amenity, because he felt that in the long run this would contribute to his making the largest profits. In the pursuit of this end he set up in Belgravia, as the Duke of Bedford did in Bloomsbury, tollgates around the outside of the area so that traffic which was not approved would be discouraged from moving through the area. So the profit motive, at least in the middle of the nineteenth century, was capable of producing examples of what might be considered excessively interventionist planning. Cubitt's forms of intervention are precisely those which we may now, after Buchanan and all that, want to bring to the attention of such planning authorities as the G.L.C.

Now for the particular ways in which the failure of the price mechanism affects the efficiency of the use of the road system.

(1) I have referred to the pricing of roads, and I would like to say a few words about that. The case for 'road pricing' is quite simple. It is clear that, in congested situations, as the amount of traffic on a section of road increases so does the cost, and in particular the time cost to the driver. The existence of congestion shows clearly that the driver is willing to pay those costs which he incurs directly (the average congestion cost). But it is not so clear that he would be willing to pay those costs which are incurred by the rest of society (i.e., the extra costs, particularly time costs, of other road users), as a result of his decision to use that congested facility. The logic of the road pricing model is simply that the appropriate price, the market clearing price, should be that where the user is charged an amount equal to the marginal social cost rather than simply to the average social (congestion) cost.

It may well be technically possible, by means of electronic devices, to obtain a system which approximates to this theoretical ideal. But I think it is also useful for us to have a look at some of the difficulties which arise in the application of this theory. The most obvious problems, of course, are those of enforcement. They are not particularly within the competence of the economist to discuss, though they are clearly substantial problems. But there is just one comment I would like to make on this subject. There is a commonly held view, particularly by the police and administrators, that any device of this kind should be enforceable, preferably at 100% efficiency, and should be equally enforced on all sections of the community. It is frequently thought unfair and impracticable, and therefore not to be recommended, to use something like special licences, in which you are only likely to catch about 10% of the offenders.

But first, everyone knows, for instance with regard to the 30 mile an hour speed limit, that we do not have even 10% of the offenders against the law caught and convicted. So, if all the dire consequences with regard to general disregard of the law are to follow for a law which is not totally enforceable, then they should already have occurred with regard to speed limits. It is not clear that this is the case.

Secondly, in any case the object of the exercise is to produce a particular result, a lower traffic flow. In order to obtain a given level of results, it would be possible simply to impose higher fines for those people who are caught. There must be some combination of levels of fine and levels of enforcement which will give the desired result. So this is a possible line of approach in traffic management. Instead of setting fines low and trying to enforce the law at very high cost, we might possibly set fines at a very high level and rely on fear of being caught to keep observance levels high. I don't want to expand on the income distribution and equity effects of that, but I simply leave that as a point which might be usefully thought about.

The second point I want to make about road pricing is that an absolute optimum is not possible by this means. I think some over-optimism was shown by those who first produced the case for road pricing with regard to the degree of precision with which it could be applied. The main reason for the impossibility of an absolute optimum relies on the way in which human beings respond to the price mechanism. After all, a price is only useful in so far as it is a signal to behaviour. There is no point in charging a very high price for vehicles using Oxford Street when the street becomes jammed if the nature of the situation is that they cannot possibly do anything about it. The price is only useful in so far as it can be foreseen and the road user can adjust his behaviour accordingly. This means that to be effective the prices have got to be known in advance and they have to be publicised in order to have the appropriate effect on behaviour. This means that we cannot adjust our prices effectively with any great frequency and any great precision. Economists have tended to overlook these sort of problems by virtue of simplifying the situation in static examples.

There are, indeed, a number of other criticisms which might be made of the 'road pricing' technique. The fact that we cannot attain the perfect application of the theoretical design so frequently specified by economists leads us therefore to the consideration of some practical proxies for pricing devices.

Probably the most common and the most popular of such proxies is the use of parking policy. Now, without doubt, this means can be used to control traffic in some kinds of towns. But it does have its own disadvantages. For instance, it tends not to affect through flows. Thus, in the case of Central London for example, if we had parking restraint which prevented or limited the journeys made by people working in Central London the effect might simply be to improve the situation for other kinds of traffic. Thus we might finish up with Central London being used much more predominantly than is presently the case for through traffic flowing through the West End to the docks. This clearly would not seem a very sensible or attractive solution. Nevertheless, if it is combined with other measures of traffic management in a sensible way, parking control may provide a reasonable approximation to what one would expect with a proper road pricing policy, particularly in towns with a suitable road layout.

(2) Similarly for public transport, as with roads, partly because of practical difficulties of implementation and partly because of the conservatism of the transport operators, there has been a tendency for prices to be predominantly based on average cost. Where there are very substantial differences in the marginal cost of provision of services, this has led to an inefficient and uneconomic provision and use of public transport facilities. The failure to charge an appropriate price for the peak is a particularly important case. One of the results of this is that there is insufficient pressure put on firms to relocate their activities and to reorganise them in order to make efficient use of transport facilities. Similarly with public passenger transport, if fares are averaged over journeys of different length, there is an increasing tendency for people to live further and further away from their jobs irrespective of the true cost to society of this decision.

(3) Our present system tilts the balance in favour of the private car and away from public transport. This clearly results from a lack of congestion charges because, even if the bus was to be charged the appropriate road price in the same way as the car (i.e., in fact say 5 times the charge for a car), the incidence per passenger would be very much less, because it carries many more people. The alternative is to subsidise public transport, which obviously makes sense in a given situation, but the thing you have to beware of is here again the encouragement that you give to employers to mislocate their activities because of the lower costs of transport for their employees. Indeed, it might be much more sensible to make a levy on employers in central areas to pay for these subsidies; that would be the right way in principle to mitigate some of the bad effects of a subsidy paid by the tax-payers or the rate-payers.

(4) Finally I should say something about pedestrians and cyclists. I am glad that Professor Williams has mentioned them, because they are so often forgotten. If you look at these vast traffic surveys, they tell you very much less about these types of movement than about other (vehicle) movements. Yet they are cheap and easy forms of transport, particularly in smaller cities. (It is easy to forget the small cities. Obviously, a large proportion of our population do live in larger cities; but there is also a large proportion living in smaller

cities where the problems are very different and where the contribution that pedestrian and cycle movements can make is much greater.) An example of this bias is the way in which traffic accident figures tend to be presented. It is often suggested that an unduly large proportion of traffic accidents involve cyclists or pedestrians. The implication that often seems to be drawn is that pedestrians and cyclists cause traffic accidents and that, if only we could get rid of them there would not be so many accidents. Well, I must admit that that is in some sense true. (Though the only case I know of a pedestrian actually damaging a car was in the case of a daughter of mine who at an early age walked into a moving car, damaged it, and benefited to the extent of a large box of chocolates from the driver of the injured vehicle. But that I think is a rather rare case.) The important thing is that there is very little knowledge of the costs to pedestrians of traffic management measures; of how you could minimise pedestrian costs; or of how you could minimise total traffic cost by the encouragement of pedestrians and cyclists. It is interesting that it seems very rare in this country to allow bicycles to move against the general flow of traffic in one-way streets. This is done, for instance, in Italy where they have gone much further in favouring bicycles through traffic management measures.

Having talked at some length about the price mechanism and the ways in which we might approximate to its use, one must admit in the end that cities provide situations in which it is not always possible to adapt at the margin and where it is sometimes necessary to pursue all-or-nothing solutions. If you adapt at the margin, there is a danger that you will continue to favour the private car and to tolerate the decline of public transport and that there will be no break in this vicious circle. To deal with this problem we would have to compare alternative systems, as wholes. This is completely compatible with economic thought and there is no reason why one should not make these comparisons. However, in so far as one does continue to have to make day-to-day decisions and to make adaptations at the margin, it is appropriate and proper that we should try to make them in a way which would reflect the operations of a price mechanism if one were to exist.

13

Public and Private Transport in Towns

D. W. Glassborow†

IN THE GREAT days of the Windmill Theatre, there was usually a resident comedian, whose task it was to fill the intervals when the girls were changing clothes from one state of almost nothing to another. I do not know why it took so long. In the planning of the programme for this symposium, I feel I have been cast for a somewhat similar task. I hope that, unlike a typical Windmill audience, you will not feel that this part of the proceedings is too long.

I am well aware, however, that if I were conscientiously to try to cover the whole of my subject, I would be stopped by our chairman before I had properly begun. So I will not try. I would add that nothing I have to say would have seemed new to transport men ten years ago.

In real life the link between short term measures and long term solutions is a most important one—and in a very real sense the task I have been given is to ask how far the action which town planners and traffic engineers take today is compatible with a civilised way of life in ten, twenty or thirty years time.

In previous papers a town planner, a civil engineer and an economist spoke about short term management. But, management of what? And what role can they, when practising their professions, play in management? My answer to the second question is, of course, precious little. I am sure, from what they have said, that they agree. None of the three really talked about management and Mr. Bayliss's contribution might more nearly have been that of an economist. So far as the first question is concerned, I do not believe the transport system of a town can be managed at all, in the business sense and I think it is wrong to apply such terminology. Users of transport in towns can be manipulated, confused, frustrated and cheated. But management of the transport system? We need first to agree the objectives.

† Chief Planning Officer, National Bus Company.

When I consider the question of how the overall transport system of a town might be run by a benevolent dictator, I am reminded of the day in 1954 when I joined the British Transport Commission to head the newly formed economics department, full of enthusiasm, sure of the answers and not properly aware of the important questions. I did however ask one question, which I still believe to need answering. I tried to find where the managers were, because there were engineering departments, a commercial department, an operating department, a finance department, a legal department, a public relations department, a manpower department. That list is not exhaustive, but when I looked for a management line all I could find was a vacuum. Nearly twenty years later after a series of re-organisations, disorganisations and re-disorganisations, some of them based on the most expensive management consultancy advice, I still cannot detect a real management line actually at work in British Railways.

This is not meant to be a criticism. I think it really reflects the intractability of the railway management problem; one serious consequence is that inevitably each of the major railway departments believes that, if only it were left to them to decide, they would make the right decisions and run the show properly.

I come back at once to the urban transport problem. In the absence of someone properly in charge, the various interested professionals, the planners, the engineers and the economists each believe that they should be in control, because theirs is the true faith.

I would not myself like to say that expertise in any one of those professions is a bar to those possessing it being successful overall controllers of movement in and into towns: if such a function were given to an individual, I see no reason why a professional expertise in town planning or in civil engineering should, in itself, prevent a man from carrying it out successfully. I am, however, sure that neither the planning department nor the engineering department of a city is the right department to exercise such control, nor should the man responsible overall be head of the highways department, if the city has one. Partly because it seems to me that the idea that the ordinary citizen matters comes rather late in their thinking.

What about the economist? Here I am, I suppose, inevitably prejudiced. I do not think that the attention devoted by economists to transport questions has been of real value to the management of transport operations in the time I have been concerned with them, though their activities may perhaps have been of modest net benefit in the formulation of government transport policy. Their public utterances and published works have, I believe, tended to cause practising transport men to believe their expertise to be of little value.

Whatever the role of the economist is in the context of urban transport problems, it is certainly not a management one. But at least economics has the advantage that its starting point is the study of human behaviour in the context of the ordinary business of life and it recognises the constraints imposed by financial and physical resources. It is particularly valuable because it recognises the importance of the time-scale and the problems and possibilities of the transition from short term to long term solutions. As an economist, however, his approach is not conducive to decision-taking, which is the basic function of management. Economic studies can assist decision taking by providing an evaluation of the choice between charging or tax systems and physical controls intended to have similar effects. Economic advice might, I believe, be of particular value in the choice between road pricing and other means of influencing the use of urban road networks.

Management requires an autocrat, subject to broad direction and to accountability and to ultimate removal if he is judged to have failed. I find it difficult to see how such a post can be fitted into our concept of urban government. I doubt whether elected representatives would wish to give anyone the necessary power in such a politically sensitive context.

We nevertheless require someone to sort out the conflicts between the town planner and the highway engineer, since both of them, to judge by the contributions this morning, think they are responsible for amenity, traffic management, parking, public transport and the rest.

I do not feel we can trust either of them on their own to produce decent long term solutions, if we are to judge from the many mistakes of the past, which continue to be repeated today. Town planners in the past seemed to have ignored the transport problems their land use plans create. Even now much of what is being done suggests to me that they do not yet comprehend transport problems. There are, of course, exceptions. What seems not to be understood is that the solution to individual transport problems is only simple when you really accept that it is complex—and too complex to be handed over to computer models, in which many now seem to have almost blind faith.

Traffic engineering techniques are, of course, fallible because they seek to improve the wrong measures.Too much of their working is based on counting vehicles and measuring speeds, not people and goods and start to stop journey time and costs. They do not seem to count pedestrians very often—do they believe pedestrians do not count?

The pace of physical change is slow. Even more important, once they have been approved, plans for re-development based on faulty techniques continue, because of the inertia of the administrative machine, long after the mistakes have been recognised by the leading authorities in the planning and transport field. This makes it all the more important to provide the autocrat—or local government committee attempting to carry out his function—with a framework of future objectives and sound advice on the extent to which short term solutions may hinder their achievement. At present we seem to have a fundamental difference of view between those who believe we should spend large sums on improving roads in cities and those who feel public passenger transport to be an alternative.

I thus come to the heart of my subject—public transport and the role it can and should play in urban travel. I would like to remind you that just 70 years ago in September 1901, a Colonel Crompton addressed the British Association on the subject of street traffic. He proposed, I gather, the construction of new main roads with motor-buses travelling at 10 m.p.h. and carrying 14,000 passengers an hour. This would have needed a flow of 540 buses an hour of the then current seating capacity. A Mr. Robinson (of London United Tramways) perhaps better known as Sir James Clifton Robinson pointed out that such a flow of buses would require a reserved road to achieve even 8 m.p.h. He also pointed out that 120 of his tramcars could carry 8,400 passengers an hour. Mr. Robinson conceded that the future might well be with motor traction on special roads, but that for the time being it was the tram plus the tube railway in co-ordination which was the answer. The motorbus of that time was, of course, a very unreliable vehicle.

The bus versus rail argument is thus by no means new. A fairly recent study in which the same argument came up was that into various rapid transit proposals in Manchester. Rapid transit is of course a most misleading term because, whatever advantages most reserved track systems have in urban areas, the overall door-to-door journey speeds achieved for short distance travel cannot be termed rapid. It must be accepted that for a flow above about 15,000 passengers per hour, a conventional rail system is at present the only one which has been properly tested, though one can question whether town planners who in their land use plans propose to create or continue even higher flows really accept a civilised urban life as one of their objectives.

If one can accept that peak flows of more than 15,000 passengers per hour in one direction are incompatible with the planning of a civilised urban environment, the choice of a tracked system does not appear essential. A study of a reserved bus lane project, undertaken by a group of British firms, showed the possibility of carrying up to 14,000 seated passengers in one direction. Mean journey speeds were affected by the number of stops and the distance between stops. By arranging for stops to be by-passed by through vehicles, higher mean speeds could be obtained at the expense of longer waits at stops.

The practical safe maximum flow, allowing for stopping and merging was some 300 vehicles an hour, in view of the particular signalling system to control merging which was proposed. The bus considered was one in current production. For non-stop operation on a 12-mile route, mean journey speeds of over 40 miles per hour appeared possible, while those which stopped at intervals of one mile would average about 30 miles per hour. The results of these studies show, I think, that operated to serve a similar part of the travel market, buses can provide for large flows at more frequent service intervals than is normal with urban train services.

Next, the bus compared with the car. I have recently seen a report that a race between a bus on a reserved lane and a car using the normal highway system on a 14 mile trip into Washington D.C. was won by the bus. Both vehicles started at 8.00 a.m. The bus arrived at 8.35 a.m. and the car at 9.07 a.m. The same article also reported that during a two day rail strike in May this year an extra 102 express buses were used on an exclusive bus lane into New York and the service carried an additional 14,400 passengers between 8.00 a.m. and 9.00 a.m. I am not advocating planned continuation of such excesses. I think, however, that these examples show there is an important role for the express bus on a reserved track in planned urban transport.

This leads me to refer to a paper presented by Professor Smeed to the Manchester Statistical Society in February, 1961, entitled 'The Traffic Problem in Towns'. Other pre-occupations have prevented me from keeping in touch with further work developing the approach he then adopted.

In one section of the paper he produced a measure of methods of movement of people at peak times, which might be used for ranking. This was the area of the track divided by the passenger throughput. This he presented as the area required for a single journey of one mile at peak periods.

I believe this concept a useful contribution to understanding and to planning, because one of the problems we now face in towns is the encroachment of travelling and parking space on expensive land required for other purposes.

I recall when I first saw Professor Smeed's paper I had some doubts about the absolute values he had calculated and some further doubts about the assumptions he had made concerning the technical characteristics of the methods he compared and in particular the passenger loadings of the vehicles. I think he was probably too generous in his railway assessment and too limited in his view of bus loadings.

The methods he has assessed were pedestrians, urban and suburban railways, mixed traffic of cars and buses on urban streets, showing narrow streets and wide streets separately, and cars on urban motorways. He did not include an assessment of buses on urban motorways. Nor did he consider bicycles.

You will note that the assessment was only related to the movement function and did not take account of the differing convenience of access to the ultimate destination which the use of that particular method provided. In the ranking in terms of space economy for movement the urban and suburban railway line came first. Next came the pedestrian footway requiring about 3 times as much space, followed by buses in mixed traffic on urban streets, which required from 4 to 10 times the space, according to the movement speed assumed and with a relatively low assumed average load. On urban streets the space requirements of car use ranged from 10 times that of the railway, with a wide road and 4 occupants, to 100 times with a narrow street and only the driver. On the urban motorway because of the higher speeds, the car with 4 people required only 5 times the space of the railway.

To me one of the big gaps is the absence of an assessment of the bus in a reserved lane, where as I mentioned earlier, the practical throughput of a bus only lane is greatly influenced by the stopping pattern required for picking up and setting down passengers—that is by the convenience of the particular service from an access point of view.

I will not therefore attempt exactly to place the reserved lane bus service in Professor Smeed's ranking list, but it must be better than the ordinary stopping service in an all-purpose road.

I will rather next turn to discuss how convenience of access affects the desirability of facilitating the use of any one method. Clearly the pedestrian footpath network performs the access function with almost no loss of the movement capacity of the area. The other modes require varying additional amounts of land to permit the access needs of the travellers to be supplied. Buses, if they are allowed to stop to pick up and set down are the next best means of providing access with economy of land use. Cars in urban streets seem to me to create appalling movement problems if they are used to provide convenient access for the car owner, while much of their convenience to the user is lost if they have to be left in a car park for a short stay. Railway services, while apparently economical of space for moving people, seem to occupy large areas of land other than for track; which Professor Smeed did not bring to account. So far as access is concerned, rail seems to me to be worst of all, and will usually require a secondary journey by some other means of movement. Where an area is completely re-developed to accord with an urban rail system this may not be so—but the same results could then be achieved with a reserved bus route.

Amenity is very much a matter of personal judgement. My own view is that pedestrian movement is the least destructive of amenity, given adequate space, while car and bus movement at the higher speeds is particularly destructive. One-way streets are, I believe, particularly undesirable. Parked cars are generally bad, except where underground space is provided—which is, of course, costly. I have yet to see a multi-storey car park with an attractive appearance.

Surface railways again are destructive in amenity terms—being bad or worse than dual carriage roads—and underground ones are expensive.

I will not go into the argument about the amenity aspects of building urban motorways, except to say that those who plan the sequence of pulling down and re-building sub-standard residential and industrial areas of cities should not work in isolation from those planning the new road networks, and both should ensure that the necessary finance is certain to be available. It is, in my view, not so much that Westway should not have been built, though there may be ways in which its design is deficient, but that its construction ought to have gone hand in hand with re-development along its route.

It is not only in terms of access, however, that one must be careful of misusing Professor Smeed's concept as a means of ranking the alternative ways of travelling. The speeds normally attainable and the physical effort involved are also very relevant to the planning and use of an urban travel system made up of a combination of them.

It is obviously important to take account of the traveller's attitude to what is an acceptable throughout journey time. We know that cars on urban streets at peak times rarely average more than 10 miles an hour, unless one way systems are in operation which often involve higher speeds over longer (because indirect) routes. Bus journeys in similar circumstances may be performed at 6 to 7 miles an hour and urban rail journeys at perhaps 15 miles an hour. Suburban railway journeys and urban motorways provide speeds of 30 to 45 miles an hour.

In terms of space requirements, access and amenity, I therefore conclude that a form of private transport (that is the pedestrian) is the most appropriate means of catering for peak hour city centre movements. It is clear to me that planners and traffic engineers together must plan for pedestrians to have priority. Because of low speeds, the objective must be to give pedestrians the most direct and unhindered passage. Particularly harmful are large urban roundabouts, pedestrian bridges and subways and junctions where pedestrians are prevented from following their natural path by railings or other such barriers.

If I plump for private transport for the shorter journeys, I think it is equally clear that for the longer city centre journeys some form of public transport is desirable. My own preference is for the bus, which can provide better access to a greater variety of different destinations than can a rail system, and more frequent services for a given volume of flow. I believe it also in practice to be superior in terms of operating costs. Complete pedestrianisation of streets is not always desirable; I can think of cases where the balance of advantage is in permitting buses to pass through such streets at low speed.

I also believe that there is an important role to be played by the taxi in city centres. I put the taxi in the public transport category. Its virtue is, of course, that it does not create the parking problems which are associated with the private car.

I have already pointed out that I regard as uncivilised an urban environment which requires urban railways—though new urban railways used to less than capacity can be attractive, if costly. Where railways already exist, it would not in my view be sensible to abandon them. But I am sure we should avoid developing urban type railway services to provide for suburban travel needs or for the longer journeys in the larger conurbations. Is it really sensible, in long term planning, to expect air passengers to travel between Heathrow and London on the Piccadilly Line instead of by direct service? However sensible it may be for airport employees to travel shorter distances to and from work in this way, instead of adding to car congestion in the central airport area.

So far, I have been putting a very simple case for planning the travel to work system as a combination of private walking and public transport, in quite a conventional way, though with the emphasis on the use of buses rather than rail. It is, I think, likely that by this means we would avoid the need to create more city centre road space and also the building of new underground railways at a very high cost.

There is, however, a very large gap in the argument. Roads currently perform a number of very important functions quite apart from helping to supply the needs of travellers to and from work. The life of a city would quickly come to an end if there were no provision for industrial and commercial goods traffic, ranging from raw materials, intermediate products and fuel going into factories, to the onward movement of finished goods from wholesalers to retailers—and ultimately local delivery to houses.

There is in my view no substitute for roads for these functions. Such movements can usually be performed outside the absolute passenger peaks, but in many areas today the existing roads are unsuitable for much of this movement of goods. There is a need on amenity grounds to take this traffic so far as possible away from streets where people live and from the main shopping and office areas. This requires the creation of a primary road system and, in some instances, the building of urban motorways. It is an illusion to believe that the need for such road construction can be avoided by the improvement and the subvention of public passenger transport.

I would finally draw attention to the fact that there are many minor traffic flows which cannot economically be catered for by stage carriage or contract buses. A complete ban on cars for such journeys would mean they could not be performed. I would add that the carrying capacity of urban roads is often well in excess of requirements, if all passengers went by bus. A bus lane carrying 5,000 passengers an hour at the peak will look quite empty. Put the same passengers in cars at 2 persons per car and there is an intolerable situation. But in addition to the buses, there could be about four times as many cars without serious congestion—if you could only keep the numbers down to that level. Herein lies the political problem of the reserved bus lane alongside congested lanes used by all other vehicles. The traffic problem comes back to enforcement.

The economists present will probably particularly have noted the absence of costs figures in the comparisons I have made. This is not because I do not think costs to be important. I believe that costs figures on their own are misleading and incomplete costs figures to be worse still. And, in view of the difficulty about assessing land values in cities and the link between such land values and accessibility by the various means of transport, any cost figures must be incomplete.

I also am aware that, from the user's point of view, the quality of the service is of vital importance. It can well be the case that a transport user values the more costly service much more than it costs but would only use a less costly one if he were handsomely paid to do so. This is one aspect of the choice between alternatives which I do not believe to be properly brought to account by the still fashionable cost/benefit analysis.

I must now conclude. If I had tried to cover the whole ground, I might perhaps end by summarising my main points. There are inevitably so many gaps, however, that this would be wasteful. I will content myself with a question. When you have agreed on your objectives and prepared your plans based on your own value judgements, how will you get the ordinary citizen to behave as you think he should?

14

Desirable Characteristics of the Main Road System

R. J. Smeed†

Editor's Preface

PROFESSOR SMEED, who was invited to give a paper at very short notice, decided to give a summary of a paper, not separately published, that he submitted to the Public Enquiry on the Greater London Development Plan.

Introduction

The desirable layout of the main road system of a town is a subject of great importance but has not received the attention that the subject deserves. Some aspects of the subject were, however, tackled in a recent paper,[1] and the object of this note is to summarise those conclusions considered particularly relevant to the long term road planning problems of a large town like London. That paper concentrates on two criteria for assessing the desirability of a given type of urban road system:

(i) The minimisation of the total cost of all journeys for a given origin-destination pattern.

(ii) The minimisation, for amenity, social economic or other reasons, of the distance travelled in selected parts of the towns, especially in the town centre. The technique employed for considering this aspect made use of the concept of the distance travelled per unit area. Since, however, this quantity has large values on the road system and is zero at other places, the quantity is calculated over an area containing both roads and other places and over an area sufficiently large to give meaningful values, sufficient, in fact, to

† Professor of Traffic Studies, University College, London.

[1] R. J. Smeed. *The effect of the design of the road network on the intensity of traffic movement in different parts of a town with special reference to the effects of ring roads*. Proceedings of Tewksbury Symposium, Melbourne, 1970. Construction Industry Research & Information Association, London. Technical Note 17.

reveal tendencies for traffic to concentrate at some parts of the town rather than others. The distance travelled per unit area, calculated over a sufficiently large area, is called in the paper 'the intensity of travel'. It was found that:

General

The type of road network and the routeing methods used have much less effect on the average distance travelled than on the intensity of travel. For the usual urban journey patterns some routeing systems result in high intensities of travel near the town centre and low intensities at the outskirts. Others result in low intensities of travel at the town centres and relatively high intensities at the outskirts.

Effect of route on intensity of travel

(a) Travel in a town via radial routes, i.e. routes in which travel takes place from origin to town centre and thence to destination, naturally results in a high intensity of travel at the town centre.

(b) Ring routes, i.e. routes in which travel takes place from origin to the nearest point on a single ring road, then along the ring road to the point on it nearest to the destination and from this point to the destination, result in a relatively low intensity of travel in the region surrounded by the ring road, especially when the ring road has a high proportion of trip ends outside it.

(c) Routes approximating to direct ones, i.e. those in which travel takes place on roads as near as possible to the straight line joining origin and destination, are often used in real road systems. The intensity of travel due to such routes is intermediate between those for ring and radial routes for parts of the town within the area bounded by the ring road.

(d) Routes based on a number of radial roads together with a number of ring roads result in intensities of traffic within the town higher than those due to single ring routes, except in the neighbourhood of the ring road itself, but lower than those resulting from direct or radial routes near the town centre.

Choice of route by drivers

Since there is often a social requirement for low intensities of travel at some parts of a town, especially near the town centres, the conditions under which drivers will, of their own accord, use ring roads require consideration.

In an area containing a series of concentric approximately circular roads together with the usual type of road system, drivers choosing the quickest route generally choose a route involving a circumferential road, provided that the speed on the circumferential roads is more than 60 per cent higher than on the ordinary road system.

In an area with a single approximately circular ring road together with a normal type of road system the drivers using the quickest routes will use the ring road if both trip ends are external to it, and if the speed on the ring road is more than 60% higher than on the normal road system. Such drivers will not use the ring road if both origin and destination lie approximately within a circle concentric with the ring road and of radius half that of the ring road.

The effects on average distance travelled and on intensities of travel of drivers selecting the cheapest instead of the quickest routes when they have the choice of circumferential and radial routes may be deduced from the results of drivers choosing the quickest route by substituting for the ratio of the speeds on the circumferential and radial roads a quantity equal to about 0·75 times this ratio. The effect of drivers choosing the shortest routes may be obtained by substituting unity for the ratio of speeds.

Average distance travelled

On most types of ordinary road systems the total distance travelled from any set of origins to any set of destinations is about 27 to 31% greater than the total airline distance between the same set of origins and destinations. With a road system consisting of radial roads plus concentric ring roads, however, the total distance travelled is only about 10% greater than the sum of the airline distances between the origins and destinations, provided that drivers select the shortest routes.

Some effects of a single ring road

Ring roads can have a major effect in distributing traffic whose destination is within the area surrounded by it as well as diverting by-passable traffic. Since a relatively fast ring road tends to result in a low intensity of travel in the area it surrounds, the provision of such a road in a road network not possessing one can often be used to effect an appreciable reduction in the amount of travel in the region that it surrounds provided, of course, that the consequent reduction in travel time does not itself result in the introduction of an equivalent amount of new traffic.

There is a large difference in the intensity of travel on the two sides of a ring road if it is at all near the centre of a town.

General

The above qualitative results and the corresponding quantitative ones given in the paper referred to above lead to the conclusion that London, which has a predominantly radial road system, would gain greatly by the addition of a series of ring roads. This conclusion is made even stronger by the fact that any newly constructed road is likely to generate new buildings near it, and thus increase its use. It is presumably better to increase the intensity of development on ring roads away from the centre than on roads passing through the centre.

It therefore appears that in the long run the general concept of a series of circumferential roads as proposed in the Development Plan would be of considerable benefit to travellers in the London area.

The above arguments do not, of course, discuss the question of whether the proposed system of the London plan is economically justifiable, and this point must be considered separately. It should, however, be realized that to a considerable extent the financial and social costs of a new road system must be borne by the existing community; the benefits from it will not arise for some years. A new road system is therefore of more benefit to the young than to the old. Many of the latter will suffer loss of amenity and some even homes and will not gain the benefit. The question of whether to build a new road system is, therefore, considerably bound up with the question of how far it is reasonable to cause losses to the old in an endeavour to benefit posterity and the young.

15

Problems of Building Roads in Towns

C. W. Wolley†

Some Definitions

FOR THE purpose of this paper the roads considered are urban motorways and other principal roads. Estate roads and district distributors, etc., construction of which no doubt has its own problems, are passed over. Towns are conurbations of, say, 100,000 population and upwards.

Building is taken to cover the whole sequence of detailed planning and design through the actual construction period.

The Problems

Life, as we know, is full of problems and they come frequently. All work contains its own special problems. The ones involved in building roads in towns that I propose to discuss are not those of a technical or mathematical nature which occur in analysis and design, but the wider ones, which, due to their breadth, involve other people. Indeed, many of them are created by other people.

When a road is to be built in a town, as elsewhere, the engineer's position is different from that of many of the other people involved. The engineer has executive powers and responsibilities. The engineer has to produce a structure which is acceptable to the public aesthetically, which is functional and carries the expected traffic volumes adequately, and he has to do all this within the limits of standards and restraints laid down by others. On top of this the work has to be done economically, within the framework of what is politically acceptable locally, and what can be afforded locally, the cost being approved, ultimately, by the Treasury. In all this many are involved, or involve themselves, some having no responsibility and only

† Engineer in Charge, Bristol: Freeman, Fox and Partners.

pseudo-authority. It is necessary to face up to the maxim that one is not going to please all of the people all of the time, and, in particular the small, but vociferous band of people, found in all towns, who object on principle to everything in a negative way and rarely, if ever, propose an acceptable alternative. These people seek to maintain the *status quo*, which in an ever changing and expanding world, is impossible.

A few years ago, as the use of the motor car increased resulting in traffic congestion in towns and between them, there was a great outcry, led by the Press, for the construction of new and better roads. Efficiency and safety were two of the major advantages expected from these new roads. Over the past decade or so, about 1,000 miles of rural motorway have been built with a marked improvement in transport efficiency and a reduction in the rate of accidents, but very few motorway type roads have been built in towns and most now suffer severe congestion. The time has come when the emphasis is changing and towns will be in the forefront of the road-making effort. However, this changeover period has coincided with a period when we have become environment conscious and public opinion, once again led by the Press, is questioning whether new and bigger roads are the answer. There are alternatives to the private motor car but none offer the convenience and essential economic advantages of the motor car and convenience is the most easily saleable and most sought after commodity of this decade. The social desirability of mobility is beyond question, the desire to travel is inherent in the average man, who, being an individual wants to go where he wants, when he wants and how he wants. It opens his horizons and enables him to enjoy the environment as a whole. The average man would prefer to live on a normal housing estate and be able to motor into the country at his convenience, rather than be told we will improve your environment by taking away the roads and you must stay there.

This has created a situation where the biggest problem for many road builders is in not building any roads. All their energy is spent in considering what is possible economically and acceptable socially. The alert planners saw the expansion in the use of the motor car before it was politically accepted. Their overall plans of the 1950s were as forward thinking as they were allowed to be, but they were fluid and allowed for adjustment as the facts proved that which they already envisaged. The planner is probably looking 20 years ahead overall, but knows he can only execute for 5 years ahead. We are, in general, going through a period of re-appraisal of our requirements. We need better roads. We want to preserve that part of our community life that is worth keeping. We also have to consider what we can afford to do and we must consider what we can't afford not to do. In making our choice we must keep in mind the possible results of our decisions. I am sure we would all prefer to have busy, bustling but prosperous cities and not be left with quiet, pleasant, sleepy cities with everyone unemployed. These questions are all the more difficult in that there is no absolute answer, it is all a matter of degree and opinion, and what suits one situation may be quite inappropriate elsewhere. I hasten to add that some towns and cities are getting on with the job steadily without fuss and if not beating progress, at least keeping up with it.

Preserving the Environment

In considering the question of preservation of the environment, we have to think with 'town' in mind. We cannot and indeed it would not be desirable to, make the centre of towns as quiet as a country lane. The character of a town is based partly on a certain amount of rush, crowds, hubbub and a sense of speed and urgency. This is the essential character of a town, and by contrast, why we enjoy the countryside. The centre of a town at 5.0 a.m. on a Sunday morning can be quite depressing, although the beauties of Westminster Bridge at that time have been expressed poetically.

The usual basis of the objections to new urban roads is that they concentrate the noise and fumes in one area. It is often overlookd that the diversion of traffic onto a new road will free other roads of traffic and can thus improve the overall environment at the expense of one corridor. Careful planning can remove traffic from residential areas and route new roads through industrial areas or over and alongside railway complexes which already have low environmental values. The result is to improve the environment. An alternative is to route the road through areas of obsolete housing and take the opportunity to replan a whole area with a suitable buffer area between the road and the new development. This approach can also help to separate residential areas from industrial areas with great overall benefit.

It is now accepted for urban road construction that we can afford to elevate roads, so as to avoid the formation of environmental barriers. This was not so in the early days, and many an elevated road being built or about to be built, appeared on development plans as improvements to existing streets. Lucky is the town that had a planner with the foresight to route these roads so that construction as elevated high capacity roads is possible. However, we only elevate our roads the amount necessary to give minimum headroom to provide grade separation at road crossings. This puts them at a level to cause maximum nuisance in residential areas, just about level with the bedrooms. There is a case for elevating them to a much greater height, say 80 feet to 100 feet. The area underneath would be of much greater value and would keep the noise and fumes away from the houses. Interchange problems would be greater but not insuperable, although an adjustment of detailed design concepts and standards would be required. The costs would be higher but so would be the gains.

Tunnels are becoming fashionable as a means of routing urban motorways without interfering with the environment. Undoubtedly this move to tunnels is now more viable because of the thought and energy that have gone into the design of tunnelling machines—there are now six that I know of—with a resulting improvement in the economics of tunnelling. In some situations the cost of a tunnel can now compare with the cost of an elevated road. Tunnels, of course, have their disadvantages and even simple breakdowns can cause severe congestion.

Having said that tunnels are fashionable, several factors must be kept in mind. Entrances and exits tend to be large and straggling and sterilise more land than does an elevated interchange and also the sterilisation is more complete. Secondly, tunnels are not the panacea of all ills, as in certain localities they can be prohibitively expensive if not impossible for geological reasons. Additionally the expense of a tunnel is not justified if a route can be found where an elevated or ground level road is not going to cause unacceptable intrusions on the life of the town. A tunnel can be justified in certain topographical conditions, and in particular social conditions, such as the avoidance of a public open space or similar.

While on the subject of tunnels, and the advantages thereof, we could revert to the methods of Stephenson and have elevated tunnels. The railway bridge across the Menai Straits was an example. This would increase the visual impact of the structure, but radically reduce the pollution caused by noise and fumes, the latter being extracted at suitable points.

Economic and Administrative Constraints

At all stages, whatever other considerations there are, cost must be borne in mind. The road that gets early priority in the programme is the one where a cost–benefit analysis shows a good-financial return and we have no way of assessing, in cash terms, the value of quietness and clean air. Attempts to 'evaluate the environment', though laudable, have been very unconvincing.

The line for a new road is normally chosen at the time the town development plan is drawn up and this corridor is then protected. At this stage it may not have been decided whether the road is to be at ground level, elevated or in tunnel. After a decade or so the corridor becomes fairly well defined by new construction. The engineer then has a problem because the road has to be made to fit the land and surroundings, often recently built, which are available. In practice this has some minor advantages because, although on occasions it necessitates the use of much ingenuity to keep within the permitted area it obviates the wasteful use of valuable land.

A further problem is the services which are spread abundantly in, through and under cities. I find it disappointing that, although the line for a new road is made public on the development plan, there is not a follow up of co-ordination by the public utilities. It is only too common to have to divert co-axial cables and similar at great expense, laid in the past few years, from the line of roads where the line has been public for many years. I know of one job in London where the cost of services diversions were twice the cost of the road. I also feel that more could be done in the way of 'services reserves', along, near or under new roads, which would enable the utilities, over a period of years, to rationalise their apparatus. I think that no city has services which were rationally planned; they have all developed over the years haphazardly and must be very uneconomic. Ring roads could provide the basic line for new ring mains. Unfortunately, the statutory undertakers are partly beyond the planning laws and so work unco-ordinatedly in a way that seems expedient at the time.

I have mentioned that the engineer has to fit a new road into land reserved before detailed design is undertaken. I mentioned an advantage that stemmed from this procedure. There is another facet to this problem. The alignment standards for urban roads are a reduction of those standards which have evolved for rural highways. However, their application needs a lot of care and thought. They are not capable of automatic application. As well as keeping in mind the new road that is being built, it is necessary to strike a balance with the standards of the existing roads to which connection is to be made. At present we try to keep high standards throughout a new road and on all slip roads to the point of connection with the present road system. Often a real saving could be achieved by keeping the high standard, a high speed of, say, 50 m.p.h., only on the main road and a short distance along the slip road, then reverting to normal city street standards and speeds of less than 30 m.p.h., over a transitionary length. I think it would also be safer by ensuring that traffic speeds be reduced before joining the city streets.

An example: the Merits of Elevation

I revert now to a point I made earlier, and that is the question of how high is an elevated road. We have, in London, an example of an urban motorway going over factories. The road was lifted to clear the factories, but is still low enough for noise and fumes to be unpleasant. Other elevated roads are so low that they create a rather dark area underneath. Of course, a lot can be done by careful landscaping and, with imagination, use can be made of the area underneath. How much better though, if the road were 80 or more feet up in the air, the area under is light and the noise and fumes are up and away. Of course, all roads cannot be lifted this high, but many could, in cities with suitable topography, and the increase in cost would not be prohibitive. However, I think tradition would prevent such a construction. Only the shipping interests in this country have the power to insist on high clearances, and then they are achieved without problem.

Let us now take this concept a stage further. We support elevated roads on columns, which for aesthetic reasons we keep as slim as possible, and they serve a single purpose, to support the road. Suppose we made these columns bigger, in fact so big that they can be made use of for another purpose. Perhaps big enough to form offices, or a multi-storey car park. In other words, a series of multi-storey buildings, at say, 100 m. intervals, connected by single span bridges and with the roof carrying a road. Near the centre of the town these 'piers' would make ideal car parks. There would be a problem of finance as different interests would be involved, but these problems should not be insuperable.

Yet another solution would be to reserve ground level completely for transportation and parking, and elevate everything else. This would include pedestrians, shops, etc., and would require a complete redevelopment of the area.

Reverting again to the more traditional, if, when a new road in a town is planned, consideration of the whole redevelopment is given, a route can be chosen where the road construction is only a part of the whole. Lengths of elevated road can abut, cover and even form warehouses or factories. Other lengths give the opportunity for public open space with covered play areas. For this to be achieved comprehensively, all should be planned together from the word go.

Similarly, with a tunnel, or a road built in cut and cover, the cover could be in the form of a building over the top. The cover would not need to be continuous; there could be park areas where ventilation shafts could be formed. This is not by any means a new idea in itself, the District Line in London is an example of how our forebears solved the problem.

The main difficulty in the implementation of such ideas, apart from the break from tradition, is the splitting of responsibility. In this country too often the engineer, who is responsible for building the road, has only that to consider. Redevelopment of the area is undertaken by others. Also the financing is from separate sources, but if co-ordination could be arranged and the design and construction of the road made part of the design and reconstruction of the area, we might see some very imaginative solutions. Incidentally, much comment is made of the detrimental effect of motorways, but it is very common to see that when a motorway is built, new houses are built as near as possible to it. Undoubtedly, the construction of major new roads has an inflationary effect on land values adjacent and near, particularly near to interchanges.

Progressing to the more mundane, the actual period of construction of a road brings with it problems, most of which affect the general public. There are traffic diversions, hold-ups, noise, dirt, mud on the road, piling, etc. All these problems can be reduced or alleviated, but in almost all cases only at extra cost and at the expense of prolongation of the agony. It is necessary to strike a balance. A big inconvenience for a short time or a lesser inconvenience for a longer time and at greater cost. Also, the degree of such inconveniences are a matter of opinion and will be looked on differently by a contractor, paying proper regard to the economic aspects of his endeavours and his responsibilities to his shareholders or a Member of Parliament or councillor assiduous in protecting the interests of his constituents.

A further detail problem of construction is in the provision of suitable and adequate working space. Land and space is so valuable in a town that it is very easy to put a value on the provision of working room. It is not so easy to assess the value of having adequate space; even a contractor tendering would be hard put to arrive at an adjustment to his rates to allow for inefficiencies in working and inconvenience.

Finally, the question of the detailed appearance. At present we elevate roads in towns on viaducts we have to live with all the time (tunnels are out of sight and out of mind). Generally we use concrete because it is durable, economical and maintenance free. If we use steel we paint it, often in bright or pastel colours. I feel we should be prepared to paint concrete also. Concrete is a material which can be designed to be pleasing in form, with good design, but I am not too happy with it as a material to live with at close quarters. Almost all new concrete buildings are adorned in one way or another and when we have, in a City, a structure like a viaduct under and around which people are going to move, sit, play football, etc., then the treatment should be more than just concrete. For the traveller on the road, alright. He sees the concrete at 40, 50 or even 60 m.p.h. The pedestrian lounger, football player, is in closer contact. The modern epoxy-based paints have a long life, are available in pleasing colours and have been used extensively to admirable effect in Holland and elsewhere. Concrete sculpture, an alternative, may not suit everyone, but is certainly a change from flat grey concrete, but has the disadvantage of being very expensive.

Conclusion

My personal thesis can be summed up in the single word, co-ordination. Building of roads in towns is only part of the overall continual evolution of a town, its services and way of life. If all aspects of development could be covered under a single authority, money would be saved, inconvenience and heartache lessened, and the final result would be seen to be acceptable at a much earlier stage.

16

Project Selection and Social Welfare

M. E. Beesley†

IT MAY BE agreed that project selection has two main objectives; to increase the total welfare of those affected by projects and to affect the distribution of welfare between them. Governments in particular in assenting to, or financing projects, are not indifferent to the question of who gains and who loses as a result. Evaluation in these senses involves the measurement of costs and benefits associated with projects, both to compare projects and to judge to what extent resources should be devoted to them in total.

The typical urban road investment includes prospective benefits such as time savings and accident savings, and may impose environmental costs, which are not the subject of market (cost) transactions, though some elements—for example savings in vehicle costs—are correctly measured by their prices on the market. The problem thrown up by measurement is then threefold: it is possible to get relevant evidence in cases where prices are no sure guide; can one get agreement that evidence is relevant, i.e. secure a consensus that valuations are reasonable; and, where measurements are agreed, how can one arrange that conflicts revealed by them can be resolved? (A potential conflict arises where for example a project which benefits some is costly to others.)

Taking first evidence: there are three possible sources from which to draw:—first, and directly relevant only to some benefits and costs, is the evidence of prices; second, inferencces from situations in which choice involving cash transactions is observed, as in valuing the time saved in travelling; and third, the implications about values which can be derived from the past actions of authorities operating in a relevant sphere—as, for example, by inferring from the money devoted to safety projects what the implied value of life saving was.

† Professor of Economics and Dean of the Faculty, London Graduate School of Business Studies.

These sources of information, even if available and deemed good sources, usually do not exhaust the information needed for measuring prospective benefits and costs. With any current choice among projects, unmeasurable costs and benefits will remain. These, in effect, will be added to the measured benefits and costs when decisions by the responsible authority are taken. There will thus be a 'bureaucratic residual function' of valuing benefits and costs.

One very widely held opinion is that, in looking to improvement of methods of project selection, the 'bureaucratic residual' should be reduced. In one sense the ambition of developing cost-benefit analysis is to correct for, and narrow the scope of, bureaucratic influence. Also there is wide support for the view that project selection should be more amenable to direct public influence. The latter could be accomplished, but encounters difficulties of principle: voting directly on projects may well lead to results oppressive of minorities which nobody intends or wants; and, more frequently, using elected representatives—e.g. a Minister—to decide, imposes costs in terms of over-loading a decision centre more heavily, with possible general loss in the quality of the decision making.

Cost–benefit analysis was essentially developed to narrow the 'bureaucratic residual' and indeed started in a situation in which in effect almost all the benefits and costs were the subject of bureaucratic decision. Its scope in measurement grew essentially by appeal to individual consumer behaviour. Thus the information sources now available for cost–benefit analysis show a distinct bias towards the revealed preferences of individuals. Items of benefit implying an individual's valuation of *other* people's welfare have not been greatly developed. (An example of the latter would be the valuation set by a person on saving another's life.) Also because increasing information is costly, there is a tendency to apply valuations established in one area to other situations, and not necessarily appropriately. (Thus there is considerable scope for debate about applying valuations of time derived from commuter choices to travellers to airports.) But in terms of establishing a consensus about the correctness of valuations, evidence based on individual choice has been relatively successful. Values of time they derived are now widely accepted for a variety of urban project valuations.

Cost–benefit analysis has developed hardly at all in respect of the second major objective noted at the outset, namely the distribution of income. This is partly because of the very high cost of investigation—

the technical problem of measuring the impact of a project on any but the immediately affected is severe. More important, those responsible for evaluation are very reluctant to assert a consensus, as the Roskill Commission's refusal to take a judgement on such issues showed, in spite of the fact that it was frequently pressed to do so, and had the means to investigate quite deeply had it wished. In this, it was responding to the traditional economic view that direct measures to redistribute income are to be preferred to indirect; and it was reluctant to take on what it regarded as a Government responsibility.

Hence the development of cost–benefit analyses has in many respects not made decision making easier. It has tended to detract from bureaucratic discretion; though welcoming valuation exercises which are founded in consumer behaviour, administrators have encountered consequent pressure to rationalise further. The distinction between the measurable and the unmeasurable has sharpened: decisions are less easy to defend. The pressure to recognise distributive issues has increased. Those initiating projects have also gained in insight; ingenious discoveries of new forms of benefit lead to what is sometimes called 'control-loss' phenomena. All this has tended to hamper the realisation of what may well be the greatest advantage of CBA—to influence the initial selection of projects through applying what is found out about benefits and costs in the analysis stage.

To realise CBA's potential contribution to better decisions, one has to look at the whole decision-making context in which it takes place. The interaction of CBA with its decision-making context is an uncharted area of analysis. To begin the discussion, a distinction may be made between large scale, ad hoc enquiries like the Roskill Commission on the third London Airport and the Greater London Development Plan enquiry, and the on-going organisational process, where CBA has to be used as routine, as in much of local authorities work in roads. In the first, there is an exceptionally large, irreversible decision; it is much more possible to use the political decision making system; the 'residual' problems are large; and there is little prospect of using further investment, by adjusting the budget allocation system, to correct for mistakes as information gets better. There are advantages and disadvantages in each type of situation from the point of view of improving the quality of decisions, and we should focus developments in CBA accordingly.

Taking Roskill as an example:—a major failing, in my view, was first, not to allocate funds to increase information about key elements in the evaluation—notably to examine closely the valuation of time for airport travellers, and their reducing reliance on valuation by analogy e.g. with commuter travel. More important, the form of decision-making imposed on Roskill (the particular form of public enquiry) drastically reduced the proper consideration of alternatives. Good evaluation depends on exploring alternatives. In the Roskill case, 78 sites were initially considered, but only 4 were subject to detailed public debate. There was a considerable learning process in reducing the 78 to the 4; and much evidence was taken about them, but there was no way of feeding this information back into a consideration of the 78. In short, iteration was extremely limited. It would have been impracticable to have had a detailed public scrutiny of many more than 4 sites; so that inherently the aim to include public influence directly conflicted with the need to iterate. A consequence of the publicity was probably also that the Minister, when finally taking the decision against the Roskill recommendation, took the line of minimising costs to persons affected adversely, not of maximising net benefit. He did not rationalise his decision in the Commission's terms, even though the Commission took great care to set its measured costs and benefits alongside incommensurables such as amenity losses, and come nevertheless to a conclusion. It might have been preferable, in this case, to have reverted to an old style public enquiry on one site only, but preceded by a thoroughgoing but non-public cost–benefit analysis, or, alternatively, to have put the result of the analysis to a Parliamentary debate, with the implication that a failure to make a socially acceptable decision would be held accountable at the next general election. The decision might also have been improved had compensation for those adversely affected been available, prospectively, on a more generous scale than it was.

A further alternative way for dealing with conflict might have been to have left the final decision to the Commission itself. This would have had some precedent in the old-style nationalised industry board, where a number of 'good men and true' were selected to represent the public interest. But it would not in practice be adopted, first because responsibility for living with the consequences of a decision is held to go with the power to make it, and second, because of the impossibility of ensuring a truly representative set of decision makers.

With the on-going process, more attention is possible to the learning process; valuations may be more standardised, and it becomes possible to emphasise the initiation of projects rather than sophisticated techniques of ranking them. It may also be possible to work with generalised weighting systems to represent distribution objectives. By continual exposure to choice, the implied preferences of top decision maker, for example the Minister, in this respect can be discovered and applied. Thus, in a sense, one is operating a system in which each element in the organisation—the decision maker and the analyst, the engineer who designs projects, the consultant, etc., can learn from interaction. Improvement of the process then hinges on improving the inducements to learn. Thus the problem becomes a general management one—of rearranging rewards and the system (for example promotion, prestige or pay) in such a way that the total task/performance is improved. Thus the development of cost–benefit analysis and indeed any other analytical device has to be evaluated in terms of its impact on the total management system. This is an area in which analysis has barely begun.

Finally, it may prove that most important gains in welfare from altering the decision making process may simply come from attention to bureaucratic boundaries and budgets. Thus measures designed to increase safety span many agencies. There is a great difference in the implied valuation of life in their present activities limited at different levels by available expenditure. A reallocation of budgets and agency boundaries with reference to a relatively crude pay-off measure such as lives prospectively saved per £ spent might well substantially improve welfare.

17

Traffic and Towns: An Overview

K. M. Gwilliam

I. Introduction

THE INTENTION HERE is to summarise the wide ranging discussion which followed the presentation of the papers and to attempt to discern the major areas of agreement and of disagreement amongst the wide range of disciplines represented.

On one matter, at least, early agreement was reached. The distinction between the short run and the long run, from which we started, did not appear in the discussion to be a particularly useful or manageable categorisation. The first major conclusion which we were able to draw was that planning, as a very complex on-going process, was not conducive to any practical partitioning of this kind. Thus, while it is useful to examine the logic of specific management measures in a static context or to presume a fixed management scheme in initial appraisals of investments, the ultimate formulation of policy requires the full complexity of the short term–long term interactions to be taken into account.

As the period distinction withered away so a different distinction imposed itself on the discussion. It seemed both sensible and manageable to distinguish between the discussion of *objectives* and the way in which objectives were adduced and formulated on the one hand and *policies* available to achieve specified objectives on the other. This synthesis is, consequently, arranged on that basis.

II. Objectives

We started by considering the planning process as analogous to the operation of a business. In this model the population at large fulfil the role of the shareholders. It is in their interests that the business is to be managed but the nature of the information system is such that they are only able to control its operation by the periodic selection (or rejection) of directors. In the analogy the politicians are the directors whose general stewardship is thus periodically put to account. They are responsible for the general lines of policy which will be implemented by executive officers, represented in the planning process by planning officers and technicians.

As a model of the *formal* roles of the parties in the planning process this analogy raised no great controversy. But when the analogy was pressed to analyse the actual operations of the planning process it began to break down. In particular, the respective roles of the technicians and the directors in the planning process was a matter of dispute. Whilst it was agreed that management is, to some extent, essentially an autocratic function, and that the business model assigns this function to the directors, it was suggested that in the planning process this autocracy is frequently exercised by the technician in the interests of solutions which appear to him to be technically attractive.

Both the planner and the engineer resisted this suggestion as being an ill founded caricature of the real planning situation. They insisted that their powers are in fact closely circumscribed by the need to refer to the appropriate committee of the council. Whilst the politicians must inevitably rely on the technical judgement of their advisors, and the technical advisors have in this respect a responsibility to make proposals and judgements which they cannot evade, nevertheless there is a very close and continuing check on the activities of the technicians in this need to convince the public representatives of the desirability of their proposals.

In some respects, indeed, it was suggested that the essentially political role of direction was too strong and resulted in inconsistency and hence inefficiency in operation. The treatment of public transport in Washington D.C. was quoted as an example of an issue which became a political shuttlecock with consequent disastrous effects on the efficiency of policy implementation. In the face of political instability, or in the face of a strong confrontation of dogmas applied in the transport field, it might therefore be the case that too clear a role for the political director and too subservient a role for the technician would be positively inimical to the public interest.

We may be encountering a very similar difficulty generated by the confrontation of political dogma in our present treatment of urban public transport in Britain. For some time politicians of the left have advocated free or subsidised municipal transport as a means of bringing about some degree of redistribution of income. This pressure has been resisted by conservatives partly on the grounds that such redistribution was not desirable and partly on the grounds that even if it were desirable to redistribute income the subsidy of public transport services is not an efficient or desirable instrument for such redistribution. More recently, however, the interaction between private and public transport in towns has been the subject of more searching investigation by the technicians. A case appears to be emerging for some subsidy of selected public transport services as a proxy for the proper road pricing scheme which does not exist. The argument is one of efficiency and does not depend at all on views about the desirable redistribution of income. But, because of the entrenched position which the political parties have tended to adopt on the income distribution front, it is extremely difficult to achieve a dispassionate consideration of the efficiency arguments for subsidy.

It thus appears that there is an inadequacy in the analogy between the business process and the urban planning process over the respective roles of the director (politician) and the executive officer (planning technician).

The Role of Public Participation

Even more difficult than this, however, is the role of the shareholder —the public at large. Recent planning legislation has attempted to provide a much more direct role for the public than merely that of electing councillors who will in their turn direct planning through their council committee structure. It was this question of the role of public participation in the formulation of plans that caused the greatest difficulty in the discussion.

Firstly, there was the question of how interested the public really is in the planning process, particularly at the strategic level. The construction engineer suggested that the available evidence of public inquiries indicates that deep interest is only shown when very immediate and personal matters are at stake, and that the traditional local planning inquiry is a perfectly adequate vehicle for handling such concern. Even if it is not, because all the crucial decisions have been made at a strategic level *before* the local issues are taken, it does not necessarily follow that the way to improve the procedure is to insert another level of public inquiry. Unless the issues before an inquiry are of a kind which can be adequately comprehended by the public then a public inquiry process gives merely an illusion of participation. Some evidence offered in support of this thesis was the very low attendance at the strategy hearings of G.L.D.P. and the very great attention apparently paid to objections, not from the public at large, but from other planning authorities.

This assertion was resisted. It was argued that London was a very bad example because of the complexities, both technical and institutional, stemming from its sheer size. In smaller cities there frequently exist groups with a continuing, well informed interest in the planning process, well capable of formulating and representing their views as consumers. For instance, the Oxford Preservation Trust has taken a leading part over the years in opposing certain transport schemes and promoting others.

Clearly a number of elements would contribute to a lively and productive participation process. A limited physical planning area, an alert and responsible local press, and the presentation by the planning authority of a range of alternative schemes were all suggested as means of adding to the value of a strategic planning inquiry process. None of these were believed to exist in the London situation and therefore it was felt that it would be premature to write off the structure planning inquiry on the evidence of the G.L.D.P. example alone.

The second fundamental problem, however, was to determine what was the purpose of the inquiry. A range of alternative philosophies existed, which were not mutually consistent, but amongst which neither the statute, nor in the case of G.L.D.P., the practice, made clear selection. Four main alternatives were canvassed:

(i) The process was one of *goal formulation.* In the course of an inquiry objectives of fundamental public concern would emerge for subsequent incorporation in plans.

(ii) The process was one of *goal evaluation.* The role of the panel of inquiry was to 'judge' the desirability of the goals built in to the plan presented and to report to the Secretary of State accordingly.

(iii) The process was one of *technical appraisal.* The role of the panel was that of ensuring the internal consistency of the policies proposed and the consistency of the policies proposed with the objectives explicitly stated.

(iv) The role was one of *conflict resolution.* The purpose of the inquiry in this sense might be seen as that of providing a forum for the resolution by discussion and negotiation of conflicts.

Each of these philosophies has its difficulties. With respect to *goal formulation* the major difficulty appeared to be one of equity. Whilst, in a continuous planning process, some feedback from the public may be a desirable check on the designs of the planners, it is a quite different matter to rely to any large extent on the goals formulated in the course of an enquiry process. For, as Professor Beesley argued, the process inevitably emphasises and weights heavily the benefits and detriments of a relatively small number of immediately identifiable gainers and losers. One of the advantages claimed for the Roskill Inquiry, in contrast, was that the research team, largely composed of economists, acted as a balance against this tendency and acted, in effect, as guardians of the interest of the 'diffused beneficiaries'. We return to this point later; suffice it at the moment to note that the presentation of formal appraisal procedures, whether in cost–benefit form or otherwise, does avoid this sort of problem.

The difficulty of regarding the inquiry itself as a *goal evaluator* is a fairly straightforward political one. The urban planning process, of which transport planning is a part, inevitably involves many value judgements. The purpose of any degree of local autonomy in planning is to permit local sentiment, as ultimately represented by the elected representatives of the people, to be translated into practice. The principle that any group of experts, however dispassionate and independent, should over-rule such judgements seems to be contrary to the fundamental purpose of the whole exercise.

The third role, that of *technical appraisal* seems least controversial. The principle of employing independent experts to subject the structure plan to such a searching check seems perfectly acceptable and highly desirable. The difficulty here is one of cost. Planning is becoming a highly complex activity. The data and research foundation for a major structure plan is immense. Whilst at the moment, by dint of very hard work, it may be possible for a public inquiry to understand all this, Mr. Bayliss foresaw the possibility that, in five or ten years time, no inquiry of reasonable size and duration would be able to disentangle it. He drew two conclusions from this. Firstly, if we are to be satisfied in the beneficence of the planning process we must have, and be able to have, more faith in the elected representatives as guardians of consumer interests. Secondly, on the technical issues, appraisal must become a much more continuing activity than hitherto if it is to be meaningful.

The problem of the fourth role, that of *conflict resolution* seemed to be that it was more of a pious hope than a role. Indeed, it was suggested that the public examination of the details of a plan was much more likely to disclose and focus conflicts than to resolve them. In this event, it might also be the case that recourse to a formal appraisal, such as cost–benefit analysis, further accentuated conflicts rather than contributing substantially to their resolution in the sense of persuading disadvantaged parties to withdraw their opposition. This, of course, might be a very useful function, clarifying the 'residual' issues on which essentially political judgements need to be made. But it is not conflict resolution.

It is difficult to reach any firm conclusion from this discussion. The public inquiry into strategy or structure plans is in its infancy, and because of its complexity the G.L.D.P. inquiry may not be a good test of its value. But there was agreement that to some extent we are still in search of the correct role for participation.

Techniques of Participation

It is extremely difficult to separate a discussion of the *role* of participation from a discussion of *techniques* of participation. Nevertheless an attempt was made to appraise existing procedures.

It was readily recognised that the statutory provision for structure plan inquiries represented a serious attempt to overcome one of the most difficult of planning problems. The feeling that public inquiry is held too late in the planning process for any fundamental changes to be made has been widespread and has given rise to much dissatisfaction with the procedure. In principle, at least, the new procedures were welcomed.

The main concern arose over the means of converting this principle into sensible practice. This concern took a diversity of forms. At one extreme the view was expressed that there was little wrong with the formal arrangements for inquiry into planning decisions but that the lack of co-ordination in the planning process itself made it extremely difficult to conduct a sensible appraisal. Unfortunately whilst the desirability of co-ordination can be agreed in principle it is a very elusive characteristic in practice. Planning situations are extremely complex and sensible arrangements for the co-ordination of one set of decisions or policies may be disruptive in other areas. It is not the nature of the activity that all inter-related decisions can be taken simultaneously. Perhaps the best that we can hope for is that, by experience, the most appropriate boundaries will become apparent. The formulation of the objectives and policies of the planning authorities within some formal framework, such as the P.P.B.S. scheme now being introduced by G.L.C., may contribute to this.

A second point of concern was the availability of data and the level of understanding of the data. For instance, it was Professor Smeed's view that we were still a long way from understanding the nature of traffic demands and the technically efficient ways of satisfying these demands, and that in this state of ignorance it did not matter very much who made the choices—they were all likely to be equally inept. The conclusion that would follow from this line of argument was that further research was of paramount importance.

From a planning officer's point of view Mr. Bayliss expressed an almost directly contrary opinion. Whilst he would agree on the importance of improving the data base on which decisions are founded, he saw the major difficulty of participation as that of an already unmanageably complex proliferation of data. His fear, which has been mentioned previously, was that neither the private objector, nor indeed an *ad hoc* panel of inquiry, would be capable of comprehending what was already known. Thus, for him, a consideration of the data situation led to the quite different conclusion that sensible public participation or public inquiry might only be achievable in a continuous form.

A third matter of concern was the quasi-judicial nature of the existing planning inquiry process. Whilst the great merits of the legal profession in examination and advocacy were recognised it was felt that the formality of the proceedings sometimes inhibited inexperienced objectors and witnesses and frustrated their attempts to contribute usefully. Moreover the adversarial procedure itself might lead to a resistance to modification and compromise in a published plan whereas it might be one of the functions of the inquiry to resolve conflict by seeking such compromise.

A fourth problem of techniques of participation related to the distinction between matters of general strategy and matters of local detail. The success of the structure plan inquiry as a means of contributing to a feedback to the planning process from the public on matters of general strategy depends very much on our ability to make a sensible distinction between local and strategic issues. Unfortunately, it is almost inevitable that objectors whose interests are essentially local will wish to be heard at an early stage in order to try to affect strategic decisions. The distinction between the two types of issue is difficult to draw and unless there is a very strong secretariat able and willing to refuse objections at the strategic stage there is likely to be duplication of hearings and undue prolongation of strategy inquiries.

Two institutional matters contribute to this problem. Firstly, so long as the inquiry is seen partly as a public relations exercise there will be an inevitable tendency to 'lenience' in the classification of objections. Secondly, so long as compensation provisions are felt to be inadequate—both by objectors and in some respects by planning authorities—inquiry procedures at all levels will be overwhelmed with objections, phrased as strategic objections, which are really compensation arguments.

One final problem, raised directly by Professor Beesley's paper, merits discussion in this context. This concerns the need for feedback from the inquiry process to the planning process. The importance of such feedback is readily agreed by the planners; indeed, G.L.C. evidence to the G.L.D.P. inquiry specifically refers to it. But the 'one shot' inquiry does not permit an iterative procedure to be adopted. Even Roskill, with a fairly precisely defined objective, with a fairly long inquiry and with its own research facilities, was not able to revise its initial selection of possible sites in the light of the criteria and information that ultimately emerged at the later stages of the inquiry.

If we summarise and list these criticisms we find that they do show a certain degree of mutual consistency. It has been argued that plans do not shown evidence of internal co-ordination; that the data basis is unintelligible to the layman; that the judicial procedure further inhibits the consideration of the case of objections; that participation is only attempted at a detailed rather than at a strategic level; and finally that the procedure does not provide adequately for feedback even where reasonable objections are lodged. They are all points relating fundamentally to the capacity of the planners and the planned to communicate with each other in a productive way.

Three different, but not incompatible, devices were seen as possible solutions.

The first possibility suggested was that the planning authority be required to prepare and present for public choice a range of feasible alternatives. The South Hampshire study was quoted as an example of such a procedure. It does seem very doubtful, however, whether, in a very complex interdependent plan, the public can appreciate fully the implications of widely defined alternatives. This would be particularly problematical if any of the plans contained significant elements outside the existing experience of the public (as for instance the inclusion of new modes of transport). On the other hand, it is only in this way that we may be able to evaluate alternatives which, because of the existence of external effects, would not be properly evaluated by any market mechanism concerned with evaluation of marginal changes.

The second suggestion, canvassed initially by Professor Williams, was the provision of a preliminary phase in the inquiry process at which the 'boundary conditions' of the plan were clarified and at which any defects of data would be established. Such gaps in data could then be filled, as far as possible, by an independent research team which would provide information to all parties. This might be associated with a specially appointed group of planning experts able to advise and inform all objectors and assist them to present their arguments in the best informed and most telling manner—a sort of planning legal aid. Although this function was undertaken effectively on occasions by well advised private societies and might even be fulfilled by a sympathetic inquiry secretariat or by the planning authority itself, it was not at present done systematically. The existence of such a team might prevent undue repetition of poor objections as well as contributing to the efficient presentation of well founded ones. This is one way of attempting to bridge the gap between the enormous complexity of the planning process and the level of understanding of the general public.

The third possibility attempts to bridge this gap in an even more radical manner. It was suggested by Mr. Bayliss that we might sensibly recognise the impossibility of providing the bridge on an *ad hoc*, once and for all, basis and seek instead to develop what he called 'intermediate institutions'. He recognised the very serious and valuable work attempted by such groups as the London Motorway Action Group but argued that they inevitably suffered from lack of resources and lack of continuity. He pointed to the example of the Model Cities programme in North America, as part of which resources were made available by the Federal Government to selected local groups. These groups were then held responsible for disseminating information about plans at a local level and for providing feedback to the planners on a continuing basis. Such a device, Mr. Bayliss argued, would only be possible on a long term basis which would imply abandoning the principle of major set piece inquiries.

Conclusion

To conclude the discussion of objectives let us return to the simple analogy between the planning process and the business. Although the analogy may not be entirely appropriate for the relationship between the politician and the planner, its major defect lies in its description of the relationship between both planners and politicians and their shareholders, the public at large. Whilst in the business situation it is fairly easy for the directors to know what the shareholders want (usually profit and security) and therefore to get on with the pursuit of these ends with only occasional reference back, this does not apply to the planning situation. Instead, the politicians and planners are faced with responsibility to a public pursuing a variety of ends (some of which may be mutually inconsistent) with fluctuating levels of energy. If their aim is to limit public criticism by conflict resolution procedures, they are condemned to an existence shying at a constantly moving target. Moreover, as there are questions of income distribution involved, they cannot conceivably satisfy everyone. They can never succeed; they can only hope to fail creditably.

Expressed in these terms the task appears thankless and frustrating. It can, perhaps, only be made more amenable by redefining it in more concrete and stable terms. Here the economist's approach of obtaining, or seeking to obtain, behavioural rather than political evaluations may help. A formal appraisal of alternatives in terms of current evaluation conventions may be a very useful way of providing a workable basis for practical planning by drawing the value judgement fire on to the conventions themselves.

III. Policies

The discussion of contemporary transport policies disclosed three areas of major interest, namely:

(i) System design and the urban environment.

(ii) The role of public transport.
(iii) Traffic restraint.

Though these matters are very closely inter-related we may usefully and helpfully consider them *seriatim*.

System Design and the Urban Environment

The importance of preserving—and indeed in many cases improving—the environmental standards of our urban areas was readily agreed. The proliferation both of defects identified and solutions offered in almost any planning inquiry testify to the importance which is attached to this problem in the public eye.

We already know a good deal about the ways in which the internal environment, both in the home and the vehicle, can be improved by design features. There are also a number of self-evident road and traffic design features which can improve the external environment in particular respects. The existence of this basic technical know-how serves more to accentuate the problem than to resolve it, however. For whilst the problem may superficially appear to be one of aesthetics and technology in essence it is one of economics.

Whilst we know that noise, fumes, visual intrusion, community severance, pedestrian delays and so on are disliked, we can also see that, except for a small range of design improvements, the amelioration of the detriments is not costless. Thus, in order to convert our growing recognition of the importance of the environment into sensible design guides we need to quantify and evaluate. At this level, unfortunately, our understanding is presently inadequate. Although recent research work has produced some useful information about the relationships between traffic levels, the physical design of roads and buildings and the physically measured levels of noise and air pollution, this is only a small part of the information which we need. We are not able at the moment to quantify in physical terms what we mean by visual intrusion and community severance, much less to relate them to traffic or road design characteristics. Even for a fairly straightforward effect like that of pedestrian delay, where the techniques of measurement and research are fairly obvious, the research has not been done.

Even if we had solved this set of problems, and could precisely and accurately forecast the physical effects on each of our environmental characteristics of a proposed investment or management measure our difficulties would not be over. The various effects would still have to be evaluated. Clearly we would only wish to expend resources on physical improvements insofar as such improvements were of value to their recipients. Even if we are unable, in the event, to obtain behavioural evaluations which will allow environmental aspects to pass out of the class of design problems to which we can only apply informed judgement, and into that class which can be based on quantitative criteria, we shall still need some means of checking the general acceptability of the judgements made by architects and planners. One of the great difficulties in this field is inevitably a fear that professional and public opinions of what is desirable may diverge substantially.

The instinctive reaction of the economist faced by this sort of problem is to look for behavioural evaluations in markets or in the quasi-markets represented by individuals' personal trade-off possibilities. It is by this means that progress has been made in the treatment of the value of time savings. So far, however, the search for easily interpreted trade-off situations involving environmental effects has not been very fruitful. Examination of variations in house prices, which might be expected to reflect the capitalised values of differences in environmental standards, has so far proved most intractable yet more direct trade-off situations are extremely difficult to find.

An alternative approach which has been suggested is similarly based on the analysis of individual behaviour. This is to simulate market situations in laboratory experiments, offering individuals choices between different sets of characteristics associated in the purchasing of a house and recording their preferences in a series of choice situations. Analysis of this type of experiment so far has shown that individuals do display a degree of consistency in their implicit valuations which is perhaps surprising. Whilst this approach is attended by all the usual difficulties of simulation of complex social and psychological phenomena it does seem to offer some possibilities.

A third much cruder approach to the same problem is simply to offer, for appraisal by the public, a number of planned solutions involving different environment and cost mixes. Whilst such a choice situation offers the greatest realism it also incurs all the difficulties of the individual's inability to appreciate the full implications of a complex and interacting situation.

Consideration of the necessary data base to enable environmental characteristics to be continuously appraised in the design process led to the conclusion that a good deal more research was necessary before a satisfactory position could be achieved. But planning is a continuing process and the best must not be allowed to be an enemy to the good. Hence it was agreed that practicable approaches were necessary in the interim. Four instruments of design were discussed in this context.

Firstly there is the concept, commonly associated with Professor Buchanan, of *environmental areas*. The recognition and delineation of areas of common character forms the basis for decisions concerning the type of transport and traffic conditions permitted. The logic of this approach is that some land uses are more sensitive than others to particular elements of the external environments. Once these elements of special sensitivity have been recognised design can then proceed on the implicit understanding that high value will be attached to avoiding transgression of them. Viewed in this way the concept of the environmental area is a proxy for a presently very inadequate evaluation process. It may thus act as a bridge between the design skills of the architect and planner and the economist's search for behavioural guides to evaluation.

The second instrument, that of *minimum design standards*, is closely related to the first. It is conceptually clear that the application of rigid minimum design standards irrespective of cost could result in an uneconomic use of resources; it is also clear, however, that in the absence of the necessary information for a continuous variation of environmental characterising in the design process, the minimum design standard may be a very reasonable second best. The use of this instrument does not, of course, remove the need for evaluation. The standards themselves must be determined in ways which recognise economics as well as aesthetics. In the design process, however, they do permit a consideration of external environmental effects to be injected in a way to which the engineer and the architect are accustomed and can operate.

The third instrument discussed was that of establishing, for design purposes, a *hierarchy of roads*. It was agreed that part of our present environmental trouble stems from attempting to use the same type of road to meet all our needs. Taking an extreme case, it is clear that one would design roads which were exclusively for vehicles travelling at high speed quite differently from roads which were exclusively for pedestrians. In principle, of course, there might be a very large number of situations lying at different points between these extremes and we must avoid the danger of creating unduly expensive nonsenses by too rigid an application of hierarchical systems. But so long as we recognise this danger, the device could be a most useful way of contributing to environmental improvement. One interesting and important example of the kind of problem in which careful relationship between the function of a road and its design might bring about significant benefits is that of ribbon development of shopping centres in urban areas. It is often the case that major shopping centres are strung along the important radial traffic routes out of town, involving a fundamental conflict of function. The case for separation of these functions by a design device is extremely strong.

Thus, perhaps the best way to look at the issue is to regard hierarchical form as a 'design style'. It is a means of avoiding the need to re-examine recurring aspects of problems—a technique commonly adopted in architecture. Whilst we must be cautious about assuming that it is a solution in itself it does offer a means of incorporating into our designs the existing body of knowledge on certain broad and generally experienced problems.

The fourth instrument discussed was of a quite different order from the rest. One of the problems of the planning situation is that not only do environmental improvements usually have a resource cost, thus presenting efficiency problems, but they also involve substantial redistributive effects. Cost–benefit analyses commonly assume that the role of the economic appraisal is to deal with efficiency of resource utilisation on the assumption that considerations of equity will be handled separately—perhaps by general fiscal policy means. Unfortunately it may not always be easy to separate the issues clearly in this way.

Given this interdependence one of the causes of difficulty may be the way in which the experts put forward their opinions. Both engineers and economists (in cost–benefit analysis) tend to present a single technically or economically efficient recommendation which frequently ignores, or obscures, the distributive implications. In contrast with this, the *planning balance sheet* approach, associated particularly with Professor Lichfield, sets out in list form not only the component effects but also a list of those who benefit and those who lose. This permits him to offer alternatives to the politician, and reserves for them the ultimate distributive decisions which neither the economist nor the engineer is particularly competent to make. Whilst the details of the Lichfield approach may be criticised, it was agreed that it offers a framework which potentially recognises not only the difficulty of evaluation of environmental items but also the redistributive implications of alternative plans. This instrument appears to be well worthy of further development on this score.

To sum up; problems of environment offer the most rigorous test to urban transport planners. In the long term a much stronger data base is needed for design guidance. In the short term, however, the problem can be to some extent systematised and simplified by the instruments discussed.

The Role of Public Transport

One of the most difficult and paradoxical of situations in the urban transport field is that of public transport. For whilst both planners and the public testify to the important role which it must play in urban areas it nevertheless continues to decline both in quantity and in profitability. The economist rationalises this in terms of the disparity between marginal social cost and price for the use of road space in urban areas which, he claims, inevitably results in an inefficient use of resources. The engineer and the planner, whilst not seeing the problem in the same terms, increasingly recognise that marginal adjustments of use, made as a result of the inducements of the market mechanism, are not leading in the direction of what they would recognise as an efficient solution. Hence there is a growing agreement amongst the technicians from various disciplines that specific action will be required if the proper role of public transport is to be achieved.

Though this does represent a gratifying degree of agreement between the disciplines, there are still many issues on which agreement cannot easily be reached both concerning the level of public transport which it is desirable to provide and the means whereby this objective is to be achieved.

Let us first consider the desired level of public transport. Although public transport is at present provided on a commercial basis the existence of substantial externalities and the inadequacy of the price mechanism for road space means that the market mechanism does not necessarily produce an efficient solution. Thus it appears that the 'balance' between public and private transport will appear as one of the elements of the urban transport situation which will have to be planned. Where this point of 'balance' lies, however, is not easily determined. Conceptually, the economist would say that it is represented by that modal split which would exist if prices were made equal to marginal social cost both for road use and for public transport. But as he does not know where this point will lie in fact, the conceptual statement is of little help. All that is clear is that it will involve *more* public transport than a market mechanism will produce with the present road charges regime and public transport operations appraised on a commercial basis. It is readily agreed, however, that this point of balance needs further clarification.

Notwithstanding this element of uncertainty about how much public transport to provide, a number of means have been suggested for improving the split of traffic between public and private transport.

The first possibility lies in better planning of public transport services, and particularly in improvements in the interchange between modes. It was suggested that in most towns the interfaces between various public transport modes and between public and private transport were extremely poor. This stems from a number of causes. Historically, bus and rail companies have found themselves in direct competition and market pressures sometimes encouraged them positively to resist good interchange between modes. Moreover, institutional and educational traditions have created a wide gulf between planners and public transport operators which has only recently begun to narrow. Whilst further developments in physical co-ordination may be expected to increase the attractiveness of public transport, and should certainly be encouraged, of themselves they are likely to make relatively little impact on the modal split situation.

A second instrument of a rather similar kind is the introduction of new techniques of public transport by the planning authorities themselves. It was suggested, for instance, that travelators might eliminate, or at least reduce, the disutility attached to inter-modal transfers and to journeys on foot. Or, more likely, that measures of traffic management or road investment specifically directed at public transport could improve the relative attractiveness of buses. Special bus tracks, exclusive use of bus lanes, traffic signals biassed in favour of bus operations and the like are increasingly popular with transport planners. The advantages of such measures are that they can be presented, appraised and justified in the same terms as other road investment or management schemes and, (unlike subsidies), do not involve any obvious major conflict with the political dogmas of either political party.

The third instrument, and that which is becoming the most popular candidate as a means of significantly altering the situation, is the application of physical restraint on private vehicle movements—particularly for journeys to work at peak periods. We discuss this in more detail later. There is no doubt that the use of such measures as restrictions upon car parking can force traffic from private to public transport. The difficulties here seem to be whether sufficiently stringent measures to achieve the desired balance by this means will prove to be politically acceptable. In the large conurbations, such as London, it is already beginning to appear that parking restrictions of an unprecedented severity would be required. Especially where it appears that there are substantial real benefits attached to private transport (even if this is merely an illusion created by the inappropriate pricing system) it is doubtful whether we will be able to find the political will to implement the restraints. This suggests a set of possible instruments involving changes in the relationship between the prices charged for public and private transport.

This change in relative prices can be achieved in two main ways. Either we can increase the charges for the use of congested roads by private vehicles (the road pricing approach) or we can reduce the prices of public transport (the subsidy approach). Whilst road pricing is undoubtedly the conceptually correct solution it is not yet clear that it is practicable. Though we know that it is technically feasible there is still much that we do not know about it. We are not sure how precisely we should apply it, nor what it would cost to make it effective in a large urban area. We do not know what effects it would have on the distribution of welfare or on the effectiveness of policies to protect environmental areas. Above all, it would be an extremely unpopular measure politically in the short run. Thus whilst some form of change in the pricing system for urban road space is likely in the long term, it may not be available for our immediate problems. The Department of the Environment has suggested, in connection with the G.L.D.P. inquiry, that it will be another ten years before it is ready for widespread application. This seems to leave us with a subsidy of public transport as the only viable economic instrument to affect the balance in the near future.

In its most extreme form there is presented an argument for free urban public transport. For instance, the recent G.L.C. discussion paper on London transport set out this case. The main objections to such a scheme are well known. It may encourage some wasteful use of transport facilities (although the extent of this defect is very much a matter of argument); it leaves the operator without any financial criterion as to what services to provide; and, for large conurbations with many visitors, it offers subsidies to outsiders and produces difficulties about the allocation of the financial burden. Above all, however, it is extremely doubtful whether it would do the trick. Research work in this country and the U.S. has suggested that the bulk of journeys would still continue to be made by private transport even if public transport were completely free. Another way of stating this is to say that the difference in the value attributed by the consumer to private and public transport is too great to be out-weighed by the complete subsidy. It is primarily for this reason that it was agreed that free public transport was not the complete solution of the problem.

Notwithstanding this conclusion there do appear to be some rather more narrowly defined circumstances in which subsidy was deemed to have merits. Insofar as the problem is one of relative quality of service there would seem to be a particularly strong case for capital grants to finance improvements in public transport service. There may also be a case for subsidy, on distribution of welfare grounds, to support the continued operation of unremunerative services if the desired redistribution cannot be achieved in any more effective way.

To sum up; there is a clear consensus of opinion to the effect that some stimulus is needed to the provision and use of public transport in urban areas. A number of instruments are available none of which, by themselves, are likely to re-establish the desired 'balance' between modes. Above all, however, we still need by research to clarify the position substantially both with regard to the balance to be sought and with regard to the likely effectiveness of individual instruments.

Traffic restraint

The final topic discussed, that of restraint, disclosed two areas of disagreement. The first concerned the way in which we should define the amount of restraint applied; the second related to the adequacy of the range of instruments of restraint presently available.

First of all we tried to define an optimum level of restraint. The strating point which the economist would adopt in trying to answer this question is that it would be the level implied by the traffic flow obtained when the charge for road use was always equal to marginal social cost. In other words, even if road pricing is not physically practicable it should be the conceptual reference point for determination of restraint policy. This differs, clearly, from the obvious engineering benchmarks of free flow speed achievement or maximum flow, both of which the economist would reject as economically inefficient. The very fact that these possible engineering targets are unacceptable to the economist explains the importance of the conceptual point that is being made.

If efficiency in the use of road space were the only target and there were no external effects on non-vehicular road users or on environmental standards this initial benchmark might be adequate. Unfortunately it was widely agreed that the matter is not as simple as that. Effects such as those on pedestrian delay and environmental quality are not easily evaluated and our appreciation of marginal social cost is likely to be to that extent deficient. It is because we are unable, at the present, to rationalise all the variables that a political decision is necessary. Thus it might be that we would justify the complete closure of a street to vehicular traffic on something looking more like an intuitive appreciation of the aesthetics of the issue than a careful economic appraisal. This is not to say that the decisions presently taken in this area are necessarily right. Indeed, one of the present problems may be that the corporate political mind is insufficiently aware of interim possibilities. Moreover, the larger the town the more difficult it becomes to grasp the implications of radically different solutions. A good deal thus remains to be done in the presentation of real alternatives in a meaningful manner.

The second subject of discussion was the adequacy of the instruments available. It was agreed that a wide range of such instruments does exist,ranging from road pricing at one extreme to direct prohibitions at the other. For small towns it was felt likely that some combination of these measures was almost certainly capable of achieving any level of restraint likely to be deemed desirable. Experience in London suggests that this is not necessarily the case for large cities. Beyond a certain level the restriction of journeys by parking restraint becomes increasingly unpopular and difficult to enforce whilst more draconian measures such as restriction on car ownership are unlikely to be politically acceptable. Thus, for the large conurbations further work on means of restraint, including further investigation of the practicability of pricing solutions appears necessary. One of the tragedies of transport planning in the sixties is that we have collected vast amounts of data in the conurbation transport studies, at great expense, without significantly improving our ability to answer some of these essentially practical problems.

With restraint, as with the other policies which were considered, we therefore concluded that whilst there was sufficient basis for formulation of policies in the short term, there was need for substantial research to improve the basis for future policy formulation.

IV. Epilogue

The discussion began with a consideration of the objectives of urban transport planning, in the course of which a wide range of different, and sometimes conflicting, views were expressed, particularly about the role of public participation in the planning process. It concluded on a similar note of disagreement with respect to the nature and extent of the support which it was desirable to give to public transport. But sandwiched between these disagreements on policy objectives there was substantial agreement about the various planning techniques considered. Engineers, economists and planners not only appeared to understand a good deal about each other's disciplines but also were agreed that all had a part to play within the planning process as presently understood. Even on such delicate matters as the treatment of environmental standards, where much further research was deemed necessary, it was agreed that the problem called for the combined skills of a number of disciplines.

It was clearly believed that we either have developed, or could develop, both the analytical skills to forecast future developments in the urban transport situation fairly accurately and the instruments to affect or redirect that future. What we do not appear to have done is to arrive at any clear consensus concerning what the objectives of planning should be, nor to have decided how such objectives should, in future, be determined. Thus, if we were to attempt to elicit a single statement to summarise our thoughts on the state of the art it would be that transportation planning, so long regarded as an essentially technical exercise, has now clearly shifted from the area of civil to that of social engineering.

Index